Peter Harcourt was born in Toronto in 1931 and
studied music at Toronto University before coming to
England to study English literature at Cambridge under
F. R. Leavis. From 1962 to 1965 he worked on the staff
of the Education Department of the British Film Insti-
tute, during which time he also contributed occasional
talks to the B.B.C. and articles to *Film Quarterly* and
Sight and Sound. He then joined the Film Department at
Hornsey College of Art, and also lectured at the London
Film School, St Martin's School of Art, and the Royal
College of Art. In 1967 Peter Harcourt returned to
Canada to establish a programme in Film Studies at
Queen's University, Ontario.

Peter Harcourt

Six European Directors

Essays on the Meaning of Film Style

Penguin Books

Penguin Books Ltd, Harmondsworth, Middlesex, England
Penguin Books Inc., 7110 Ambassador Road, Baltimore, Maryland 21207, U.S.A.
Penguin Books Australia Ltd, Ringwood, Victoria, Australia
Penguin Books Canada Ltd, 41 Steelcase Road West,
Markham, Ontario, Canada
Penguin Books (N.Z.) Ltd, 182–190 Wairau Road, Auckland 10, New Zealand

—

First published 1974
Reprinted 1976

—

Copyright © Peter Harcourt, 1974

—

Made and printed in Great Britain by
Cox & Wyman Ltd, London, Reading and Fakenham
Set in Linotype Pilgrim

Earlier versions of Chapters 4 and 6 were published in *Film
Quarterly* (Berkeley), Spring 1967 and Spring 1966 respectively
(copyright © The Regents of the University of California, 1967
and 1966).

for Marilyn
who could have improved everything

CONTENTS

PREFACE

The debt I owe to all those who have helped me in my thinking about the cinema is too far-reaching to be documented in detail. It really begins with R. E. Keen of the British Broadcasting Corporation, who first encouraged me to take my ideas seriously by putting me on the air; it extends through my years at the British Film Institute, where, for a time, Stanley Reed and Paddy Whannel provided me with a base from which to operate; it continues now at Queen's University in Kingston, Canada, where for the past six years I have been allowed to continue my work.

Nevertheless, I would like to mention certain individuals who have offered me encouragement: Andrew Brink and Paddy Whannel in the past, and more recently Norman MacKenzie and George Whalley here at Queen's. I am especially indebted to both George Whalley and Doug Bowie for their helpful reading of my typescript; to Stuart Samuels, who helped me disentangle some of the conceptual confusions of the conclusion; to Carolyn Hetherington, who typed the bulk of an early draft of this book; to the Canada Council, who helped me return to England for the final stages of it; to Nikos Stangos of Penguin Books, who has been most patient and helpful throughout the years that he has been kept waiting for the delivery of my typescript; and to Judith Wardman, who prepared the final copy for the press.

Finally, however, I must thank my students, who have always made me feel that my work was worthwhile.

Peter Harcourt
Queen's University
Kingston, Canada
1972

I

INTRODUCTION

a note on film criticism

One has no right to love or hate anything if one has not acquired a thorough knowledge of its nature.   *Leonardo da Vinci*

There is to my sense no work of literary, or of any other, art, that any human being is under the smallest positive obligation to 'like'. There is no woman – no matter of what loveliness – in the presence of whom it is anything but a man's unchallengeably own affair that he is 'in love' or out of it.   *Henry James*

These two quotations represent the twin poles of critical method. They define both its purpose and eventual limitation.

On the one hand, works of art exist as objects in their own right. They possess a reality independent of our observation of them, a value, possibly, independent of our response to them. If we wish to understand the world and the objects in it, we must be attentive to it. We must examine it closely, asking ourselves how *this* object can be related to *that*. We must be sufficiently open to experience to be capable of learning from it.

For small children, this is rarely a problem. A child's mind seems open to all kinds of observations, without feeling the necessity to be constantly preferring one experience over another. But as the process of formal education begins, filters are slipped in front of the mind. Experiences become increasingly screened, and strong imaginative and emotional preferences begin to assert themselves.

What the Leonardo quotation implies, it seems to me, is that we must guard against these preferences getting in the way of our further observation of the world outside ourselves. If we allow our preferences too soon, too strongly, to assert themselves, they will get in the way of further experience and may restrict our development. The Leonardo quotation embodies the ideal of the scientific method – an ideal somewhat fallen into disrepute these days in the hands of the technologists, but valid nevertheless: valid as an *ideal* more than as an attainable goal, as something we strive for from time to time but not to the exclusion of other, competitive aims in life.

In order to observe something accurately, we must have a kind of detachment from it. But the degree of detachment is the crucial factor. Without the point of view of the observing self, we could make no sense of experience. Without some sense of purpose or ulterior curiosity to give momentum to the adult observations of life, there would increasingly be no observations at all. More simply, we require a bias to be sure of where we stand; but at the same time we must try to avoid prejudice if we wish to be able to see over the next hill.

This leads to the reference to Henry James. His quotation speaks for what might in this context be taken as the antithesis of the scientific method. James is alluding to the most private, apparently irrational, element in our response to art and life, the element that finally determines why we prefer one thing to another, why a given woman or work of art *speaks* to us in some immediate and overwhelmingly personal way, transcending detached observation, scarcely allowing analysis. James rightly values this highly. Without these inner, most private, allegiances, we wouldn't be capable of an emotional response to life at all. Yet without the maturity to be able to suspend these responses from time to time, or to give ourselves to experiences that are not so overwhelmingly personal as our most private ones, we are not likely to continue to grow.

Why it is that a given woman or work of art 'speaks' to us in this immediate way has to remain a mystery. It springs from something too private in each individual for us to be able to grasp its origins with any certainty. It not only explains the emotional content which remains at the core of all value judgements concerning works of art, no matter how objective they may try to be, but it also relates to less serious matters, like why we prefer one colour to another or dry wine to sweet. It obviously has to do with past associations, associations probably not consciously remembered but in the mind nevertheless, waiting to be called upon. It has to do as well with the assumptions of our culture and the way we learn to *read* experience within a given time and place. It may also have to do with the mysteries of psychological types, the basic trend of our particular temperament, perhaps even with our zodiacal sign! However, the basic point about these personal allegiances is that to ignore them is to deny our emotions; but at the same time, the feeling they can give us of being absolute and unalterable is undoubtedly an illusion.

We can be 'in love' in a variety of ways, even though each way seems absolute at the time. Similarly with works of art: we can be excited by an artist with such a passion that it seems to exclude other experiences for a time. But if we cling to that excitement, or shun the possibility of allowing new excitements, we may limit ourselves and stop developing.

Balance is the ideal, of course, perhaps simplistically: unless we remain detached to a degree, we will lack the flexibility of movement necessary to gain a broad view of things, but unless we take root, we might not fully blossom, we might fail to become what our culture or our temperament wanted to make of us.

We require both detachment and involvement at one and the same time. We need to be able to 'bank our fires without extinguishing them', as George Santayana has said of the Greeks. So the opposing quotations from Leonardo and Henry James should be securely placed over every critic's desk: they both have an equal right to appeal to us, as we have a responsibility to honour them both.

*

How do these notions relate to the problems of criticism? The critic/journalist might not be too aware of them, working in isolation as he does, evaluating works of art chiefly in the light of his own responses. He is liable, in fact, to mistake the Jamesian quotation for the Leonardo – to assume, that is, that a strong emotional response is *proof* that he has 'a thorough knowledge of its nature'. In my view this is a perversion of critical method.

The critic/teacher, on the other hand, is in a more privileged position. Through his students, he has a constant testing ground for his own responses as well as for his own attempts at descriptive analysis. And as the students are always changing, they are perennially young. The critic who is working out his own position in the classroom has psychological research facilities at his disposal that are an incomparable advantage, especially if he is concerned, as I am, with striving to distinguish between his own most private, subjective allegiances and the more public elements that can be described as valuable in any work of art.

The Leavisian belief in criticism as a corporate activity can most readily be put into practice in the classroom. The prototypal question 'This is so, isn't it?' ceases to be rhetorical when it is enthusiastically answered over the decades by a multiplicity of cries, 'Yes, but . . .!'

In the classroom, therefore, the critic/teacher has the opportunity to test his ability to *describe* a given work of art in a way that gains some measure of agreement from the group, and then to talk of *how he feels about it* as a somewhat separate matter, inviting the students to accept his description, or so refine it that, in the case of film, both teacher and students have an agreed description of what has happened on the screen. The students can then offer their own responses, responses that will no doubt be different from his, representative as they are of their own cultures and age-groups, of their own different experiences of life.

I recognize, of course, that one cannot totally separate elements of response from elements of observation. How we respond determines what we observe just as much as what we observe determines how we respond. At the same time, the classroom critic does have a recurring opportunity to test these different elements, to preserve the most private part of his imaginative allegiances so highly valued by Henry James while simultaneously having the opportunity of refining them – certainly of refining the descriptions he might offer as in some way *standing for* the particular film.

As with painting, unless we can translate the multi-sensorial experience of watching a film at least partly into words, we have nothing we can talk about. One cannot quote from a film except by accurately describing it (or by striving to) – one of the reasons why film criticism remains at such a primitive stage in comparison with literary criticism, for example. Any critical method concerned with film must begin by offering some kind of description of what the critic proposes to criticize, an observation of what has appeared on the screen. This does *not* mean that he should recount the story of the film (as film reviewers are invariably obliged to do) or say in a nutshell what the film is about. Rather he must attempt to describe how key moments in the film actually have been organized, how they appear, how they sound, how they move. Only if these three elements are described accurately is the critic in a position to say what the film is about – in no way an easy task!

Like consciousness itself, art begins with observation, with each individual's subjectivity. The challenge, in understanding art as in understanding life, is to reach out from one's own subjectivity towards the subjectivities of others, to the point where, as Merleau-Ponty has put it, 'the paths of my various experiences intersect, and also where my own and other people's intersect and engage each other like gears'.[1]

By this intermingling of our own subjectivity with the subjectivity of others, we can move towards a notion of a greater objectivity, towards the ideal represented by the Leonardo quotation at the head of this chapter, towards a greater awareness. Critical discussion, meaningfully engaged in, can provide incentives towards this development of awareness.

To refer to Henry James again:

The effect, if not the prime office, of criticism is to make our absorption and our enjoyment of the things that feed the mind as aware of itself as possible, since that awareness quickens the mental demand, which thus in turn wanders further and further for pasture. This action on the part of the mind practically amounts to a reaching out for the reasons of its interest, as only by its so ascertaining them can the interest grow more various. This is the very education of our imaginative life . . .[2]

In any case, only with such a belief in the value of discussion and thoughtfulness and in the possibilities for growth do teaching and writing become meaningful. The alternative is solipsism, or, worse than that, narcissism – a turning in upon the self.

*

In criticism, while we are working towards some degree of objectivity, striving to honour the spirit of Leonardo's insistence before we make up our minds about what we finally think of a given work of art, there are three subjectivities that we are dealing with: the subjectivity of the work of art as we perceive it (which is not necessarily identical with the subjectivity of the artist involved, not necessarily the one-to-one correspondence of his intentions); the subjectivities of our neighbours; and finally, primarily, our own subjectivity. The point of teaching or writing about art at all is that through discussion with others we can possibly refine our own response, certainly our *understanding* of our own response.

It is doubtful if a full response to anything has ever been immediately altered through discussion or criticism. But both these activities can sow doubts in the mind which may have a delayed effect upon us and thus ultimately alter response. My own experience is that, after I have seen a film, no amount of discussion or criticism will immediately alter how I feel about it, but discussion can make me aware that someone different from myself saw different elements in it. Sometimes these are elements not even seen by me, or, more frequently, they are elements which I did not feel particularly central in my viewing of the film at the time. However, if the criticism is thorough and demanding, these elements may take on greater importance in a subsequent viewing of the film, and this change of perspective may alter my response. At any rate, this has been my own experience of the personal value of the critical method, clumsy though it can be at times when applied to film, so bound up as it is in words and concepts borrowed from other arts.

The same applies to interviews with a film director (or any other member of the film crew, for that matter): while we are in no way restricted to understanding anything in art in terms of what the artist or artists might happen to say about it, such comments can be helpful in resolving doubts that might exist in our minds. Access to direct comment can be most useful in works of art that seem unclear in some way, where we sense inner inconsistencies or breakdowns in form, where we cannot fully *appropriate* the work either in our response to it or in our understanding of it. Not that such external information, even when helpful, will settle these matters for us; but it may help us in deciding what we can think about them, it may give us some intellectual guidance in our own speculations about what seems to be wrong.

This perhaps implies a fourth subjectivity, the subjectivity of the artist himself. But I don't really think so. Our basic responsibility, as critics, is to the work itself, to the responses of our neighbours (or students), and to our own innermost feelings. Criticism consists of a dialogue among these three things, with references to additional information like the personal comments of the artist himself when it appears to illuminate something that we ourselves cannot easily understand.

In the classroom, this dialogue is actual. In written criticism, however, certainly in my own, the dialogue is implicit in all the questions that I keep asking myself, and the answers are partly a transcript of the many replies I have heard. Some artists, like Eisenstein and Resnais, initially made very little direct appeal to me. Through discussion with others, however, in this case particularly with art students, elements in their work began to take on meaning and I then began to relate them to other works that I personally, instinctively enjoyed. Thus one moves forward and is stretched a little, as one gains a broader base for one's own critical position.

In criticism, it is essential to strive to separate what a particular film *actually* is from what we *feel* about it, especially from what we feel about it after only one viewing. In my own work, I have also been concerned more to *elucidate* a given work than to *evaluate* it firmly in the Leavisian sense. Evaluation may be criticism's ultimate goal as it certainly is implicit to a degree in everything that we do and say. But to be able to practise it at all with any judicial authority seems to depend upon two crucial factors: we must, in Leonardo's sense, feel that we have indeed a thorough knowledge of the nature of the

work of art we are proposing to evaluate; but, more important
than this, we must be able to refer to a stable scale of values in
the world outside.

I have few quarrels with the traditional Leavisian values of
maturity and seriousness as they have been used, certainly in
Leavis's earlier work, to present his own position. My quarrel
with these terms as they have found their way into film criticism, principally in the work of Robin Wood, is that they tend
to stress unduly the narrative and psychological virtues in any
given film, virtues that though always valid may not be primary, as in artists as diverse as Resnais and Fellini.

Similarly, I read with admiration John Berger's concise statement of his own position in the preface of his collected essays,
Permanent Red: 'What can art serve, here and now?', he initially asks; and then in a way that more clearly defines his
ideology, he asks 'Does this work help or encourage men to
know and claim their social rights?'[3] These are useful questions,
it seems to me, and certainly provide the strength and distinction of so much of Berger's writing on art. However, it is
doubtful whether the answer to the second question if applied
to Fellini's $8\frac{1}{2}$ would be too unambiguously affirmative. It still
seems to me, however, to be a pretty fine film!

My own questions, then, may seem slightly evasive, but they
reflect my understanding both of the nature of film and of the
world we live in – huge questionable factors, it seems to me, in
the light of recent history. If art is ordered reality, as Wilfrid
Mellers has said, then criticism can evaluate the nature of the
order with some confidence, but nowadays must be less certain
about the nature of the *reality*.

My own critical approach is to begin with questions that
elicit descriptive answers, reflecting the need to know more
before we decide. I am continually asking 'What is going on
here? What does this moment in the film seem to be communicating? What is it celebrating? What do I really feel about
it? What do you feel?' In criticism the tone I most admire is that
of an inquiring tentativeness, reflecting the difficulties of knowing with certainty anything at all in a world in which the traditional values have either gone soft and hypocritical or else

have actually dwindled away. In my writing, I am thus constantly trying to challenge the confidence that people often feel in their own responses; while in my teaching I am particularly excited when discussion has been so rewarding that it has challenged the confidence of my own responses.

*

As we strive to honour the twin poles of respect for the artefact and respect for our own response represented by the Leonardo and James quotations that opened this chapter, so too it can be valuable to approach works of art from two different positions. If we wish to acquire a thorough understanding of the nature of any given thing, we can bring to that pursuit all the materials we can find that might prove helpful. This is the impulse towards research, which, in spite of the flood of written material currently available, has scarcely begun as yet in the cinema. The more we know about France, the language, the cultural customs, the works of art in all fields, the better we will be able to *know about* the films of Renoir or Godard. Such knowledge as we possess will undoubtedly put us in a better position to answer such questions about these works as we might ask ourselves.

However, helpful though scholarship can be and necessary to a degree, I must insist as well on the validity of its dialectical opposite. It is perhaps badly timed to insist upon it here, in a book of film essays, when ignorance might seem to reign supreme amongst many professional commentators on the cinema. Nevertheless, scholarship, at least initially, does not necessarily increase one's ability to *respond*; it does not automatically increase that most extreme and private pleasure that Henry James was at pains to defend. In fact, if knowledge is imposed upon us, it can get in the way of a really personal response.

This again is more a teaching consideration than a strictly critical one. But it is important, nevertheless, to emphasize the validity of *ignorance* when discussing critical method. Our imagination works in mysterious ways. The experience of, say, a Japanese film for someone who knows nothing at all about the country and who has never previously seen a Japanese film can be overwhelming. Speaking personally, one of the most electric cinematic experiences of my life occurred while seeing *Sansho Dayu*, without titles, without any idea of what was really happening, without much experience of Mizoguchi previously, but during which the images, sounds and inner rhythms affected me like music.

In the cinema, the danger of too much knowledge (or knowledge too mechanically acquired) is that it can concentrate attention too exclusively on the conceptual aspects of the film, that it might encourage us to intellectualize our experience to the detriment of our response. More about this later. Right now, I am simply concerned to point out what I take to be a perceptual fact: the *less* we know about the culture from which a given film springs, the more we might instinctively respond to the inner form of the work itself, undistracted by familiar surface details.

The present critical climate has changed a good deal – for critics like Andrew Sarris and Robin Wood have helped us appreciate the artistic values of the American cinema; but for the most part, it has been easier for English-speaking critics to perceive the artistry in European or Asian films than to see comparable qualities in the Hollywood product. Faced with a Howard Hawks Western starring John Wayne, most viewers, and reviewers, would be more aware of the all-too-familiar elements of the Western genre and of Duke's personal mannerisms than they would be of the personal, stoical world view of Howard Hawks. Faced with *Ugetsu Monogatari*, on the other hand, who has read anything by Ugetsu in English? Who has ever seen any of these actors before? Who knows much about the traditions of Japanese theatre, from which some of the conventions in this film undoubtedly spring? In our ignorance, then, we are better prepared to respond to the film as a film, to its own particular form, even though a subsequent search after knowledge, especially the knowledge of more Mizoguchi films, would help us more perfectly to understand the film.

What these last few paragraphs boil down to is this: we undoubtedly need scholarship to help us *understand* a given work of art, to help us to honour Leonardo's ideal. But scholarship in the arts is secondary. Response is primary. The facts that are most useful to us are those which help us to answer the questions about a given film that we are asking ourselves, questions always related to those primordial ones: What does this mean? Why is it affecting me like this? How does it relate to other films that I have seen?

So when discussing films, we can approach them from two contrary directions – the direction of knowledge and the direction of ignorance. Knowledge will certainly help us more perfectly to understand our own experiences and may lead us through the superficialities of an intellectual curiosity about something to a deeper, more personal involvement in it. But generally, it seems to me, knowledge about a work of art becomes most meaningful when it *follows* response, when it illuminates the instinctive obscurities of a personal involvement.*

While not primarily scholarly, the essays that follow are the result of my own initial self-questionings about my response to the various directors considered, directors all chosen from cultures foreign to my own. These self-questionings often began in a totally uninformed way. However, as it is impossible in a book to embody the results of an ignorant response to the cinema, I emphasize its validity lest some readers might deduce from what follows that one needs reams of information and an extensive experience of the cinema in order to enjoy foreign films. I don't think this is so. In fact, sometimes it is the reverse. The film is a particularly powerful art form and can speak to the most uninformed amongst us, often across decades and cultural

* When I speak about knowledge, I am referring here *not* to the instinctive knowledge which we inherit through our culture but to the knowledge which we acquire through reading and education – that is to say, to scholarship. As a Canadian, however, I can understand a Canadian film with an intimacy impossible with a Japanese film, no matter how learned or thoughtful I might be. While it is true that surface familiarity can blind us to the essential form of a work of art, that same surface familiarity can make for an intimacy of understanding impossible for someone outside the culture.

barriers, with a power and an immediacy that no other art form can count upon. Knowledge becomes important when we want to *understand* what we have experienced, understand more about the work of art in itself and about our own response to it.

At one time I was keen on relating individual works from an unfamiliar culture to other indigenous artefacts in the effort to create a background for the work in hand. Reasons of space and a gradual shift of interest have all but eliminated this anthropological element from the following essays. Certain vestiges remain, like the references to de Chirico in the Fellini essay, or to the climate of Surrealism in my account of Buñuel, or to Bergman's cultural origins.

When considering the mysteries of response and why it is that we can give ourselves so easily to one kind of art and not to another, I have also had occasion to invoke Herbert Read's seminal examination of the relation of children's drawings to psychological types in order to help us to understand why, for instance, we might *refuse* to respond to a film conceived in a particular style.[4] Expressionism, for example, is a historical term that can be related to a particular period of time and to a peculiarly Nordic style. But it can also be related to a particular cast of mind.

There is a kind of person who, for whatever reasons, is attracted by the distortions of Expressionism, by the urgency towards personal expression characteristic of this school of art that tends to break apart external forms. Such a person would obviously be sympathetic to the excesses of, for example, von Sternberg's *Blue Angel* or to Bergman's *Sawdust and Tinsel*; and the stylistic characteristics of films like these could be related not only to other works by the same director in the best *auteur* tradition but also to large segments of an entire culture. Thus, even more than with Fellini and de Chirico because far more directly, aspects of Bergman's work could be illuminated by detailed references to the painting of Munch as much as to the plays of Strindberg and Ibsen. There is a whole field here that could profitably be explored, a field that, as I have said, touches upon anthropology. Although only a sketch for such an approach is offered in the essays in this book, I mention it chiefly because of my early admiration for Bergman. In the initial reviews that he received in the British press, I often felt that the most virulent critics (like Penelope Gilliatt) were attempting to dismiss an entire culture and possibly as well a psychological type. Such opinionated criticism does not ask itself why a given film-maker works in a particular style but chiefly resents the fact that he does.

Faced with the complete rejection of an artist's style, the critic/teacher can invoke stylistic elements in common with other works from the same culture that the viewer might feel less hostile towards, or, following Herbert Read in his defence of the distortions apparently natural to children's art, he can try a more psychoanalytical approach. For all different styles are not only the projection of particular cultures at particular moments of time but also represent particular psychological trends. The styles we most instinctively respond to may well be those that most appeal to the bias of our particular culture but also might be those that appeal to our basic temperamental needs. If we are innocent about these matters, we might even be tempted to describe the styles we most instinctively respond to as the most *natural* styles, most natural because requiring the least conscious effort on our part in order to respond to them.

But there are no rules about this. There is no simple way of understanding the apparent mysteries of response. As I have said, total ignorance of Japanese art may in one person actually facilitate the intensity of response to a distinguished Japanese film while the same ignorance might leave another baffled and at sea.

It is the baffled spectator that the critic/teacher is most concerned to reach. While mental concepts will not necessarily increase our ability to respond, they may help a little. To this end, the critic/teacher needs to call upon whatever might seem helpful to explain the characteristics of a film that is not speaking to a particular spectator, whether it be the collective characteristics of a particular culture or, more personally, a particular psychological trend. All the critic can strive to do is to make works of art more accessible to people who have not instinctively responded to them. Certainly, this is the lecturer's credo.

He can have no other. He must try to cultivate James's 'further pastures'.

*

... films cling to the surface of things.[5]

... the photographer's selectivity is of a kind which is closer to empathy than to disengaged spontaneity. He resembles perhaps most of all the imaginative reader intent on studying and deciphering an elusive text. Like the reader, the photographer is steeped in the book of nature.[6]

If film is an art at all, it certainly should not be confused with the established arts.[7]   *Siegfried Kracauer*

The movies are part of my culture, and it seems to me that their special power has something to do with their being a kind of 'pure' culture, a little like fishing or drinking or playing baseball – a cultural fact, that is, which has not yet fallen altogether under the discipline of art.[8]

One way or another, the movies are always forcing us outside the boundaries of art; this is one source of their special power.[9]

Robert Warshow

The film isn't an object that films nature, the camera isn't only a reproduction apparatus that films nature, the two together are one and the same thing. Cinema isn't an art that films life. Cinema is something that comes in between art and life ... In comparison with a painting or literature both of which are arts from the outset insofar as there is a choice, an independent life, the cinema on the contrary simultaneously gives to and receives from life ...[10]

Jean-Luc Godard

What, then, is film? How does it work upon us? How does it build up its own kind of subjectivity, as if a living thing? How do we go about acquiring, again in Leonardo's words, 'a thorough knowledge of its nature'?

Just as there is a cast of mind that tends to reject anything that seems like stylistic self-consciousness in a work of art and would therefore tend to dismiss the whole school of expressionism, so there is a cast of mind that resents any all-embracing attempt to define the *essence* or the *nature* of the medium of film. Pauline Kael simply mocked Kracauer's theoretical ambitions when she reviewed his book in *Sight and Sound*.[11] Nevertheless, as the quotations that head this section demonstrate, it is not only Kracauer who has been concerned with the Nature of Film and its 'special power', who has been aware that the appeal of the cinema is somehow rather different from and more inclusive than the appeal of the more established arts.

In discussing these matters within the classroom situation, I have found it convenient to speak of three levels on which films may affect us, levels which are actually inseparable in the most successful films in the immediacy of our response to them but which after the event become separable in speech. Yet great art is not necessarily synonymous with perfect art; and if photography and film have 'an affinity for the indeterminate', so a good many *great* films, in my view, are demonstrably imperfect. There are hiatuses in their forms. Hence (*pace* Susan Sontag) the need for interpretation,[12] for offering suggested readings of a particular film. Hence too the miracle by which films, the *great* ones, manage to stay alive. Although fixed on celluloid in time and space and irretrievably a part of the moment at which they were made, it is often the unclear, or imperfect elements in them that keep them alive to succeeding decades, that keep us, well after the event, still trying to understand.

So when I speak of three levels, I recognize on the one hand that I am producing a fiction and that the different levels are ideally inseparable in the fact of response; yet, on the other, I also recognize that few films are ideal and that the three levels can often directly parallel the co-operative nature of film production, a nature which criticism scarcely knows how to deal with and which, for the most part, this book too ignores.

Few films are made by only one man. Even Godard and Bergman, who almost totally conceive and execute their films themselves, have other people shoot them and others too who edit. And Fellini, whose work is as personal as anyone's, always has a team of writers with whom he works closely, who help him to compose the dialogue and over-all structure for his films.

In the American cinema, which works much more on an assembly-line basis and is much more firmly married to a narrative tradition, the personality of the writer is often much more noticeable, even in a film by a most personal director, than it would be in a European film – or at any rate, in the kind of European film discussed in this book.

The case of Resnais is relevant here. More than with any other of the major European directors, the elements in his work remain separable to a degree. We can certainly sort out the very different contributions made by his different writers, whether Robbe-Grillet, Marguerite Duras or Jorge Semprun. In fact, the comparative slightness of *Je t'aime, je t'aime* could well be attributed to the inward-turning and simplistic story provided by Jacques Sternberg. Resnais, of course, was *involved* in this: he approved the script and worked closely on it; but the fact that one can with some confidence talk about the contribution of the writer to a given Resnais film is one of the reasons why Resnais remains, for all his distinction, more an interpretative director than the directors discussed in this book.

Popular film reviewing, often quite unreflectively, acknowledges these different levels when it talks about good photography but silly story; fine acting but clumsy directing. More often than not, these comments are just column-filling, for the reviewer has no real idea *who* is responsible for *what* in the film. Certainly he is rarely aware of the epistemological problems implicit in talking about a fine performance in a film at all!

Here, then, are the levels that I have been referring to, whether fictional or actual:

1. *The level of incident:* this level basically refers to the plot, but it also refers to the persuasiveness of characterization. If you like, it is the most literary level, the level that most closely binds film to the techniques of the novel, that most easily allows the established literary-critical vocabulary to be employed in the discussion of it. It is also, or tends to be, the most naturalistic level, concerned as it is with psychological realism and narrative plausibility.*

In some ways, in discussion it is quite easy to be objective about it, especially concerning films from cultures familiar to

---

* Victor Perkins's insistence on the primacy of this level is the one characteristic that unbalances somewhat his otherwise excellent account of film theory in *Film as Film* (London, Penguin Books, 1972).

us. Think of Pauline Kael, at her very best, in my view, in her discussion of *Hud*, relating the failures of the film to the culture it purports to be embodying, a culture familiar to her personally from her own childhood.[13] This is a world that she knows, and the film is found to be wanting, though distinguished, in relation to that world.

In other ways, however, subjectivities intrude themselves, especially when we talk about characters, about our response to the people we see on the screen. We are back to Henry James again and to the mysteries of psycho-physical response. It is, indeed, a very private matter whether we find one body beautiful and compelling or remain indifferent to it, a matter which is only partly controlled by the form of the film. A novelist traditionally creates his characters through his description of them, of their appearance and their actions, and in this way to a large extent guides our responses towards what he feels it should be. The film-maker can do the same, of course, but often the casting alone overwhelms these other matters.

Put Duke Wayne in any Western at this moment in time and we all know what the audience's response will be. Especially in the American cinema but to a certain extent everywhere, our response to a 'star' in a given film will tend to carry over somewhat to our response to the same star in what may be a totally different film. In a solidly narrative cinema, like the bulk of the English-speaking product, where there are lines to speak and a recognizable characterization to be built up, it is possible critically to sort these matters out, somewhat independent of our private response to them. But the less narrative the cinema, the less language plays its part in building up our sense of character, the more difficult it becomes to distinguish the part from the actor playing the role.

When we see Christopher Plummer as Hamlet, we have all kinds of ways of evaluating his performance. It may well be our unchallengeably own affair whether the performance pleases us or fails to, but in discussion of it we can refer to all sorts of things. We can, for example, refer to other Hamlets we have seen, to Olivier's or Gielgud's, but above all we can refer to our own sense of Hamlet that we receive from the text.

But what do we do when faced with Monica Vitti in *L'Avventura*, to take the most interesting and (in my view) most misunderstood case? How do we evaluate such a screen performance? There is virtually no text, there have certainly never been other Claudias created for us on the screen; it is practically impossible to separate out the character of Claudia from the physical characteristics of Monica Vitti as we see them in the film.

If we see Monica Vitti as a beautiful, graceful, vital, alive human being, we will almost inevitably transpose these elements into the character of Claudia that we see on the screen. So thin are the narrative elements of Antonioni's characterization and so mechanical his method of directing his actors, there are always huge spaces to be filled in by us in our response to what we see. A source of richness in his Italian films, this characteristic of his work is also a source of immense ambiguity. For if we see Monica Vitti as essentially a somewhat clumsy, irretrievably self-conscious young woman (think of that laugh!) who is trying desperately to pass herself off as someone who is graceful, vital, and alive, then our whole response to the Claudia character will be different and our sympathies for the apathetic Sandro thereby increased.

However, I don't mean here to be scoring back-handed points against Miss Vitti or offering a corrective interpretation, much needed though it may be, of *L'Avventura*. What I *am* concerned with is the perceptual difficulty of evaluating a screen performance at all, a difficulty that increases in proportion to what we might call the narrative thinness of the film. One of the reasons why we can speak with some confidence about performances in Bergman's films, especially in his early films, is that (a) within his repertory company we get a strong sense of the variety of roles that, say, a Gunnar Bjönstrand can so magnificently handle; but also (b) they are all such *written* films. Their densely dialogued quality gives us a strong sense of theatre and of characters assuming roles, which also accounts for the fact that Bergman's early scripts are – if we like the films, that is – such a pleasure to read.

The level of incident, as I have chosen to call it, is conventionally the primordial level to which most of us respond. Judging from popular film reviewing, it would often appear to be the *only* level. Films are so often talked about as if they were visualized novels, which, to be fair, is frequently the case. However, there are also two other levels equally important in terms of our response. Next in order of priority might be:

2. *The level of argument:* this level involves the dimension in a film that, explicitly or implicitly, is concerned with philosophical implications, with social or political references that have a life of their own beyond their presence in the film. In one sense, Miss Kael is in this territory in her discussion of *Hud*; for this level refers to the structure of thought behind the work. Sometimes, as in Godard, this structure can be quite open and intrusive, which is when we would refer to a work as didactic in some way. More often, however, it represents the sum total of all the things said and done in all a director's films – in short, his world view.

This is the level that I am very much concerned with myself in the essays that follow, attempting to deduce from recurring images or patterns of speech the total implications of an artist's work, both moral and philosophical. In one way, being the most abstract, the most concerned with 'ideas', it should be the easiest level to be objective about; yet my experience has encouraged me to feel that many highly intelligent critics practise their unformed art with their ideological preconceptions unarticulated in their minds.

Take the case of Fellini. Surely he is demonstrably a master of the cinema, a *maestro* of images; yet in England at least, he has had a somewhat lukewarm following. Why is this? I cannot know, of course, without extensive research; but when I contrast the tepidity of the English response with the immense enthusiasm of the American response and think then of the idealist philosophical tradition in the States and the (alas!) widespread faith in all-or-nothing solutions to the problems of life, then the case of Fellini begins to make sense. His world is too transcendental for the empiric British taste, his mind too irrational, his affirmations too mystical. At least this seems like a plausible speculation from which research could begin.

If we voice the problem this way, then critically we are sound. But critics often mistake the artist's world view for his skill in film-making, rejecting his work because they cannot accept his world. Well, as James has put it, that too is their unchallengeably own affair; but how we articulate these matters to ourselves makes all the difference if we are intent on acquiring a thorough knowledge of the nature of film.

I am in dangerous territory here, for there is rarely a case where the ideological implications of a film can be filleted neatly from a work of art without a sensitive response to all the other elements; yet a sensitive response to all the other elements is also partly dependent on the ideological preconceptions that we bring to the work. Our expectations affect what we observe, in films as in life. So we come full circle, like a dog chasing his own tail.

The solution is dialectical: we must sometimes lean one way and sometimes another. For instance, the dilemma of sociology so far, it seems to me, is that it has not developed tools of analysis sensitive enough to be able fully and profitably to use works of art as evidence: in his useful but simple-minded study, George Huaco is forced to reduce the implications of any given film to the implications derivable from a summary of the plot.[14] Skills of analysis must be more subtle than this before the work of art can be offered as understood.

Whether we accept or reject a work of art whose world view is opposed to our own will depend on different things. It will depend, first of all, on how dogmatic we are about our own views of life; but it will also depend on the skill with which the artist creates his world that then may be seen to have certain philosophical implications.

Bresson is a case in point here. His films embody, with increasing skill and a sensuous awareness of other kinds of life possible in the world, a Jansenist determinism that is to me totally hateful. So his films virtually paralyse me, stringing me out as they do between images and characters whose screen presence makes them seem compellingly alive, and a series of events that Bresson has selected for them that makes their lives seem from the outset irremediably doomed. Thus, there is little 'interpretation' required in the sense that I offer it in the various essays in this book. Bresson's work can be analysed but not really interpreted; for there is no discrepancy between what he appears to be offering and what we really find is there. His moral position is both too consistent and too absolute to allow for much imaginative shaping on the part of the critic.

Sometimes, however, the implications we might gather from the films of a particular artist may run quite contrary to what the artist consciously intended, even quite contrary to his conscious ideology or view of life. In fact, it is this kind of discrepancy between conscious intention and actual presentation that creates the real job of interpretation and requires tact and flexibility on the part of the critic.

These comments lead me to my third and final level, which I have chosen to call:

3. *The level of imagery:* on this level I mean to include all the aesthetic elements of a film, elements not only of things seen but of things heard as well – the basic movement and rhythm and formal pattern of a film. This is the level on which a film, being organized rhythmically through time, can most approach music, requiring something like a musical vocabulary to explain its effects. At the same time, it is the level that can most securely unite a densely realized film to a complexly organized poem or novel; and one must speak, without apology for the literary analogies, of metaphor and symbol, of all the visual, verbal and aural implications beneath the surface of a film. This is the level, of course, that elevates a statement on film into a work of art, that is largely responsible for its ability to move us. It is in this sense the most important level, yet the most difficult to analyse precisely. It is difficult to analyse partly because we lack a vocabulary adequate to describe the possible richness of the many visual, verbal, psychological, balletic, and musical effects. We must constantly be analysing by analogy with the traditional arts, switching back and forth between these various elements and changing our critical vocabulary as we refocus our attention on a particular aspect of any given film.

But this level is also difficult to analyse because it is the most subjective. It is the most dependent on what used to be called matters of taste, which is to say it is dependent on the individual sensibility, educational and cultural background of the viewer, *and* on his experience of cinema. In fact with many untrained viewers it is a level that they are scarcely conscious of at all.

In one way, this is as it should be. With works of art attuned to our own temperament or cultural training, it seems to me a good thing that we can be moved by experiences on the screen without any conscious awareness of the elements of form. This is the position of ignorance that I talked about earlier. The most delicate aesthetic effects can reach us in what is almost a subliminal fashion, while our conscious minds are taken up with elements of plot and character, the elements that constitute my level 1.

The educationalist or critic here has a delicate job to do, a job requiring great tact if he is not to destroy the purity with which we can quite unconsciously be enthralled by what we see on the screen: in the effort to reach students (or readers) who have been less affected by the same experience, he must strive to make them more *conscious* of these elements of form without making the others *self*-conscious at the same time. In every work of art as in every human being there is something that is irreducible, that eludes analysis. We should not ask of criticism, is it right or wrong, but more pragmatically, is it helpful?

I have myself found no easy solution to this problem, to the problem of conveying to others *why* and *how* a work of art moves us in a particular way. The technical account of editorial rhythm as found in Karel Reisz's and Gavin Miller's *The Technique of Film Editing* seems to me, useful though it might occasionally be for aspiring film-makers, about as meaningful emotionally as the standard academic analysis of a piece of music which, for all its technical accuracy, is completely unable to convey why a particular modulation might be felt as meaningful.[15] Nor are Richard Roud's footage counts and seconds breakdowns in his Godard book really very helpful, interesting though they may be too in their own way.[16] What is most worrying about attempts at this kind of accuracy is that one suspects that, with the possible exception of Eisenstein, none of the film-makers discussed by Reisz and Miller ever conceived their films in so arithmetical a way.

In film criticism one has to work by analogy, pointing out some elements of visual design that one might want to relate to a painting, some element of rhythmic construction that one might want to relate to music, all the while bearing in mind that on the primary level, for most spectators, the film is chiefly about characters who are doing things and saying things – characters in action. The other elements seem secondary, at least on the conscious level. One draws attention to them always at the risk of an interference with a private response, a private and mysterious response to the world created on the screen.

All three levels fuse together in the most successful works of art to become the content of that work. John Berger has made a useful distinction: 'content is not the same thing as subject matter: it is what the artist discovers in his subject'[17] – and we might add, moving on from painting which is largely Berger's concern, what he *does* with it. All these levels, the different elements of plot and character, of philosophical implication, and aesthetic design, are part of the film's total effect on us. Both in viewing and in talking about a film, we focus on one level that seems striking, and then another, and then on the relationship between the two.

Indeed, with sophisticated viewers, this constant searching can virtually constitute the content of the film, which is to say the centre of attention. The real subject of a work of art, as W. K. Wimsatt has suggested, 'is an abstraction, a certain kind of thrill in discovering . . .'; or, as R. G. Collingwood might have said, in achievement. When we are knowledgeable about a given medium, indeed 'in love' with it in a Henry Jamesian way, part of our delight with any work of art that pleases us lies in the admiration with which we see what the particular artist is doing with his chosen medium. On this level, it is not unlike our admiration for skill in acting or in performing music, or, for that matter, in playing baseball! If we know a bit about film and are aware of its potentiality from the fine films that we know, then a new film that excites us will invite us to applaud the skill with which the director holds the many elements together. Wimsatt quotes Coleridge: a work of art is 'rich in proportion to the variety of parts which it holds in unity'.[18] Although this is a specialist's point of view, it is certainly true.

When discussing films in terms of their different levels, levels 1 and 2 ask to be related to our experience of life, while level 3 asks to be related to our experience of other works of art, or other films. If we appraise characters and situations, we do so in relation to what we know about people away from the screen. Similarly, our response to the implied philosophy of a work of art will depend upon our own historical situation, on what we feel is affirmative or relevant at the present time. But the third level, the aesthetic level, will depend more directly upon our artistic education, on how knowledgeable we are about any given medium, on how sensitive we are to its many possibilities.

The more advanced the critical work we are doing, the more we might tend to talk about works in terms of level 3; the less advanced, the more we would have to talk about the primary level of plot and character and then the level of philosophical implication in order to engage with the level upon which most people begin to respond. Yet all our criticism must strike a balance between formal appreciation and response to subject matter.

In the essays that follow, there is very little explicit concern with these levels at all. Nevertheless, I mention them here because they are always at the back of my mind: again and again it is rather as if I were focusing through the first level to bring more clearly into view what the basic philosophy of a film-maker's work seems to be and to make more explicit the details of the form that convey this philosophy. With some directors, like Bergman, Buñuel, Godard, and Fellini, this method seems to work well, bringing us close, I hope, to what might be agreed upon as the centre of their achievement. With others, like Eisenstein and Renoir, my method might seem to falsify their basic achievement, taking us off centre. Nevertheless, I trust that there are insights to be gained along the way.

Criticism is not the search after truth but is a voyage of discovery. It is a series of probes into the work of a number of different directors from a consistent point of view to see what we can find. In the essays that follow, it is the elusive implications of the third level and its relationship to level 2 that I am primarily concerned with, the relationship of the space within the frame and the rhythm of the sequence to the subject matter of the film, the accumulative meaning of all the structural effects. Yet this emphasis is not intended to deny the importance of the narrative and psychological elements in a film, of the subject matter, in fact. As Kenneth Clark put it several years ago:

Now it is an incontrovertible fact of history that the greatest art has always been about something, a means of communicating some truth which is assumed to be more important than the art itself. The truths which art has been able to communicate have been of a kind which could not be put in any other way. They have been ultimate truths, stated symbolically.[19]

If this is so, then what are the 'truths' that the cinema can convey, and what is the nature of the 'symbols' which convey them? This is the kind of question that has arrested my attention. Yet in striving to answer it, I recognize that there are difficulties. If in the finest art the third level is primary, it is also the least amenable to convincing analysis or critical exegesis, the least available to words. The atmosphere or 'feel' of a film often depends upon just *hints* of metaphorical complexities, seeming like a transference of resonance from unconscious to unconscious – the dimension in art that is very difficult to talk about but is its living core nevertheless. The more this level of imagery, as I have called it, submerges the other two, the more the work veers towards mystical non-communication except for the elect – indeed, the more it may slide towards insanity. Hence Fellini's films, which depend so much on the building up of a metaphorical resonance but in which there are so few explicit ideas, are more difficult to talk about than Godard's, which abound in literary quotations and scraps of ideas, all of them inviting a deliberately intellectual response.

*

All art is intrinsically subjective in its appeal. The cinema seems to offer as well, with its peculiar intensity of vicarious reality, the possibility of a fantasy world. If we are inclined towards objectivity in our discussion of the medium, there is no more effective research tool than an ever-changing classroom of attentive students against whose subjective experience of the cinema we can refine our own.

This book has been written over the last ten years. While I have tried to keep myself informed about the major writings on my chosen directors in both French and English, if this study contains an element of research it lies less with the written sources consulted than with the breadth of response offered, as I have said, by my different students throughout this period. Some of them, like Suzanne Budgen and John Ward,[20] have themselves found their way into print; but there have been many others the results of whose comments have directly or indirectly found their way into this book.

What *Battleship Potemkin* was for Ernest Lindgren and *Citizen Kane* was for Penelope Houston, *La Strada* was for me. It represented the moment in time at which I became *consciously* aware of the artistic and expressive potentialities of the cinema. That was the first film which, as kids say nowadays, actually 'blew my mind'.

2

The Reality of

SERGEI EISENSTEIN

What we want most, that cinema rarely gives us: some hint of the mere reality of the events it deals with.   *Robert Warshow, 1955*[1]

There can be no understanding of the European cinema unless we come to grips with Sergei Eisenstein. Yet to come to grips with Eisenstein could be a full-time job. One could spend one's life following up the master's footnotes, relating his many theoretical comments about art and life not only to his own work but to the intellectual climate of his time. One would need to know Russian and have a considerable command of subjects as diverse as Pavlovian psychology and the then budding study of linguistics. One should also be familiar with the Constructivist theories of sculpture and with Meyerhold's principles of 'biomechanics' in the theatre.

For Eisenstein lived in an immensely theoretical age. At a time when the politicians felt that they were remaking Russian society, the artists and intellectuals were excited by the possibility of refashioning the mind of man. It must have been an exhilarating time to be alive – if one were spared the executions, of course. It is certainly a time that we need to know more about, to understand better not only the historical situation that made the revolution possible but also the aesthetic climate that produced such powerful art. It was a time that produced what many people regarded as the first *real* examples of the cinema as art.

Film theory began there, or so it appears – not only from the prodigious writings of Eisenstein and his colleagues but also from the excitement they created in others. The films themselves seemed to invite an intellectual response. So different were they from anything seen before and so unfamiliar was the society they apparently depicted that they called forth a spate of theory to explain and to justify. As the term 'montage' was lifted from its humble French origins and sanctified into English, it acquired a mystique that for many people for many years was synonymous with the Art of the Film. Montage – the principles of editing – became the centre of film art, the justification of the respectability of the medium, its only defence (so the argument used to run) against the intrinsic limitations of photographic naturalism.

Complicated though these theories can be, and interwoven as they are with the intellectual history of Soviet Russia, at their centre lie two basic concepts. There is first of all the Hegelian idea of two opposing forces acting to produce a third force which is to a degree independent of the two original forces, offering a unique synthesis of the original thesis and antithesis. This concept forms the core of any discussion of montage. Secondly, there is the Pavlovian belief in the possibility of re-conditioning the reflexes of man to lead him in a desired direction, away from out-worn 'bourgeois' prejudices towards new, affirmative goals. Although this Pavlovian belief might strike us as encouraging the crudest forms of propaganda, it could also provide the basis for a fresh idealism. Perhaps with the right kind of conditioning one could change human nature. Perhaps at last the millennium might arrive.

The quality that most pervades Eisenstein's own writing is the quality of excitement. Inaccessible as much of it appears to us now, pedantic if you will, it is important to stress his intellectual curiosity, his promiscuous hunger for insights from all previous civilizations that might help to produce the revolutionary art of this new, exciting world. Like the revolution itself, the cinema was a fresh creation. 'All the roads of that period led towards one Rome', as Eisenstein has said.[2] It is only natural that he and his colleagues should think of film as being *the* art for the world they wished to create. 'For us, the cinema is the most important of the arts', Lenin had said,[3] thinking of its ability to reach the vast masses of illiterate Russia; while, for Eisenstein, its chief importance seemed to lie in its ability to synthesize all the arts that had preceded it.

In fact, one of the most appealing characteristics in the re-

Sergei Eisenstein

lentlessly intellectual Eisenstein is his slightly simple-minded way of seeing all former art as the imperfect manifestation of what the cinema could be. Flaubert becomes one of the originators of montage[4]; and Eisenstein reveals an acute eye for the cinematic potentialities of Dickens and Zola.[5] If all history with its exploitations and pointless class struggles led to Communism, then all art led to the cinema. So it was possible to believe in those days.

Yet, intellectually exciting though much of the theory is and illuminating as it may be for those able to read it closely,[6] it has two great disadvantages. First of all, in its abundance and obscurity it can have an intimidating effect. In our efforts to understand it, it can take us away from the films themselves – as, indeed, it did Eisenstein. There is a sense in which the writing can become more interesting than the films. It is certainly more indicative of the far-ranging curiosity and intellectual energy of Eisenstein the man. Yet this same quality leads to the second disadvantage: I cannot myself see how the writing *really illuminates* the films at all. So available have all the concepts been, especially as they have been filtered through to us by popularizers like Lindgren and Montagu,[7] that the theoretical framework traditionally offered as justification for the achievement of the films has in a sense kept us from looking closely at the films themselves. Personally, I have always felt a certain sadness at the spectacle of the prodigiously energetic Sergei Mikhailovic, reduced to an academic by the political climate of the time, as late as 1939 *still* writing articles on the achievement of *Potemkin*, explaining the intricacies of that film which he had conceived fifteen years before.[8]

From the writings themselves, one might get the impression that they held Eisenstein back from developing fully – except that in his films, when he was allowed to make them, he *did* develop. The films actually display a far greater diversity of approach than his own theory has encouraged us to recognize. The concepts, so ideological in their implications, have blinded us to what, in the films themselves, Eisenstein and his colleagues have actually done.

Part of the anger, I am sure, that Eisenstein detractors like

Robert Warshow and William Pechter have expressed comes from the gap that exists between what these Soviet films *claim* to be doing and what has actually been done.[9] If the films fail to give us 'some hint of the mere reality of the events they deal with', what do they give us instead? If we throw away for the moment all references to theoretical explanations and to political ideology, what are some of the characteristics we might detect in the films as they now exist? What are the elements that seem most striking in Eisenstein's silent films when placed alongside the work of his two great contemporaries, Pudovkin and Dovzhenko? What, finally, can we mean by montage?

*

'Montage structure', Marie Seton quotes Eisenstein as saying, 'unites the objective existence of phenomenon with the artist's subjective relation to it ...'[10] In *Film Form*, Eisenstein explains that '... montage is an idea that arises from the collision of independent shots – shots even opposite to one another'.[11] In different places, he says different things – offers different explanations. Just before his death he suggested that 'Montage ... was no more (and no less) than the fixing of an artist's perception of events around him'.[12] At different points in his career, Eisenstein also speculated about the origins of montage, this supposedly all-governing concept. Not only did he find it equally in Flaubert and in the principles of dialectical materialism, but in even more ancient sources as far apart as Japanese hieroglyphs and the tradition of the circus and music hall.[13]

All true and not true, simultaneously exciting and exasperating, these are the kind of comments that have teased us away from a consideration of the films themselves. What can we really *mean* by montage? How does it reveal itself in the films of that time? Is the term as applicable to Pudovkin and Dovzhenko as it is to Eisenstein? What are the characteristics that we might observe in their films?

To begin with, we observe not a single concept determining the style of the films but an immense diversity. If we take Pudovkin's *Mother* (1926) as perhaps the most conventional of the films of the time, how does that film work? For the most part, it seems to stress the traditional theatrical virtues. The film revolves around a compellingly realistic portrayal by Vera Baranovskaya of the Moscow Art Theatre, and in many of the sequences the style of the film itself seems subservient to the quality of this performance. The film really alternates between a conventional narrative style that serves to stress the personal elements in the story and a more rhetorically poetic style that seems intended either to project intense personal feeling or to underline the ideology.

The bringing in of the murdered father provides a scene of immense force and classic simplicity. The sequence begins with the mother on her knees before her icon and ends with her on her knees before the authority of the Tsar – two false gods that govern her life and make her actions false and obsequious. These framing shots are both long-shots, and their symmetry serves unambiguously to define the space in which the action takes place. As the sequence unfolds, every editorial or optical effect can be explained in terms of the mother's psychology. The close-up of the father's boots as he is carried through the door serves both to emphasize his deadness and to convey the mother's concentration on the inertia of his lifeless body. Similarly, the series of dissolves through the floorboards revealing the guns beneath provides our cue for her memory of her son hiding the guns.

This sequence provides a perfect example of a classically narrative style, a style that later became the text-book classicism of technically expert 'thriller' directors like Carol Reed and David Lean. We always know where we are. We know physically where the characters are in relation to one another and we understand what the issues are between them, what they are probably thinking. The editing is unobtrusive as it is subservient to the story. It directs our responses while leaving us unaware of it. Within this basic style, the cut-aways to action outside, to the military marching in on them, are still part of an unambiguous cross-cutting narrative tradition, consolidated ten years earlier by Griffith. Meanwhile, the dripping faucet that punctuates the mother's wake with an intensity that virtually creates its own sound is a perfect example of an image *intrinsic* to the scene itself yet full of poetic overtones, even to the point of suggesting the tears that she herself cannot shed.

Not all the film works in this way. The boy's imprisonment, which is perhaps best known because Pudovkin himself has talked about it,[14] is the most deliberately poetic and, I would suggest, the least successful for us today in terms of Pudovkin's intentions. There is really no place for simile in cinema.[15] When someone looks out of a window and then we see children playing, ducks waddling, and a brook running free, the cinema is so physical a medium that in such a context we must imagine that the boy himself is seeing these things, no matter what Pudovkin would have us believe. Yet from the way he has shot the sequence, we cannot know whether the scenes we see he sees as well or whether they are meant to convey, by a kind of literary analogy, the feeling of liberation within the boy's own mind.

The most rhetorical sequence occurs at the end. In fact, within the history of the cinema, it bears a striking resemblance to Resnais and works in somewhat the same way. Just as in *Hiroshima mon amour* we glimpse the iron balcony several times before we learn of its narrative significance (that it was the place from which the girl's German lover was shot), so in the final sequence in *Mother* we several times see the metal bridge intercut with scenes of the workers' procession before we see the horsemen charging across it on their way to trample the workers down. Perhaps for Russians familiar with the locale where the film was shot, there would be no confusion (for I believe Pudovkin was addicted to this kind of care). But for most non-Russians, these dramatic cut-aways create a sharp dislocation of space, making us lose our bearings in relation to the action while simultaneously increasing our sense of excitement.

For such a sequence to work, we must really be able to give ourselves over to the movement of the film, to its own inner rhythms. We must allow it to affect us like music. While I have argued that the more poetic, lyrical moments are really invalid cinematically because too directly borrowed from the devices of literature (a much less *physical* medium), such a rhetorical excitement as characterizes the end of this film seems of its essence. Not its *naturalistic* essence, but its essence nevertheless. Such an abstracted use of its materials serves to elevate the film above the personal level and imply a general statement, paving the way for the ideological conclusion that ends the film – a montage (in the Hollywood sense) of cities arising from the sacrifice of the slaughtered workers. And if the break-up of the ice on the surging river has chiefly a symbolic significance, it is also the culmination of all the water imagery that has run throughout the film.

Whether or not we accept the implied ideology is not in question here. The flourish of the ending can affect us directly and physically, like an orchestral *tutti* at the end of a symphony. Whether we are prepared to transfer our attention in this way will depend partly on who we are but also on whether up to this moment the film maker has created a sense of trust in us. Fellini's endings are dependent on much the same sense of trust, often implying a switch from the particular to the general, moving out from the defeat of one individual man towards an affirmation of life itself.

I would defend the end of *Storm over Asia* (1928) in much the same way. *Storm* also offers us a totally different general style to put alongside that limiting word, montage. The film is best known today, especially in North America, in its shortened form of about eighty minutes in length, the form used for the sound version that the Russians have made available. This is a pity, as the shortened version really leaves out many of the best things. What seems so splendid about *Storm* and so uncharacteristic of what we generally expect from the Soviet silent cinema is its great feeling for natural space and for the slow rhythms of life of the Mongol trapper, especially in the opening sequences – the sequences most cut in the shortened version. Somewhat like *Mother*, in *Storm over Asia* we are invited to share the Mongol's world very much from the Mongol's point of view, to admire his lonely skill as he tracks down his silver fox. These sequences hardly depend upon editing at all. There is as much composition within the frame as there is in any film by Orson Welles or Budd Boetticher.[16] There is also a feeling of great intimacy and appreciation of the Mongol's day-to-day life. These are the means, expressive naturalistic means, by which Pudovkin (I would argue) builds up our sense of trust.

The execution sequence towards the end of the film is also exceptional in much the same way. It is exceptional too in the way that all the characters are so personalized – the pipe-smoking British regular in charge of the shooting (one of the 'villains' in this film) as well as the Mongol himself. The sequence is full of what might strike us nowadays as Method mannerisms – little gestures and incidents that reveal Pudovkin as more the disciple of Stanislavsky than of any new school of dynamic montage. But these gestures work, nevertheless. The offer of the cigarette and the Mongol's smiling incomprehension both serve to individualize the drama, to make specific and human its ideological base.

Throughout this film, what seems most striking is this feeling for natural space, formalized just enough to make the action meaningful. As Pudovkin has put it:

Nature in the picture must never serve as a background to the scene being taken but must enter organically into its whole and become a part of its content.[17]

The execution sequence is shot largely in long-shot, with two solitary trees on the bleak horizon that parallel the two men. The execution over, the return of the British soldier is shot in such a way that one tree dominates the other – a simple, obvious device perhaps, but one that does have about it the feeling of intimacy, a feeling for the *actual* people and the *actual* space, the feeling that Pudovkin as an artist has observed and felt the characters he has created for us. They are not simply pawns within his ideological patterns as they frequently seem with Eisenstein. Such a sequence does not really work at all in terms of montage.

The rhetorical flourish at the end of the film may be considered comparatively crude. But not for me. With the switch of planes from the personal to what is virtually the metaphysical, I am carried totally along with the frenzied dash forward of Mongols uniting, not for any ideological reasons so much as for musical ones, like at the end of *Mother*. In spite of its narrative liberties, this closing sequence conveys the feeling that such a dynamic and masculine individual, were he to be infinitely multiplied, *would* be capable of cleansing this world of phoney pomp and bureaucratic cruelty. After all, it is no more miraculous than the sudden arrival of the cavalry that lends its elation to the end of so many hazardous moments in a John Ford film. If you think about it, the Pudovkin sequence is rather more nobly conceived; it is perhaps even more plausible.

It may be that Pudovkin's was a less adventurous talent than Eisenstein's. He certainly seemed less determined to break with the psychological traditions of the Stanislavsky theatre. It may also be that as an actual scientist (he was trained in physics and chemistry), he lacked Eisenstein's immense respect for the logic of science and felt less need to subject every aspect of life and art to its rigorous control. Speaking about *Mother*, he seems almost apologetic about the position he adopted:

In that picture, I first of all tried to keep as far away as I could from Eisenstein and from much that Kuleshov had taught me. I did not see how it was possible for me to limit myself, with my organic need for inner emotions, to the dry form that Kuleshov preached ... I had a strong instinctive inclination for living people whom I wanted to photograph and whose soul I wanted to fathom, just as Eisenstein had fathomed the soul of his Battleship Potemkin.[18]

Yet it is really only in *Mother* and in *Storm over Asia* that this 'instinctive inclination for living people' so beautifully expresses itself. *The End of St Petersburg* (1927) is much closer to the Kuleshov style, especially in the 'dialectical' cross-cutting between the battlefield and stock exchange. However, it is not my wish here to offer a detailed discussion of the work of Pudovkin or even to imply too directly a value judgement about his work in relation to Eisenstein's. What I am primarily concerned with is the variety of style within the Soviet silent cinema, a variety that has tended to be oversimplified when the films have been discussed in terms of montage.[19]

Even in terms of montage, however, there is still immense variety. One of the most extraordinary examples of what we might call pure montage is found in the opening sequence of Dovzhenko's *Earth* (1930). Many commentators have discussed the lyrical aspects of Dovzhenko's work, stressing his Ukrainian origins. Indeed, this element is striking and has remained so, I would argue, in his sound and colour films of the 1940s and 50s, even in those executed by his wife. Naïve though his pantheism may be, it allows Dovzhenko to create moments of intense physical beauty and to give as well the feeling of continuity among the generations of peasants that have worked the land.

This feeling of continuity is perhaps most obvious in the opening of *Earth*. There is also a certain splendour in the statuesque impassivity of the peasants, 'at once appealing and frightening in their rigidity and incomprehension', as Robert Warshow has put it.[20] In fact, Warshow is good at pointing out the timeless quality of the film, its great sense of space and of the passivity of the people. But what has always struck me most about it is the montage structure of this opening sequence. After the opening long-shot of the sky and the grain, held for what seems to be an interminable length of time, the sequence of the old man dying works entirely in single close-ups. The complete reverse of *Mother* in this, it has no sense of natural space at all. There is not so much as a two-shot to give us a clue as to where the characters are standing in relation to one another. For its sense of continuity, the sequence depends entirely on the direction of the characters' eyes.

The result of such a technique is the total dismemberment of space – curious in a film that in other ways gives us such a strong sense of the characters' relationship to the land. Perhaps the conditions of shooting imposed this technique on Dovzhenko, forcing him to shoot little bits, one at a time; perhaps it was an attempt to implement some private theory of his own. He has in fact spoken of his desire to simplify his cinematic language.[21] But whatever the reason, the results are astonishing, simultaneously very physical and personal in all the close-ups of the Ukrainian faces, yet totally abstract in the way the shots are joined together. This technique intensifies the film's lyrical air at the same time as it depersonalizes it, implying a generalized statement about *all* peasants and their relationship to the land. The nearest equivalent in Eisenstein would be some sections of *The Old and the New*, especially the much-discussed cream-separator sequence; but even this works in quite a different way. With the theatrical naturalism of Pudovkin on the one hand and this atomized humanism of Dovzhenko on the other, what generalizations might we make about Soviet film style that could provide a foil for the films of Sergei Eisenstein? Of course, there are none. Nor are there many that we can make about Eisenstein.

*

There has always been more diversity within the films of Sergei Eisenstein than we have been encouraged to recognize. Indeed, there is immense diversity within each single film. Talking about *October*, Jean Mitry has suggested a distinction between what we might call in English *intrinsic* and *extrinsic* imagery.[22] As early as *Strike* (1924), this distinction could be made. From the outset in Eisenstein, there is a contrast between imagery apparently discovered in the natural landscape and imagery that is imposed from outside by the point-making faculty of the mind. In *Strike*, the sequence of the picnic, with the longshot of the workers, arm-in-arm, dissolving slowly through the close-up of an accordion playing, is a most lyrical evocation of the mood of the moment and, like the dripping faucet in *Mother*, creates a sense of its own sound. On the other hand, the slaughter of the workers intercut with the slaughter of a bull is of quite a different order. Like Pudovkin's spring-joyous lyricism, the bull would imply a kind of simile. Though this device *can* have the shock effect that Eisenstein intended, I would argue that it is a much cruder type of effect.

By the end of *Strike*, there are other effects as well. Again like *Mother*, there is the formal symmetry achieved by the child saved from the hooves of the horses before the riot begins which is answered by the child dropped gratuitously from the top of the tenement buildings. In fact, the metaphoric potentiality of the tenement buildings provides what is really one of the strongest sequences in this many-styled film. As the horsemen gallop over the metal passageways cutting the workers down, one really gets the sense of 'the workers joined together by bonds of steel'.[23] The sense of violence here is organic to the location in which it is set, is *intrinsic* to it, and therefore has a dramatic unity of its own. We think more of the workers and of the political implications, of the 'mere reality' of the event itself, than we do of the artistic mind that has structured it for us.

Although *Strike* is obviously strong enough to contain it, the bull simile is of a different order. For its effect, it depends upon the mental connection that we must make between the two separate shots. In this way, it makes us more aware of the mind of the artist than of the reality of the event. Not that such an effect is in itself invalid – or else we would have to throw out of the contemporary cinematic canon all of Resnais and most of Godard! But it does ask for a more intellectual response. This is obviously what Charles Barr is complaining about when he writes:

A montage link ... reminds one of the children's puzzle which consists of a series of numbered dots: when they are joined together correctly, the outline of an animal appears. We participate in solving these, but only in a mechanical way, and there is only one correct solution.[24]

The complaint against it finally is less artistic than moral (if one can make such a division): it puts the spectator too much at the mercy of the artist. It imposes upon us the artist's ordering of reality without giving us a sense at the same time that the reality depicted has a life of its own.

Behind these comments, of course, is a Bazin-cum-Kracauer view of the cinema. The Nature of Film, it does seem to me, is concerned as much with the creation in photographic terms of natural space and movement, of a reality to a degree independent of the artistic process, as it is with any principles of structural montage. The editing process is the most intellectual part of film-making, the part least dependent on external reality. It is thus the part over which the film-maker has the most immediate control. It is when we feel a film-maker is using his editorial authority to underline a moral that runs contrary to the one that we ourselves might like to derive from the same material, it is when we feel we are being got at in this way that we might want to complain, with Robert Warshow, about the 'triumph of art over humanity'.[25] Depressed by the ideological insistences of a season of Soviet films, Warshow went on to exclaim: '... how utterly vulgar art and belief can be, sometimes, when measured against the purity of a real event'.[26] When we are forced to feel that something we value highly is being falsified by the insistences of a particular artist, we might make this kind of complaint. There is no better example of this kind of imposed oversimplification than in *October* (1927) and – to a degree – in *The Old and the New* (1929).

The complaints against these films are so well worn that I hesitate to make them all again. Yet distinctions can be made. Writing about the bridge-raising sequence in *October*, William Pechter asks:

To what extent do such sequences enlarge and illuminate the human experience? Rather, to what extent do they simplify and diminish such meaning?[27]

We can see what he means. The very authority of such a sequence counts against it if viewed from a social-realist point of view. The slow acceleration of its own internal rhythm, a rhythm that seems independent of the movement of the characters; the cold sensuality of the girl's hair dragging over the lip of the raising bridge, a sensuality intensified by the numerous angles from which it is shot and by the cuttings back in time; the beautiful cut-aways of dappled light on the undercarriage of the bridge alternating with the slow upward movement of the entire structure, a movement intensified for us by that solitary dangling horse – all these effects create their own magnificence that seems primarily to be making an aesthetic appeal. We think much less of the event itself than of the mind of the man that has structured it for us.

To this extent, the very splendour of such a sequence distracts us from the 'purity' of the 'real event'. Yet the issue isn't simple. George Huaco has drawn our attention to 'the socially detached, ivory-tower quality of the expressive-realist film'.[28] Eisenstein and his colleagues were less concerned with the political actualities of the contemporary 20s than with the historical struggles of 1905. They were obviously concerned to create mythological forms. Whether consciously or not, the Soviet film-makers went to the 1905 period with the same regularity as American Western directors go to that period in American history just after the Civil War. In both cases, there seems to be a desire to set their events just far enough back in time for the oversimplifications of historical fact to appear more plausible. This is frequently the way myths are made. In one sense, there is not much 'mere reality' in Westerns either, though Warshow didn't complain.[29] Still, there are differences.

In *October*, Eisenstein's most directly political film, what seems offensive to us now is not so much the formalism of the bridge-raising sequence as the crudity with which assumed political points are made. The Kerensky-mounting-the-stairs sequence is obviously not much concerned with the actual Kerensky. The sequence asks for a playful response. It is, in this way, satirical. Yet it is not subtle satire. It is the kind of satire that appeals basically to a sense of smugness, that invites us to think that *they* are in the wrong. Stupidity, pretentiousness, incapacity in public and private life become the failings of *other* people. We ourselves are exempt.

It is this *moral* falsity rather than the political oversimplifications that I find so offensive, that makes so much of this film unsatisfactory as a fully adult work of art. In spite of gross historical inaccuracies, in the most distinguished Westerns there is a kind of moral truth, an insight into the failed dreams of the American nation. Oddly enough, there is often a dialectical structure in the most interesting of these American films that allows the film-makers both to enact this dream and to criticize it, sometimes making for moral confusion but often for moral complexity as well. In John Ford's *Fort Apache*, for example, one of the most interesting Westerns from this point of view, the film allows us both to recognize the destructive limitations of Colonel Thursday as a man *and* to feel that he might have been effective as a legend.

Sergei Eisenstein

There is never this kind of complexity in Soviet films, certainly not in Eisenstein. There are some hints of it in *Earth*. For all its statuesque, lyrical quality, in the death of Vassili there is a sense that the collectivization of agriculture met with some resistance. There was opposition, suffering, pain. This touch of realism lends historical force to the rest of Dovzhenko's film. It encourages us to believe in him, to have faith in what he is doing. It helps to ballast the more lyrical moments, just as the naked anguish of Vassili's betrothed (in the uncut print of the film) provides an astonishing note of psychological realism through the directly physical nature of her grief.

We must look in vain for such ordinary touches in Eisenstein, for any sense of a truly human struggle. In contrast with *Earth* where we see shots of the fences being ploughed away, thus creating the tension to come, in *The Old and the New* we have a totally unmanned, abstract series of dissolves as the fences separating the kulaks' land magically disappear or reappear, according to the point-making needs of the film. Similarly, a moment of potential human illumination in the film, the scything contest between Jarov and the old man, is sacrificed to the slogan as the mowing-and-turning machine outdistances them both. 'Hurray for the Machine!' the title cries out; and we have a close-up of the competitors, shaking hands.

If it works at all, this sequence too works on a rather abstract level. We are invited to admire the cleverness with which Eisenstein does things, establishes equivalences between the cutting action of a grasshopper's teeth and that of a mowing machine. Whatever our ultimate evaluation of such a set-piece may be, it draws attention to what the film-maker is doing with his material more than to the material itself. The 'reality' depicted becomes more the artistic process within Eisenstein's own mind.

The real limitation in much of Eisenstein's silent films is not so much his political slogan-flinging as the absence of any probing interest in the events themselves. Prodigiously intelligent though he was, and omnivorously curious about all walks of life, there is little evidence in his films that he was attentively curious about the events his films deal with. For all his excitement about the photogenic potentiality of machines in motion, he didn't seem very interested in how a machine actually works, in what it is intended to do.

A rather touching moment in *The Old and the New* occurs towards the end of the film. For the sake of the cause, the collectivization of agriculture, Martha is prepared to sacrifice her peasant dignity and offer bits of her skirt to repair the broken tractor. It is a pleasing moment in the film, with the beautiful Martha overcoming her shyness – until we ask ourselves: what could possibly be wrong with a tractor that could be repaired with a skirt? Possibly there is an answer, but I think my point remains.

In that other set-piece from *The Old and the New*, the cream-separator sequence, there is a similar problem. 'It thickens, it thickens!' Eisenstein's titles have the peasants exclaim. But if my own boyhood farming memories serve me correctly, nothing 'thickens' in a cream-separator. It doesn't make butter: it simply separates the cream from the milk. Yet Eisenstein doesn't care about this. Nor does he care about how the peasants might really have responded. Nor does he care about how the natural light, observable in the group shots, would fall upon their faces for the single close-ups. He lights each one for its own sculptural potentiality. The actual people, the actual events, don't seem to interest him. What does then?

At times, in these early films, it would seem to be his own ideas about film form that engaged him most deeply, his ability to build up structures out of scraps of real events. He is supremely *the* intellectual director. Life itself seems to engage him less than the ideas it prompts in his mind. He may have been one of those people for whom their own thoughts provide their strongest emotions. There is certainly support for this speculation to be found in his work.

Marie Seton has suggested that Eisenstein's was actually a split sensibility. This has been resented by many Eisenstein admirers as it might seem to undermine the intellectual validity of what he achieved, making his artistic accomplishments subservient to his personal neuroses. Yet from the films themselves, there is a lot to support her point of view. Back to the Kerensky sequence in *October*: there does seem to be a contradiction between the puerile way that Kerensky is treated, the easy gags about his laurel crown and then the peacock, and the visual splendour of the sequence itself. The light reflecting within the baroque magnificence of the Winter Palace thrills the eye while the Kerensky figure, always marching yet staying in one place, provides a centre of attention within this luminous structure. Like so much of Eisenstein's silent films, the sequence works best as a kind of abstract art. Like the raising of the bridges, this sequence achieves a kind of sublimity of its own, deflecting attention from the event it is dealing with towards a contemplation of its own artistic achievement. It is in this sense grandiloquent, capable certainly of creating an aesthetic thrill and sense of awe; but it is *not* the kind of art that would encourage us to think intelligently and precisely about the reality of the time. It is in this sense *anti*-intellectual – a grotesque paradox within the work of a man who is the most intellectual film-maker the world has ever seen.

Like much of his writing, these effects in Eisenstein tend to numb the mind. They encourage a generalized, unthinking response to the reality supposedly at their centre, and *this*, I feel, is the great failing of these films. I sometimes think that my objections are not that different from Stalin's or Shumyatsky's. This gives me pause. Yet so much of *Strike* and of *October* and of *The Old and the New* seems to involve the creation of compelling patterns of line and light around a subject matter that has itself been imperfectly understood.

For all his prodigious interest in film form and his belief in the dialectical basis of art, he frequently failed to find a valid dialectical structure that might have genuinely served 'to make the final ideological conclusion perceptible'.[30] *The Old and the New* is full of moments of great charm and, I suppose, of immense hilarity. We may possibly be at fault in taking it all so seriously. Nevertheless, only in *Battleship Potemkin* (1925) did he succeed in finding images that would enable him to build up a dramatic structure in the best Hegelian tradition that might help us feel *and* understand the validity of the Communist position.

The greatest art can win us over to points of view in themselves repellent to us. Because of its opposing tenderness and intimacy of characterization, *Bonnie and Clyde* succeeds in apparently validating the violence of their lives. Eisenstein's failure to do this might be taken as an indication of his limited trust in the reality of the events. One of the limitations (one could argue) of so much early Soviet cinema is not that it is so propagandistic but that it is too unintelligently so to persuade us sufficiently. If the film-makers had believed more in the validity of the events they dealt with, they might have handled them differently than they did. This certainly seems true of Eisenstein.

If *Battleship Potemkin* is, then, the most accomplished of Eisenstein's early work, it is not just for the external, formal reasons that Eisenstein and others have so often talked about. It is not just its five-act structure with each act pivoting around a focal moment as the whole film pivots round the slaughter on the steps.[31] It is not just these classical and (in one sense) unimportant matters. In spite of the caricatured portraits of the officers on the ship, of Eisenstein's lack of interest in them as men, the film succeeds because, in the opposition of the battleship and the town, it creates for us an imagistic structure that can move us in different ways. In the heightened emotions it conveys, it might even be giving us some sense of how it *felt* to be there at the time. The Richelieu Steps, the misty harbour, the ship itself, all possess a reality too well defined and too innately physical for Eisenstein's constructivist impulses to be able to destroy it.

Eisenstein has explained how they had to work at great speed.[32] Perhaps this was an advantage for him, as it was to be in a less personal way with *Alexander Nevsky*. As Eisenstein identified himself with Leonardo da Vinci, we might adduce Freud's essay on Leonardo as a possible clarification of at least an aspect of Eisenstein.[33] Certainly, like Leonardo, Eisenstein was often distracted from his own creative activities in the pursuit of a tangential theoretical concern. He was himself aware of this.

I have a strictly academical approach to all I do. I make use of all available scientific data; I discuss with myself problems of programme and principle; I make calculations and draw inferences ... I stop writing the scenario and instead plunge into research work, filling pages and pages with it. I don't know which is more useful but abandoning creative work for scientific analysis is what I am often guilty of. Very often I settle a particular problem of principle only to lose all interest in its practical application.[34]

Evidently the filming of *Potemkin* wouldn't allow this, though the enforced professorial role later on in his career gave him the sad opportunity of theorizing about *Potemkin* for the rest of his life.

In *Battleship Potemkin*, the unifying images of the huge ship and guns are dramatically appropriate in their constant suggestion of violence and yet, like the river image in *Mother*, they seem symbolic of conflicts to come. In contrast to these masculine, assertive images constantly dominating the screen, are the gentler images of yawls in Part IV with the wind-full freedom of their billowing sails. In their surge forward out from the shore to the cruiser, in their offer of fresh food, and in the fullness of their approval, they might convey to us the feeling of achieved peace and acceptance, of freedom and joy. Unlike the multiple view-points of the dead girl's hair dragging over the lip of the rising bridge in *October*, a device that lends a distracting aestheticism to the contemplation of a human horror, the multiple lowering of the sails of the yawls increases the feeling of happiness by stretching that sensual moment in time.

In this sequence, the lyrical feeling is so intense that we are probably undisturbed by the more distant aspects of continuity – the shifts in the strength of the wind, the colour of the sky, the frequent dislocation of our sense of direction. Yet unlike *Earth*, continuity problems are rendered secondary by the sweep forward of the yawls. In this sequence, what we might feel as an over-indulgence in aesthetic effect actually contributes to the sense of celebration, creating in its way a cinematic ecstasy.

Splendid though this basic imagistic structure is in *Potemkin*, the film is not without its difficulties. Though its sense of physical reality is one of its strongest features, unlike Pudovkin,

Eisenstein is not that interested in employing his art rigorously to define a sense of space. It is not his method to organize his marching forces in such a way that their bulk and momentum might *imply* a symbolic abstraction concerning the consolidation of the masses. As he does with his sequence of three lions, Eisenstein employs his crowds *directly to make* this symbolic point.

We might be struck by the serpentining diagonal of the procession along the mole and think forward to that similar procession that ends the first part of *Ivan the Terrible*. Indeed, it *is* splendid, as long as we don't ask ourselves where these crowds are coming from. For they must be coming up out of the sea! Similarly, in Part III of *Potemkin*, the crowds marching along bridges over intersecting streets, themselves filled with crowds marching in a different direction: workers in all directions not really conveying an actual event but a symbolic one concerning the future march of history. Such a sequence contains more geometry than common sense.

There is enough actual physical reality, however, in *Battleship Potemkin* for me personally to find these moments splendid – like the end of *Storm over Asia*, rhetorical episodes that punctuate the main event. But this tendency towards symbolic insistence is the difficult one with Eisenstein throughout his silent days; and his geometric concerns often succeeded in overbalancing our sense of the reality itself.

*

From the troubling diversity of the films themselves, what seems to have been the reality of Sergei Eisenstein's silent films? Basically, it seems like a kind of abstraction, an excitement inseparable from a conscious delight in the artistic process itself. This is perhaps why art students find these early films more exciting than literary students. Literary students have a built-in bias towards social realism and psychological credibility, while few of the films really work in this way. These early Soviet films are more abstract than they at one time seemed. Even when we free ourselves from the obscurities of the theory that has tended to set up distracting expectations, we are still confronted in the films with enormous theoretical considerations, especially in Eisenstein.

Whatever the formal complexities of some of the films of Pudovkin and Dovzhenko, it is still relatively easy to locate in their work a human centre to which we can respond. It is not hard to discover something universal in their best work that we can relate to directly, even though we are of a foreign culture and foreign time and perhaps of a different political persuasion. Except for *Potemkin*, this is not so with Eisenstein. His early films really give us so little of himself, reveal so little about the things in life that actually interested him. In a sense he doesn't seem to have been interested in anything he shot at all. In this way, his films become collages, appropriating incidents and objects less for their own sake than for the formal role they can play within the total pattern of his design.

As a film-maker, John Ford, we know from his work, was interested in the vast American desert and the struggles to found a new civilization there; as a writer, Maxim Gorky, again and again, was concerned with the down-and-out, with the rejects from a self-centred bourgeois world; throughout his life, Jean Renoir struggled to believe in the purifying powers of simple friendship. Eisenstein? He didn't seem to be interested in life at all as most of us might think of it. He was interested in art, art as an activity that for him was a form of life, that might possibly have provided an escape from his personal problems. Yet speculations of this kind are not really invited by the early films of Eisenstein. Unlike Renoir, he gives us so few clues within the films themselves. There is simply this formalized surface with very little evidence of any personal pressures beneath.

Whether for personal or ideological reasons or for a mixture of both, Eisenstein obviously mistrusted unconditioned human emotions. Like much of the thinking about him in his day, he wished to reduce experience to the intellectual patterns of his mind. Again like Leonardo (and perhaps for similar reasons),[35] he felt that by a superhuman intellectual effort he could make himself anew and in the process discover the rules for the synthesis necessary to establish cinema as the culmination of all the arts. This ambition, in itself a kind of megalomania, has surely as many personal as ideological roots, even though it is difficult to say what they are. Yet it is not until his sound films that a subliminal thematic centre begins to reveal itself.

After the defeat of his American projects and the Mexican fiasco and the subsequent loss of favour at home, there creeps into Eisenstein's work the feeling of the desperate loneliness of the man who must stand alone. To a degree, this was present in *Potemkin*, in the celebration of the courage of the men who took up arms against the expectations of the officers in charge of them, who seized control to overthrow the old order and bring about the new. In fact, in the last section of *Potemkin*, I have always been struck by the scenes of disorder that seem to prevail. These scenes don't make much sense in terms of the ideology of the film but they form a part of its atmosphere nevertheless.[36] There is an attempt to build up tension as to whether the rest of the fleet will join them or fire on them; but as with the tractor and cream-separator in *The Old and the New*, in all this glistening machinery there is not much sense of what purpose it has been designed to serve. The funnels of the ship and its huge guns continually dwarf the men as if they were not fully in control.

After the achieved victory, there is a tremendous sense of release. 'Full Speed Ahead!' exclaims the final title. Yet, where to? Obviously to an abstraction – the glorious future. The final close shot of the giant prow plunging into the screen gives us a sense of force and strength in an impersonal way but no sense of direction. Forward, of course; but where to? Obviously, Eisenstein doesn't know. Unlike *Storm over Asia*, there is no sense of a mighty personal force that could sweep away the old order. In *Potemkin*, it is mechanical – the ship itself, emphasized by the fact that, after the death of Vakulinchuck, there is no other leader comparably personalized to give us the feeling of someone else carrying on, of a man's individual mind making decisions. History seems in charge, working out its dialectical processes. But even if we are Marxists, we know that it is not as simple as that.

The human centre of *Potemkin* seems to lie in the glory

granted to the man – or group – that can stand on its own, as indeed, in the person of Martha, it was the theme of what we now have of *The Old and the New*. It is difficult to draw conclusions from the fragments of the Mexican footage; and much as I admire Marie Seton's assemblage, one cannot with confidence deduce too much from it. Yet central to both the Sol Lesser version and to Marie Seton's is the *defeat* of the man who stands alone, who chooses to love against the wishes of his superiors. These fragments might help to pave the way for the extension of this theme in the sound films over which Eisenstein had a more direct control: the great and lonely burden of the man who must bring about a change in history, who must stand by himself against the accepted order.

*

At what point Eisenstein became more interested in composition within the shot than in the juxtaposition of shots according to the varied principles of montage is difficult to say. Marie Seton has suggested that Eisenstein's Mexican trip changed many things in his life, including his attitude towards filming.[37] But Eisenstein had always been as concerned with structural photography as with the principles of editing: he simply talked about them less. His essay 'Film Form: New Problems', written in 1935, seems partly a recantation of the intellectual cinema he once so strongly believed in. He seems to be renouncing the purely conceptual linking of shots such as we find in the gods sequence in *October* or to a degree in the cream-separator sequence in *The Old and the New*.[38] Yet the essay is more apologetic than affirmative. Meanwhile, as early as 1929 in *The Old and the New* Eisenstein had achieved some striking examples of spatial depth within the frame – never like *Storm over Asia*, a sense of natural space (for with Eisenstein the element of design always predominates); yet through his cunning use of serpentining diagonals Eisenstein was able to create a sense of distance that many current masters of the panoramic screen could well envy.

As it has come down to us (preferably in Marie Seton's version called *Time in the Sun*), the most striking quality about the

Mexican footage is the contrast between the passionate, physically exuberant, intensely beautiful quality of the Mexican people and Eisenstein's artistic impulse to restrain this by geometry. There is a tension established between the formal elements in the film and the observable subject matter. But as with *Potemkin*, this subject matter is strong enough to survive Eisenstein's intentions. Besides which, in his fondness for triangular patterns and circular forms, Eisenstein drew inspiration from Mexico itself, from its ancient customs and architecture. If this constant formalizing tendency *does* possess deep psychological roots in Eisenstein's own life, paralleling his own constant repressive tendencies,[39] in this particular film, the formal/physical antithesis parallels the death/life antithesis that forms such a large part of the Mexican culture. Like the guns/yawls antithesis in *Potemkin*, the constant tension between the opposing elements in the Mexican footage creates a rich experience, appealing simultaneously to the mind and to the senses.

After the Mexican checkmate and the even greater defeat of the *Bezhin Meadow* project,[40] Eisenstein didn't work again in film until he set up *Alexander Nevsky* in 1938. *Nevsky*, however, was co-scripted by Pyotr Pavlenko and co-directed by Dmitri Vassiliev. Jay Leyda has underlined the paradox concerning this film. Many critics still consider it Eisenstein's finest work after *Potemkin*, and it was *Nevsky* that finally won for Eisenstein the Order of Lenin. Yet as Leyda has explained:

Of his six completed films, *Nevsky* is, in its ideas, the most superficial and the least personal of his work ... It is also the least directly executed of his films ...[41]

It has a kind of grandeur, of course, and moments of splendour. It works best as a filmic cantata, with all the oversimplifications that one might expect in such a work. Buslai, the oaf, in his courtship of Olga, the heroic peasant girl, might be said to provide a humanizing comic contrast to the dignity of Nevsky himself (and might indeed spring from local Russian traditions). But the film contains nothing, I would argue, that isn't better done in *Ivan the Terrible* (1944–6), and done there with more feeling.

There seems a kind of emptiness at the centre of this film. It fails to sustain its epic tone at crucial moments. Even the much applauded Battle on the Ice, urged on by Prokofiev's insistent music, is reduced to trombone smears as the Germans sink through the artificial ice. It seems a boy's conception of how a battle might be fought. This boy's approach is reconfirmed by Buslai's peasant prowess as, with exuberant glee, he fells his knights in armour with no more weapons than a long stick and a wooden pail. Good for a giggle, perhaps, like bits of *The Old and the New*: but hardly defensible as an example of adult art.

The *Ivans* are different. I regret immensely that the exterior sequences which were to form a large section of Part III were never completed. Had they been so, they might have provided a contrasting framework for the claustrophobic interiors of (especially) Part II. They might have emphasized the film's more public, political level. For in spite of cautions to the contrary, in spite of the multi-cultural source of much of the material that went into *Ivan*,[42] it is impossible not to see at least the second part of *Ivan the Terrible* as a deeply personal film. It seems a kind of lyrical lament which provides us with the most personal statement on film that Eisenstein ever achieved.

As the film exists for us now, the chief unifying factor within the episodic structure of *Ivan the Terrible* is the architecture. Especially in Part II, the action seems bound together by vaulted ceilings and restricted space.[43] While Part I is divided up into seven distinct narrative sections,[44] Part II, except for the Polish court sequence that opens it, is more unified in action. Throughout both parts, there is really a greater unity of mood than is at first apparent. If one thinks in terms of mood and atmosphere rather than in terms of narrative sections, there are really three recurring modes that might be distinguished.

To begin with there is the directly ceremonial. The coronation, the wedding, the extreme unction, and the death of Anastasia in Part I; the Nebuchadnezzar and (in a more pagan tone) the coloured feast sequences in Part II – the recurrence of this type of ceremonial sequence gives the film the atmosphere of a church service, of a kind of High Mass, creating a mood of grandeur and awe. Secondly, there are the declamatory sequences, the ones that generally serve to advance the action but which often take the form of Ivan raging at anyone who might be within earshot about his own ambition and power. He would seem to be trying to frighten them all into a kind of reluctant belief. Thirdly, there are the quieter, often non-verbal sequences which are more reflective and introspective – generally a world of moving shadows and overpowering threats and worries. Figures crouch beneath arches or hide behind pillars, providing the film with a slow crescendo of paranoia which gradually builds up an atmosphere (especially in Part II) of a man most miserably and most unalterably alone, forced into making decisions greater than he can bear.

These three basic modes are confirmed and interrelated, of course, by the authority of Prokofiev's music. If Part III had been completed, much of it would have combined with the Kazan sequence in Part I to create a fourth mode of action and achievement which might have given the whole film a more courageous atmosphere. But as the film now exists, while the ceremonial and declamatory dominate Part I, the paranoiac begins to take over towards the end of this section and becomes the dominant mode of Part II, giving Part II a greater sense of unity and a more intimate human concern.

*

Though immensely exciting as graphic art, the entire film of *Ivan the Terrible* can scarcely begin to engage us on a human level until we look beneath its surface elements. From this point of view, the declamatory elements are the least satisfactory. They are generally destructive of any interest that we might have in the characters. In the assertion of their rhetoric, they tend to destroy our involvement in the drama that *does* exist beneath the stylized ritual of this film. When Ivan rails at the Boyars from his (unexplained) death-bed in Part I or when he makes his maniacal entrance into the Nebuchadnezzar sequence in Part II, it is difficult to see in these self-dramatizing declamations much evidence of Ivan the man. It is easier to see them as the outward manifestation of a kind of megalomania such as we can detect elsewhere in the scope and ambition of Eisenstein's own work.

The crucial point about these sequences, however, is that they bear a rhetorical relationship to the rest of the drama. They allow Ivan to *assert* his importance, his strength, or his rage, instead of *showing* him in action. In view of the psychological inwardness of many of the sequences elsewhere in the film, these declamatory passages might also strike us as the compensational ravings of a man *without* real authority, uncertain of himself and afraid – the ravings of an angry boy. It is difficult to relate them to any realistic picture of a truly terrible Tsar. Once again, it might seem that Eisenstein doesn't really understand this aspect of his portrait any more than he understood the workings of a tractor or a cream-separator. Like the eye rolling wickedness of Euphrosinia, especially in Part I, it is a boy's notion of evil – more like the bad stepmother in *Snow White* than any actual human villain. It springs, of course, from Eisenstein's interest in the stylizations of Kabuki, but this in turn might spring from his desire to find an art-form sufficiently stylized to disguise his own feelings. One cannot really know.

Similarly, the ceremonial sequences deflect our concentration away from the personal towards a kind of abstract awe in the face of the sublime. Marie Seton tells us that Eisenstein planned the battle sequences in *Alexander Nevsky* with Milton's *Paradise Lost* open before him.[45] One can understand the attraction. Like so much of Milton, these ceremonial passages strive towards a kind of sublimity. They achieve a grandiloquence that, while possibly moving us in a generalized way, makes it impossible to attend in detail to anything being said or done. Not that this in itself is wrong. Indeed, if these films work for us, they probably work most powerfully on this level, affecting us like a kind of mass. Processions and ceremonies and incantations abound which we cannot take seriously, to which we cannot intimately attend, which in detail we cannot understand.

Although this is certainly not a contemporary emotion, in these sequences the film is sublime. It is carried by the decor, by the music, by the stylized ritual of movement and design. Our

interest both in character and in the dramatic intrigue is super-
seded by this generalized sense of awe, of something splendid
happening beyond the reach of 'mere reality'. Whether we like
it or not, it is marvellously done. It is almost strong enough to
carry the film.

Yet finally, the asserted centre of interest in the film – the
dramatic intrigue – is too unreal to hold us. What are these
Boyars to us or we to the Boyars? Worse than that, we are not
even clear what they are to Ivan. They are no more real than
the fat cigar-smoking capitalists in *Strike*. They are, of course,
the direct descendants of these. They become more compelling
dramatically when they join with the oppressiveness of the interiors and the pervasive world of shadows to become extensions of Ivan's unshakeable dread, a dread that he cannot face
on the personal level. Ivan's fluctuations between his assertions
of power and his confessions of need are demonstrably neurotic. They make less sense as a dramatization of a character than
as a concealed (and no doubt unconscious) autobiography.

The whole of Part II is a desperate appeal for friendship, for a
collective confirmation of what Ivan takes to be his inescapable
role. This appeal begins towards the end of Part I, in one of its
most introspective sequences. In the huge shadows projected on
the wall, both of Ivan himself and of his skeleton of a globe,
there is a sense of insubstantial reality and empty conquests,
while Ivan expresses his need for outside help. 'Send this to
England,' Ivan requests of his huge chess-board, throwing back
his head in stretched despair once the courtiers have left him.
Then he goes to Anastasia in her bed. 'You look worried, Tsar,'
she says. 'I am all alone,' he complains, his head on her breast.
'No one can be trusted.' Then follows the news both of the
defeat of Basmanov and of the treachery of Kurbsky. After that
occurs the poisoning of Anastasia.

'Am I right in the hard struggle that is mine?' he asks the air,
as he pulls himself up from the floor by her coffin. Implausible
though some of these actions are in terms of the film's dramatic
structure, we can nevertheless be extremely moved by such a
sequence for the personal emotions it contains, emotions largely
of loneliness and uncertainty. More than anywhere else in

Eisenstein, in this sequence there is undeniable evidence of strong human feelings breaking through the surface of the film.

Similarly, in Part II, at the opening of the film when he is attempting to persuade Philip, his one remaining friend, to stay with him, he complains: 'I lack but friendship ... a breast on which to lay my head.' A moment later he attempts to right himself by adding: 'For myself, I fear not. Only for the cause.' As if it were the cause that lacked a breast on which to lay its head! When Philip finally leaves him, we see Ivan slouched again in his throne, abject, alone, and afraid.

Such dramatic *non-sequiturs* abound in the film, especially in Part II. Yet far from being absurd, they can be deeply moving in a quite conventional way yet in a way without precedent in Eisenstein. They give us the sense of a man unable to recognize himself for what he really is, unable to accept his own fear, whether this fear be the fictionalized Ivan's or unconsciously Eisenstein's. Certainly in Part II, this uneasy fluctuation between empty assertion and self-pitying confession to whoever happens to be about appears to have been the element that most engaged Eisenstein. Along with the ceremonial, which from this point of view might seem to give the more uncertain human element the dignity of universality, this recurring pathos is the quality that gives Part II its feeling of greater intimacy.

Certain images, too, enforce this feeling of real involvement, images more intimate than anything else in Eisenstein. There is the shot of the child Ivan's foot straining down for the bottom rung on the throne that is still too big for him; and there is the moment when Ivan's anguished hands caress the fur coverlet on Anastasia's bed as he realizes that she has been poisoned and that he himself has given her the poisoned cup.

Finally, in Part II, there is the repeated emphasis given to the fact that Ivan is an orphan, that he was deprived of his mother while still a young lad, as indeed Eisenstein himself had been. Related to this (and perhaps inviting us to further lengths of biographical speculation) is the equal emphasis given to the relationship between mother and son. First of all, there is the tenderness granted to Euphrosinia and her son Vladimir, a tenderness that deepens the fairy-tale simplicities of her witch-like role that was the mode of Part I, a tenderness made most explicit when she sings her song. Then there are the parallels between the killing of Ivan's mother in the flashback and the assassination of Vladimir. In the first, Ivan is left crumpled on the floor as his mother is dragged away from him; in the second, it is Euphrosinia, once the crown has been taken out of her now limp hands, who is left crumpled on the floor as Vladimir is dragged away with a similar stylization, to the right of the screen instead of the left.

Such a symmetry of treatment seems to suggest that the destruction of the mother/son relationship is the most poignant one that must be endured. Then Ivan's thrice repeated 'As for her . . .' which is left unresolved might suggest that such a loss will serve as punishment enough. Lastly and most curiously, in a way that lends support to Marie Seton's interpretation of this film,[46] there are the close physical resemblances between the child Ivan and Vladimir, their wide-eyed, sensual quality, which suggests a far stronger visual link between the two boys than we can make between the child Ivan and his thin-lipped adult self. These are further touches that suggest on Eisenstein's part a deep personal involvement with the characters he was creating, touches that, while troubling the dramatic clarity of the film, give it an emotional charge unique in all of Eisenstein.

*

More than any other film-maker, Eisenstein resists any attempt at summing up. For me personally, he remains an enigma – a compelling fusion of grand designs with a kind of human emptiness. Or so it appears. Until the second part of *Ivan the Terrible*, it is difficult to locate a steady human centre in his work at all, to tell from the films themselves what it was that interested him in life. It certainly was never any notion of 'mere reality'. Important as all the theoretical writing may prove to be as part of the intellectual and political history of the time, as it exists for us now, it seems like a great deflection of energies and to that extent a mammoth waste of what was demonstrably a prodigiously energetic and original talent.

If much of the work of Pudovkin and Dovzhenko seems more

accessible to us today, there is no doubt that it is also less exceptional. Even if we find it difficult to locate a centre in the early work of Eisenstein, there is also no doubt that the cinema was his entire life. Perhaps this is the core of the problem. Perhaps the only reality that Eisenstein ever fully knew was the cinema itself, its theoretical implications, its aesthetic potentialities. Perhaps it is one of the tragic wastes in the history of the cinema that his films should seem so incomplete in themselves, should still be awaiting historical and theoretical insights to explain and justify them. It seems a cruel paradox that we should still feel the need for external clarification to confirm his own contribution to what Eisenstein himself once described as 'this wonderfully beautiful and infinitely absorbing medium'.[47]

3

A FLIGHT FROM PASSION:

images of uncertainty in the work of Jean Renoir

A bit clumsy, a bit slow, a bit lost in his dreams, Jean Renoir doesn't thrust himself on people. Neither do his films. One must deserve the trust they offer. *Alexandre Arnoux, 1937*[1]

I don't believe in villains – I believe that all of us are villains. And we are also all of us good. It depends on the day, it depends on the way we slept during the night, on the quality of the coffee.
Jean Renoir, 1967[2]

There is no film-maker today more universally praised than Jean Renoir. With some forty years of film-making behind him, he is the one old-timer in France to have survived the change in taste brought about by the New Wave. Indeed, his films are more enthusiastically received today than they were in their own time. They have become more contemporary as the world itself has changed. Their uncertainty of moral position, which made them seem less forceful in the thirties when compared with the work (say) of Marcel Carné, is the very quality that today makes them seem so modern. Renoir's kind of uncertainty we now take for granted. We no longer expect art to be rigorously shaped to create a grand emotion. We have come to value works that are more tentative and self-questioning, that seem more personal in their apparent casualness of technique.

Along with those of Vigo, the films of Jean Renoir are the most tentative in the history of the cinema. They work by in-direction, implying qualities and attitudes that are rarely stated directly. Occasionally, something like a choric comment by one of his characters gives us a clue to Renoir's own attitude, a clue that we might be tempted to relate to something similar said by another character in a different film. For Renoir's films add up to one immensely rich and varied single work. Renoir himself is obviously conscious of this continuity.

Jean Renoir

He once claimed about his father that

there was a connection between all his paintings. Each painting and each stage of each painting was part of the same life-long painting.[3]

And in another context he declared:

I believe that many authors, and certainly myself, tell one story all their lives, the same one, with different characters, different surroundings.[4]

Such continuity of interpretation is especially important when individual works seem imperfect in some way, the implications of their form not fully seizable by the mind. More so than with any other film-maker, each individual film by Jean Renoir gains depth and lucidity when placed in the context of his complete works, when illuminated by the recurring motifs and structural characteristics of his other achievements.

Even Renoir's comments on life that one finds scattered throughout a number of interviews, in his biography of his father, and in his recently published novel, all tell us something about his response to life and art. In fact, working backwards in time, one might well approach the films through the medium of the novel. What characteristics can we find in *The Notebooks of Captain Georges* that might help us to elucidate some of the problems in the films? What are the values that seem implicit in this work? How do they relate to his many marvellous films?

*

Central to his complete works and everywhere in the novel is Renoir's attitude towards nature. One should really write Nature with a capital 'n', as it is repeatedly a kind of deity. For Renoir, Nature can represent a value more supreme than that embodied by ordinary men, to which occasionally it might even be necessary to make a human sacrifice. In *The River*, Bogey seems less killed by the snake than absorbed back into Nature. Through his death, he is both 'saved from the pain of adult life' (as one of the characters remarks) and yet makes way for other children to be born. The final camera movement that sweeps up over the heads of Bogey's surviving family, out on to the great River itself that nourishes and receives all – that final camera movement attempts to convey to us something of the mystery at the centre of life, at the centre of the processes of creation that renew themselves and continue.

Everywhere in *The Notebooks*, there is a similar sense that the characters in it, especially Agnes, are less important than some principle of natural goodness which, for the narrator, they seem to embody and which survives – is indeed confirmed by – any experience that might actually happen to them, no matter how much injustice or suffering might be involved.

At its most refined, this response to Nature tends towards mysticism. It implies an acceptance of the essential Oneness of all creation, a view of life that Renoir obviously inherited from his father. Although this mystical response to life is most consistently embodied in *The River*, leanings towards it pervade his other work as well. But not always in the most refined way. We sometimes get the sense in some of his films, and certainly in *The Notebooks*, that it *might* have been possible to maintain this vision of the Oneness of all creation *and* to manage the merely human business of day-to-day living a little more successfully, inflicting a little less pain. There is a sense in *The Notebooks* that Agnes sacrifices first her happiness and then her life to the Captain's ideals of goodness and 'natural' beauty. She becomes the victim of his own notions of how she ought to behave. Yet her death is the source of a mystical exaltation, of an assertion of the depth of their relationship and of the validity of their passion.

> For I alone, you must realize, I alone really knew Agnes. She lives on in me and will not be quite dead till I have died.[5]

We are not too sure that this is true. On the psychological level, the Captain might be trying to cheer himself up for the clumsy way he has treated the girl.

Throughout the book, we get the sense of the Captain's aristocratic superiority to her, of his tendency to patronize her. Although he *says* he values her for her natural, untutored qualities, for the way she is more in touch with everyday life than he feels himself to be, he takes great delight during the period they are living together in her *embourgeoisement total* as she reads her way through the respectable novelists and acquires 'opinions' about them. Earlier on, when she had just left the brothel, he is immensely relieved by the 'middle-class' appearance she has in normal clothes:

> She looked rather like a village schoolmistress, and I was relieved. I had feared that it might be more the streetwalker or maid-servant type.[6]

This kind of remark, which pervades the Captain's description of his relationship with Agnes, sits oddly alongside his declaration at the end.

The novel provides little evidence that he ever really knew her at all. Rather the reverse. This is no description of his experience with Agnes to equal the vivid exhilaration of a cavalry charge:

> I had never known that supreme sense of belonging, that exaltation that filled my lungs. I did not exist, I was lost in that glorious whole.[7]

Throughout the novel, the Captain's talk of horses seems more finely appreciative than his talk of women. It has less the quality of a boast. His passion for Agnes appears finally as a great disruption of the Balance of Nature, as indeed the Captain's father had warned him might be so when he was still a lad.

> 'You mustn't think I'm against sentiment. It's something we all need. But there's a time and place for everything. From now on I'm going to start dinning into your head the grand principle that you must never lose sight of – no passion! At all costs, never any passion!'[8]

For Renoir's Captain, passion is a disruptive force that ends in unhappiness and death, that takes man away from his capacity for affection for his fellow man and for all natural creatures – from Nature itself. Agnes's virtues as a woman are described in these terms:

She made no difference between animals and human beings, that is to say, she had no sense of hierarchy. In her eyes a man was not superior to a frog, or the frog in any way inferior to an elephant. They had different functions, that was all. . .[9]

Put this way, there is something beautiful about such a natural acceptance of all living creatures, something genuinely mystical in a very eastern way, a Hindu view of life that was central to the thinking of old Auguste as well.[10] Except in *The Notebooks*, the statement is not always that pure.

Renoir's Captain tends to *reverse* the natural western process, implying a hierarchy in which human emotions seem *less* strong and fine. One might think of Boudu and his dog when the Captain says that

in the matter of friendship, dogs are greatly our superiors. Indeed, all animals are. The links between them, the emanations, are stronger than with us. I would go so far as to say that the emanations linking me with Agnes were as strong as those linking my friend Hartley with his corgi bitch Daisy.[11]

One can detect in this passage the same kind of yearning to be at one with all Nature, except that here, in the blurring of distinctions between the kind of affection that a man might feel for his woman and another man for his dog, we might detect as well a fear of deep human involvement, of imaginative commitment – a fear of the uncertainty and pain that passionate personal relationships can inflict. Even when the Captain is closest to Agnes, he seems happiest when alone with Nature, at one with the natural world:

I tread on moss with bare feet, feeling the warmth of the sun where it breaks through the leaves. A rabbit sits watching, untroubled by my languid movements. A deer emerges from behind a bush, stops at the sight of me and nibbles a sprig of hazel. I am part of that tranquil world.[12]

As Renoir creates him for us, the genial Captain Georges is really a man who uses the love experience for his own aesthetic ends. His narrative conveys to us far less of the physical actuality of Agnes than it conveys the Captain's own elevated feelings, his refined sensibility. His affection for Agnes is portrayed chiefly in these terms and is not that different from the affection he might feel for his dog or his horse. Essentially, it is no more meaningful than the feeling of pleasure he might experience from the taste of a fine wine. Gentle, genial, or refined as he may be, Captain Georges is the complete solipsist who is never fully aware of the particularity of another person. Any real sense of love which would imply imaginative involvement with someone else is therefore impossible for him. All experiences either flatter or distress his own sensibility.

Perhaps Renoir intended to present him in this way, though it is difficult to be sure. The tone of the novel seems one of warm approval, reinforced by the personality of Hartley that Renoir creates for us at the opening of the book. Yet in spite of what I'd claim to be the moral failings of the Captain, in spite of the ambiguity of tone in the book, there *is* a tinge of something fine achieved at the end. There is a sense that the Captain's account has won Hartley away from the easy affection he has for his corgis towards a greater human compassion. He adopts an unwed mother and her daughter into his home. Although even this gesture is not without its hint of aristocratic condescension, there is nevertheless the sense of something passed on from the Captain to Hartley, a sense of continuity of experience reminiscent of *The River*, a final note of tolerance and acceptance. It is as if Renoir wishes to imply that Agnes has not suffered and died *totally* in vain. If passion has been presented as largely a disruptive force, the friendship between Hartley and the Captain has helped to restore the balance of Nature.

Passion, Friendship, Nature – these three words might serve as focal points around which we could group the films of Jean Renoir; although finally we would have to add Art as well, to give *The Golden Coach* the centrality it deserves. Renoir has many times treated the passion theme directly. In *Nana* (1926), *La Chienne* (1931), *Madame Bovary* (1934), the magnificent *Toni* (1935), *Le Crime de Monsieur Lange* (1936), to a degree in *Partie de campagne* and in *Les Bas Fonds* (both 1936), most forcefully in *La Bête humaine* (1938) and then again in *La Règle du jeu* (1939), *Swamp Water* (1941) and in *The Diary of a Chamber-*

maid (1946). The friendship motif, pervasive throughout, is most central to Renoir's two war films, *La Grande Illusion* (1937) and the curiously undervalued *Le Caporal épinglé* (1962). Nature, equally pervasive, is at its most mystical in *The River* (1950) but is also central to *Boudu sauvé des eaux* (1932), *Une Partie de campagne*, *The Southerner* (1945) and to the curiously over-valued *Le Déjeuner sur l'herbe* (1959). The art motif which has played an important if subsidiary role in *La Chienne* and *Mon-sieur Lange* has been principally enshrined in Renoir's colour films – quite prominent in *French Cancan* (1955), implicit throughout in the very style of *Elena et les hommes* (1956),[13] but supremely in *The Golden Coach* (1953). There might be other motifs, of course, as there are other films; but with these four ideas brought to bear on these films, we might be able to disentangle some of the complexities of the cinematic world of Jean Renoir.

*

If *La Chienne* were better known, its extraordinary qualities might be better understood. The film is distinguished not only for its artistic qualities, but also for its qualities of moral com-plexity – one might even want to say of moral confusion – qualities that relate this early film to *The Notebooks of Captain Georges*. As in the novel, there is in *La Chienne* the sense that Renoir may not himself be fully aware of the moral im-plications of the characters he has created. If its plot is taken from the novel by G. de la Fourchardière, the implications of its atmosphere seem very much to belong to Jean Renoir.

The film tells the story of a middle-aged bank clerk, Maurice Legrand (Michel Simon), who is married to a shrew of a wife who constantly nags him about the prowess of her first hus-band, a sailor, now apparently drowned at sea. Legrand retreats from this domestic unhappiness into an imaginative world of oil painting about which his wife nags him even more. Although he doesn't realize this himself, he is, in fact, a Sunday painter of distinction. Later on in the film, his work is compared with the paintings of Le Douanier Rousseau.

One night on his way home from a regimental dinner, he

rescues a young woman being beaten up in the streets. He takes her to her flat and begins an affair with her, a 'passionate' affair that transforms his entire life. In his romantic, impractical way, of course, he has no idea that his loved one, Lulu, is a prostitute. Her attacker was her ponce, Dédé, who is now simply amused by the old man's infatuation. Dédé becomes more than amused, however, when he discovers that the paintings that Legrand keeps bringing to Lulu can be sold for considerable sums of money. Dédé even begins to promote her socially as the painter, having her encourage Legrand to produce more and more.

Meanwhile, Legrand has encountered a sailor in a pub, with whom he begins to swap stories. They talk about the tragedy of shrewish wives, and his friend explains that he once had a wife so shrewish that he pretended to be drowned at sea just to get away from her! Bit by bit, both we and Legrand begin to realize who he is. Their talk ends with Legrand inviting him to his home, to see his paintings (if I remember correctly). Legrand gets the idea that this way he too can free himself from his shrew of a wife and skip out to live with his true love, Lulu.

Hereupon follows one of the funniest scenes in the film, followed in turn by one of the most brutal in all of Renoir. These two scenes provide the hub of the film's moral complexity, as well as of its artistic achievement. As a film-maker, Renoir has acknowledged the influence of both von Stroheim and Chaplin.[14] Each is apparent here: von Stroheim, in the sordidness of the action and in the attention to persuasive social detail; Chaplin, in the apparently effortless simplicity of the technical execution, but also in the rapid shift of mood from comedy to despair – indeed, a shift more extreme than anything in Chaplin.

Legrand's whistling delight as he is privately packing his bag in his flat, awaiting the arrival of his sailor friend; his delight at the shock expressed by his friend when he sees how Legrand has tricked him; his excited, boyish, singing, tripping down the stairs away from the nagging bourgeois home towards the true love of his life – this scene has to be seen to be appreciated. It is a moment of high comedy, really of burlesque. Then the rapid, Chaplinesque shift of mood when Legrand's unannounced arrival at Lulu's flat finds her in bed with Dédé. Confronted with this shock, Legrand has to recognize at least a part of the truth. Dropping his bag, his shoulders sloped with an Emil Jannings degree of expressionistic despair, he stumbles down *these* stairs and wanders out into the street. After a bit he returns, as if to forgive Lulu and to renew contact with her; but she just laughs at him, while manicuring her nails. The masquerade is over, as far as she is concerned, paintings or no paintings. She has had enough.

The scene of his return to Lulu begins with an organ-grinder in the street below, and a small crowd gathered around to listen to the song. This in itself could be straight from René Clair, from *Sous les toits de Paris*, except that with Renoir it is a real street with real sound recorded in it – one of the first, I believe, of its kind in the history of the sound film. Through his scene with Lulu, while he is trying to re-enter the fantasy of his love for her, we see the light from her window playing upon her eyes, intensifying the sheen of her hair, and also sparkling off the blades of her scissors beside her on the bed. In a way that anticipates a similar scene of brutality in *La Bête humaine*, simultaneously intensifying and mitigating the horror of the death, we continue to hear the barrel-organ playing outside. Finally, as much confused as really angry, in a way that seems to anticipate that somewhat similar killing that ends the first part of Camus's *L'Étranger*, Legrand picks up the scissors and stabs her, in the throat. The similarity to the killing in the Camus novel, which this film precedes by about twenty years, is just one aspect of the modernity of Renoir's films, one aspect of the way that contemporary sensibility has caught up with his kind of moral/amoral dilemmas. Legrand's killing is not exactly an *acte gratuit*, considering the motivation; yet it is not exactly a *crime passionnel* either, considering the way it is done.

After the stabbing, a quick cut to outside. With the camera tilted up to the upstairs window, we slowly move down the building as (supposedly) Legrand himself descends inside, picking up the organ-grinder and the small crowd of admirers, as we see Legrand slip unnoticed out the front door and away along the street. It is truly one of the great moments of the cinema, the force of which is impossible to convey. Renoir's style is never one that draws attention to itself. Indeed, like early Bergman, through a lot of the story-telling, Renoir's style seems in many ways perfunctory, as if simply getting on with the job of moving the plot along in as uncomplicated a way as possible, with the minimum number of shots. And yet, when a difficult moment arrives, the simplicity justifies itself and the stylistic control tightens just sufficiently to contain the emotion. We get the sense of the horror of Legrand's deed and of the depth of his despair, intensified for us by the ironic contrast of the music outside; yet at the same time, the gathering in the street places his deed within a social setting, implying a more healthy, less obsessional world where people are simply at ease together, enjoying a song in the street.

A moment later, with the organ grinder still playing for us, Dédé arrives and discovers the crime. But as he attempts to leave the building, he himself is discovered, arrested, tried for murder, and eventually executed – a brutal miscarriage of justice more shocking in its way than the murder itself. Throughout the trial as we witness the unjust conviction of Dédé, Legrand himself is there, saying nothing, doing nothing, as if stunned beyond the point where he recognizes any relationship between what is going on and what he has done. In this way too the film is very modern, looking forward to the psychopathic hero of *À Bout de souffle*, to the kind of contemporary figure who feels no moral responsibility for his own actions or any emotional relationship to his own past.

The film ends with a kind of coda, as if in recommendation of a totally disengaged attitude towards life. We see Legrand in the street, now a complete derelict, looking very much like the Boudu that Michel Simon was to embody for us the following year. He also seems to be living like Boudu, picking up cigar butts from the gutter and opening car doors for the 'swells' in return for a few *sous*. We see him looking in the window of a fashionable art dealer. One of his own paintings has just been sold for a fabulous sum. There is no indication that Legrand recognizes it as his own. Indeed, he even opens the car door for the man who has bought it and watches it being driven away.

Another tramp appears on the scene (is it the supposedly drowned sailor again?), with whom he begins to swap stories. They have both, it appears, done some dreadful things. 'I've even killed somebody,' confesses Legrand. 'Oh well,' replies his friend as they walk from us down the street for the last shot in the film, 'it takes all types to make a world'. *Il faut de tout pour faire un monde*. This comment seems to be offered as a moral for the film, as a humorous acceptance of all that we have seen.

*

Magnificent as *La Chienne* is in the execution of its central scenes and modern as it seems today in the psychological alienation depicted in its central character, the film troubles me slightly in a way similar to *The Notebooks of Captain Georges* as I get the sense that Renoir himself may not fully recognize the implications of what he is doing. The ending seems too easy. We can see how it relates to Renoir's philosophy of acceptance, to his desire to be at one with all things. Encouraged by his father, Renoir wants to be able to accept all people and all actions simply for what they are, as part of Nature's richness and variety. A beautiful view of life, so compelling a part of Auguste's sensual world, but often less compelling in Jean's as he lived in more troubled times.

Inescapably a part of such a philosophy of acceptance is an amoral fatalism that leads to passivity when faced with situations that call for decision. In his biography of his father, Renoir quotes with full approval Auguste's theory of a cork floating down a river. 'You swing the tiller over to the right or left from time to time but always in the direction of the current.'[15] You cannot stand against the march of events, this parable seems to say. Again, there is a beauty and a wisdom in such a view of life, difficult to challenge in the gentleness of its implications; and for Renoir *père*, the philosophy seemed to lend clarity to his life. For Renoir *fils*, however, its acceptance posed a moral dilemma that he was never satisfactorily to resolve. In his most complex films – supremely in *La Règle du jeu*

– the dilemma creates a tension and an urgency that are obviously a result of Renoir's attempt to sort these matters out.

For a Europe that had to witness the march of Nazi Germany across its lands, this philosophy of acceptance provided debilitative preparation. It could only be maintained at the cost of sacrificing one's intelligence, of refusing to acknowledge the implications of the facts, of the need to take a stand. In his best films, as I have said, Renoir seems intuitively to have recognized this problem. But in his comments on life – in his biography of his father, or in his interviews or his novel – he seems to have had no *mental* recognition of the dilemma at all. In *Renoir, My Father*, Jean tells about the meeting between his grandfather, a tailor, and an assistant to Sanson, the celebrated executioner. Of course they got on well together, Renoir explains:

> After all, they were two good workmen: one cut out cloth, the other cut off heads just as conscientiously.[16]

In the original French, the tinge of irony in the comment might just save it from the cynicism implicit in such a remark. But there is no irony at all when, in the celebrated *Cahiers* interview, Renoir once more puts forward his fatalistic view of history. Talking about *La Marseillaise* and explaining his gentle treatment of Louis XVI:

> Louis XVI was a loser because he had no place in the period in which he lived. I don't imply that he was evil, or good, for that matter: he was merely out of place. One may even assert that in a revolution it is not the revolutionaries who win: it is the reactionaries who lose. There's a big difference. Even if there were no revolutionaries, the reactionaries would lose and disappear unaided.[17]

As I have already said, it is part of the *intuitive* genius of Renoir to make the issues of *La Marseillaise* more complex on the screen than he apparently *understands* them to be. But the interview goes on:

> It is not a matter of superiority or inferiority. There comes a time in world history when the diplodocus – or the Jewish people – disappears and is replaced by the dinosaur which is able to live very

happily in a different atmosphere and finds food that it likes in the forests. And there comes a time when it disappears in its turn. Emotions and ideas disappear, just like the animal species, whether they are good or evil. The simple fact is that they can no longer find sustenance in their environment. I think it is a question of nourishment – of food for emotions and ideas.[18]

Just what the 'dinosaur' might have been that would have lived 'very happily' after the destruction of the Jewish people, of course Renoir doesn't specify. Here we find Renoir's philosophy of acceptance carried to a perverse degree. There is no sense at all that people can actually change the course of events by struggling to do so, even if they land up in a slightly different situation than they set out for in the first place (Tolstoy's brand of fatalism). Faced with the spectacle of Nazi Germany, Renoir's mental response could only be one of resignation and acceptance, rather like the Captain's in the face of Emilien's return to Agnes, or like Legrand's friend at the end of *La Chienne*: *Il faut de tout pour faire un monde*.

It is in no way my wish to accuse Renoir personally on any moral grounds concerning his private life or to re-examine that difficult period of his life at the outbreak of the war.[19] I touch upon this obviously sensitive and speculative area only because it seems to illuminate certain confusions in the films. There is repeatedly in Renoir's work the sense that he doesn't fully accept the implications of what he is doing, that his mind cannot accept the evidence of his senses. In nearly all his films of the 1930s, this split in Renoir results in a kind of richness, a complexity of point of view which remains perpetually intriguing, as if *because* it has not been fully understood. The very formlessness, of a kind, of *La Règle du jeu* becomes part of the strength of that extraordinary film, part of its modernity, part of its courage to leave certain matters unresolved.

In his American films, *Swamp Water*, *The Southerner*, and *Diary of a Chambermaid*, there is a much more open recognition of evil than there was even in *La Bête humaine*. And, in the light of these comments, *This Land is Mine* might seem to be one of the most directly personal, even the most confessional film that Renoir ever made. It is stiff and stilted in many of its details (as his films in English frequently are); but it contains within it a magnificent performance by Charles Laughton and it very much conveys the need to take up a position when faced with the war, to lose one's hesitations and take a stand.

Just how this film might relate to Renoir's own life, it would be difficult to say (and not really necessary). But it does contain within it a strong emotional charge concerning the need for action which refers forward to the confessional comments of Ballochet in *Le Caporal épinglé*; and in its intensity, it is unique in Renoir. His colour films, on the other hand, made after the war, are morally much simpler, one might even say simplistic. They certainly are nostalgic, as if Renoir were striving to return to the greater simplicities of the world of his father, the world he knew as a boy.

La Chienne gives us the sense of a man consistently trapped by the life that he leads. His job is dull and routine and his wife a shrew. He escapes from this bourgeois tedium by retreat into fantasy – initially the fantasy of his painting, then the fantasy of his passion for Lulu. There is a certain unreality about both these retreats. While his art is meaningful as an escape for him, there is no sense that he values it with his mind, that he recognizes its worth. He is a genuine primitive, if you like, in the manner of Grandma Moses or Le Douanier Rousseau; but even Rousseau came to know something of the value of his work and to feel himself the equal of Picasso. The salient point for Renoir in Legrand's attitude to his own work is the total absence of intellectual interest in his own ability. Renoir shows no desire to relate Legrand's artistic gifts to any decision-making powers of his mind.

This, of course, relates to Renoir's view of art as inherited from his father, his view of the artistic activity as being *solely* a matter of intuition and feeling,[20] but also to his fondness for the idea of the artist as craftsman, not as a specialist or professional in his own field. In his approach to art, Legrand is very much like the white-faced whistler that we see in the opening of *French Cancan*, the man whom Danglar recognized as an 'artist' one day when he heard him whistling at the top of his ladder and who ends this opening sequence – beautifully, significantly – by offering with outstretched arms a fragile and beautiful rose to the indifferent night-club audience, occupied by its own talk of women and war. Again, it is a lovely and deeply felt view concerning the role of the artist, but it is one that makes him totally dependent on whatever might happen to him, totally without power in a brutal world. Renoir frequently presents the artist in this way as lacking real decision-making powers of his own.

In *La Chienne*, we *see* that initially, Legrand's art meant something to him; we *see* that, with the corrupt help of Dédé, society comes to value it; but we cannot really *know* what it is that makes him fail to recognize it at the end. There are psychological speculations open to us, of course, concerning the shock of his experience or anything else we might like to imagine; but Renoir isn't explicit about this. This lack of interest in causality is part of what gives the final comment its choric, generalizing air, as if summing up the implications of what we have seen.

Legrand's passion for Lulu is similarly unreal. It is probably Renoir's natural discretion that keeps him from showing us any scenes of real intimacy between them; but from what we do have in the film, it is difficult to imagine how they could have worked. Compared with the insistence of the nagging sequences at home or with the realistic detail of the killing, this elliptical treatment of Legrand and Lulu intensifies our feeling of unreality about their love. What we do have by the end of the film is the realization that his art, such as it was, failed to sustain him in any way and was renounced with the rest of his life; while his passion, such as *it* was, proved totally destructive – not only of Lulu and Dédé but also of Legrand himself. Yet the warmth of realization of many of the incidental scenes, especially of the coda, prevents us from feeling clearly the human cost involved.

If we think about it and try to understand it, *La Chienne* really presents us with a complex experience. It takes us through a most destructive and self-destructive series of situations, apparently endorsing a totally pessimistic fatalism, yet strives to leave us with the feeling of the warmth of whimsy and with a philosophical detachment at the end – or something like it; for it is difficult to describe the mood of that final shot. It is largely a matter of tone, difficult to interpret even in literature but particularly elusive in the movies. The tinge of comedy might almost make us feel that Renoir wished to evade the tragic implications of the story he has told (as Captain Georges seemed to misunderstand his own story about Agnes). At the same time, there is the feeling of a kind of forlornness as the two tramps move up the road together, not quite the same sense of isolation that we get at the end of so many Renoir films, but something moving towards it nevertheless. Finally, the film leaves us with the feeling of many issues left unclear – in one way, a formal failure, one might say, a failure of the intelligence fully to shape and clarify its material; yet in another, part of the perennial interest in the film, one of the reasons it still seems so modern today.

*

Although a much more structured film, *Le Crime de Monsieur Lange* deals with some of the same ideas in a somewhat similar way. It again touches upon the theme of art and again presents the artist as a naïve primitive, essentially a fantasist. Monsieur Lange is a timid man who buries himself in his attic away from all the terrors of the real world, while he dreams and writes about his own fabulous world of heroic adventure, the world of Arizona Jim. When the evil Batala disappears from Lange's courtyard, Lange does indeed move into the world outside. Instead of just imagining romantic affairs with dark-haired Indian girls, he sleeps with the blonde laundress, Valentine, across the way. And his photographed comic strip becomes a great success, earning lots of money for the Co-op and making them all very happy in the most traditional 'popular front' way.

When evil returns to this universe, once again in the form of Batala, Lange actually kills him. The result of this action is an isolation from the happy world he has known and, through his 'art', has helped to create. In a way that relates back to *La Chienne* and forward to both *La Grande Illusion* and *Le Caporal épinglé*, there is a feeling of great forlornness at the end. It is true, Lange has been acquitted by the people's court and has therefore been set free. But his freedom will mean freedom in exile. The last shot is of Lange and his laundress, crossing the border into some unspecified country, walking away from the scenes of happiness in the film. The rain is falling about them on the beach, while we see their footsteps growing tiny in the sand. It is as if to act is to alienate yourself. To take a stand is to isolate yourself from society and happiness.[21]

The 'passion' in *Monsieur Lange* is the passion of evil, evil lust and greed as embodied in Batala. It has also in this film clear political implications. Batala is the capitalist exploiter who cheats and lies and so keeps the people down. In fact, in any *book* on Renoir, *Lange* should occupy a prominent part. It is the one film that links Renoir most clearly with his colleagues of the thirties. It is in a sense the most *intelligent* film he ever made, formally the most intricate, the most clearly thought out. It is certainly the most symmetrical. With the printing press on one side of the courtyard, turning white paper black, and the laundry on the other, turning 'black' sheets white,[22] it is very much one of the courtyard films of the time and is linked in this way to films as dissimilar as *Le Million*, *L'Affaire est dans le sac*, and *Le Jour se lève*. In this sense, important though it is, it is in these ways uncharacteristic. One detects the influence of Prévert and perhaps others actively involved with the Popular Front. But while the film lends itself to explanations in terms of the political ideology of the time, it is still very much a film by Renoir and still very much presents his personal moral universe, revolving round his great sense of uncertainty when faced with the need to act.

The positive values in the film are chiefly those of friendship, here given political meaning by the Popular Front atmosphere in which the film was made. The negative values, primarily embodied in Batala, are those of lust and greed. The art, such as it is, while initially a product of fantasy, is dependent upon the approval of the Co-op for its worldly success. Lange's art needs the atmosphere of approval and friendship in order to survive. The evil Batala, it appears, is capable of destroying all this.

Lange's execution of him is again one of the great moments in the cinema, made famous for all time by an intricate analysis by

André Bazin![23] But the result of the way it is shot, in a double take from the courtyard with its vertiginous 360° pan that spins counter to Lange's movement, is again (one might argue) to blur the sense of the individual decision. In this way, the assassination relates back to Legrand's killing of Lulu and forward to the death of Kostylev in *Les Bas Fonds* and of Joseph in *Chambermaid* where there is a kind of mob execution in which individual responsibility is blurred. Lange, of course, does *decide* to kill Batala. But the way Renoir *stages* the scene gives us the sense that, like Legrand before him, Lange is not fully in control of his own actions. *'C'est facile!'*, he exclaims after pulling the trigger – as if someone not himself had done it. It's easy, when performed in this single-minded way.

Yet this execution, for the sake of the Co-op, is Lange's 'passion', if you like. And like Legrand's, it ends by isolating him from the world he has known. The acquittal by the improvised people's court in the café by the border *could* have been shot by another director in such a way that we got the feeling of something quite positive at the end. We could have been left with the feeling of the triumph of the morality of the 'little people' over the outmoded laws of capitalist society designed to guarantee the property of the rich. There *is* that aspect to these final scenes; but there is also this pervasive sense of forlornness as they walk away from us along the beach. Without a doubt there is a feeling of uncertainty as to where they are going or what the future may bring.

*

With the moral pattern of *La Chienne* and *Le Crime de Monsieur Lange* in mind, some of the confusions within the many-faceted achievement of *La Règle du jeu* begin to come clear. It is perhaps wrong to describe the film as formless, as I have done, for, in its way, it is indeed a highly structured and delicately nuanced work.[24] But its form is not that of the well-made plot or swiftly-told story. As Peter Wollen has put it:

...the surface is continually fluctuating and it is this fluctuating interaction of the characters, rather than the intrigue (a kind of Beaumarchais plot), which sets the pace and holds the eye. Renoir gives his actors a great deal of room and time – by the use of deep focus and long takes – and encourages them to move about. The film is awash with movement and gesture, so that the first impression is of a continual to-and-fro combined with sharp psychological accuracy. The camera, in André Bazin's phrase, is 'the invisible guest with no privilege but invisibility.'[25]

Part of the richness of this particular film is the result of a quite unusual number of traditions being drawn upon and referred to, traditions of French farce and social satire, which are themselves being qualified and refined.[26] Thus, even more than *Monsieur Lange*, the film lends itself to a variety of interpretations and invites as many social and political explanations as it reveals characteristics of the mind of Jean Renoir.[27] Yet the personal themes are there as well, even if in a subterranean way; and the moral ambiguity of the film is made yet more elusive by the ambiguity of our response to the figure of Octave, played in the film by Renoir himself.

In *La Règle du jeu*, the passion theme is embodied partly in Jurieu, the ace aviator who is a fool on the ground, but chiefly by Schumacher, the gamekeeper. Schumacher is an outsider in every way. An Alsatian by birth, Germanic in manner when compared with this very French world, he longs to return to Strasbourg where men are men and poachers are shot. He wants to take his French wife, Lisette, away from this frivolous philandering world, while she on the other hand has no desire to leave *le service de Madame*. For those that accept the Rules of the Game, this life of idle pleasure does provide a little world that, in the film, groups itself around the Marquis and his mechanical toys (*his* kind of mechanical art, I suppose). Although a servant, Lisette is very much a part of this world and values it far more than she could her life with her husband away from the securities of this society. She is one of the insiders that honour the rules.

There are many outsiders, however, as well. In fact, it is one of the feats of this extraordinary film that, while presenting us with a highly conventionalized and artificial world, Renoir makes us feel that most of the people are outsiders in some way. The Marquis himself is a Jew. The Marquise, Christine, is an

Austrian, somewhat ill at ease within the more sophisticated assumptions of her adopted society. Octave is a mysterious figure, most ambiguously defined. But he is very much a hanger-on, a kind of go-between, meddling about in the lives of other people.[28]

It is really the servants who feel most secure, whose roles are most clearly defined. But even these class distinctions are muddled somewhat by the instinctive sympathy that the Marquis and Marceau, the poacher, have for one another. Perhaps, as a Jew, the Marquis feels he has poached his way into this society. And they are both short men!

Jurieu is an outsider in the clumsiness with which he pursues Christine, while at the same time he wants to honour the rules. But the man who is most outside and most stands in judgement on this society is Schumacher. Like Malvolio in *Twelfth Night*, he is in some ways the one sane man in a mad world, the one man who believes in old-fashioned ideas of honour and virtue. He wants to shoot Marceau for trying to poach his wife. Yet, paradoxically, he ends by shooting Jurieu instead, while he and Marceau, both now sent away from this society and so friends in exile, lament together on the fickleness of women and the injustices of life. It is a tragi-comic moment in the film that is not without its confusions, its characteristically Renoirian moral ambiguity.

But the centre of ambiguity in this film is most certainly Octave. In the opening sequences, as we see him rolling about the bed with Christine or pinching Lisette, we are never too sure whether he is a sweet old avuncular father-figure or a dirty-old-man. During the magnificent hunt sequence which, in its gratuitous cruelty, paves the way for the equally gratuitous killing of Jurieu, Octave, characteristically, goes on the hunt but without a gun. In fact, the characters reveal a good deal about themselves by the accuracy and determination with which they shoot, by their attitude towards the skills of the hunt.

There is a curious little anecdote towards the end of this sequence about some poor type who carried his gun so badly that he shot himself in the thigh during the previous year's shooting.

He died, the Colonel explains, about twenty minutes afterwards. 'Isn't that funny, Christine?' asks Octave as he comes into frame just in time to lead the laughter that follows the anecdote, whittling the stick that he carries and then slapping his arm around Christine. It is a macabre little story, really not funny at all; and the slight emphasis given to it by the acquiescing presence of Renoir/Octave serves further to confuse our moral response to the hunt. Does Renoir himself (like Christine who complains that she has lost her taste for shooting) see it as brutal and unnecessary? Surely he does; and yet . . . It is hard to know what to think.

By the end of the film, there are further ambiguities. After the chaos of the masquerade, a chaos made more chaotic by Schumacher's determination to kill Marceau, Octave leads Christine outside on to the terrace and begins to reminisce about her father's approach to conducting an orchestra, in the old days, in Vienna. Another key moment within the complete works of Renoir, it is impossible to convey in words the associations that this scene draws together. There is a piano waltz coming through the windows from the drawing-room inside, while Octave walks out along the terrace as if to a podium, in imitation of her father as Christine looks on. Renoir then cuts to a long-shot from the garden so that Octave is alone in the frame. A whisper of music is still coming from inside; but there is no *real* orchestra to conduct, no *real* audience to listen. It is as if, for Octave, this moment sums up the parasitic nature of his life, the absence of any real role to play in this society. He is unable to go on with the charade. Breaking down, he confesses his despair to Christine. This scene contains a feeling of personal intimacy which seems in excess of the part Octave has to play in the film in terms of plot, and could not be explained simply by reference to its sources. It is characteristic of Renoir's method to let such moments take on a life of their own in this way, to allow the pace of the actors to determine the pace of the scene, even though it makes for structural untidiness and a consequent confusion of feeling by the end of the film.

Christine, who had decided that she would run away with Jurieu, who then for his part demurred, now decides that it is

Octave she loves and wants to go away with. He goes in to get his hat but at the last moment changes his mind. He sends Jurieu in his place. Whether from a recognition that Christine is fooling herself, or (as Lisette insists) that the younger Jurieu would be the better man, or simply from a feeling of personal inadequacy, we never know. The last thing we see of Octave, he is confessing to Marceau that he has always been *un raté* – a failure in life, living off other people, of no consequence himself. And then, with as much ambiguity as the Fool in *King Lear*, Octave disappears. He is the only person absent from the last scenes of the film.

Throughout the film, Octave has been uttering characteristically choric comments like 'Everyone has his reasons' and wishing he could hide his head in the sand and not have to decide what is right and wrong. It is difficult not to see in these comments the personal endorsement of Renoir himself, perhaps struggling to come to grips with the moral implications of the approaching war. In any case, his final unexplained disappearance feels in the film like an act of self-banishment, almost of self-destruction. It is just one of the characteristics that gives this extraordinary film a personal charge that makes it difficult to interpret tidily in any social or political way; although obviously, as with *Lange* before it and before that with *Toni*, the social and political references are also very much there.

*

'If only the world could be made of children!' exclaims Melanie's father in *The River*, after Bogey's death. Octave, too, could have made such a remark. Indeed, Renoir himself has expressed similar thoughts a number of times:

> Today we're living at a time that can no longer produce artists like Mozart and my father and I don't feel at ease.
> It's a serious thing, this world where one cannot remain ingenuous.[29]

This longing for a simpler kind of universe, a universe where one can feel at ease with Nature and with one's friends, where one can simply *live* a child-like existence without the need for moral decision – this longing is less a theme in Renoir's films than an aspect of their atmosphere, a moral quality that is part of the mood they create.

When someone comes to write the biography of Jean Renoir, this longing will undoubtedly be a recurring motif. In his films, it contributes greatly to their human quality, to their immense compassion for all living things. It also accounts for their formal imperfections, the sense that most of Renoir's films can give us that the potential power of individual moments is often greater than the clarity of the whole.

Roger Leenhardt was on to this as long ago as 1936. He recognized that Renoir seemed to specialize *dans les films ratés* but went on to explain:

> But the powerful mood his films create, their sense of humanity, the sombre grey quality that pervades his photography and characters – these qualities always win over the allegiance of his audience.[30]

And the same characteristics undoubtedly prompted Nino Frank's often-quoted remark about *La Règle du jeu:*

> What is the impression that an audience retains after seeing this film? That it's a rich work – perhaps too rich – very complex and extremely intelligent from beginning to end; but that this very richness, this unmitigated humanity, this over-abundance of intentions has carried the film-maker too far and that he has not succeeded in controlling completely the magnificent material that he has himself invented. One might compare *La Règle du jeu* with one of those meandering streams, with many detours and wide recesses, that seem to provide us with the very image of nature's confusion.[31]

Nowadays, while we might still talk about the 'imperfection' of Renoir's films, it no longer seems such a fault. It is one of the reasons why his films are still alive for us today while those of his colleagues have become little more than skilfully turned-out museum pieces. And in spite of the pressure of personal experience that no doubt accounts for a part of this imperfection, it is also a deliberate part of his conscious aesthetic. Talking to Huw Wheldon once during a BBC *Monitor* interview, Jean explained that his father

... didn't like perfection. A perfect object is dead. He wanted to catch life through the impressions it made during one moment of its existence; the purpose of art was to catch a little bit of the truth of a tree or a human being.[32]

And in *Renoir, My Father* he quotes Auguste as saying:

The big classic compositions are finished ... The spectacle of daily life is much more interesting.[33]

All of Renoir's films, then, catch more than just a little bit of the truth of the particular time and place in which they were made, of the social and political upheavals of his day. If they also catch more than a little bit of the confusion that Renoir himself must have been experiencing at the time, this, too, becomes a part of their richness, a part of their feeling of sincerity.

As we have seen, such a longing for innocence can lead Renoir into astonishing oversimplifications in his comments on life. It is also part of his anti-intellectualism. This, too, of course, he inherited from his father. 'What goes on inside my head doesn't interest me,' he quotes his father as saying. 'I want to touch ... or at least to see!'[34] And in the *Monitor* interview, he explained how his father

... asked his children only one thing: not to be lost in deep thinking, but to be gay. He loved to be surrounded by gay people...[35]

From the evidence of his films and from many of his comments on life, it would appear that Jean Renoir himself could remain gay only by closing his eyes to many things. To think about life was to acknowledge its sadness, to experience the pain. It is part of Renoir's greatness as an artist that his innate understanding made it impossible for him to keep his eyes completely closed for too long. In spite of their overwhelming desire for the simplicity of acceptance, his films contain the tensions and uncertainties of their time.

*

Passion is the quality that disrupts and destroys. Whether it is the romantic passion of a Legrand, the anarchic passion of a

Boudu, or the lustful passion of a Batala, the even tenor of life is destroyed by its existence. Ideas can also disrupt and destroy. Ideas about class can disrupt the comradeship that should be possible among all men; ideas about nationality can cause wars. At times it seems as if any strong feeling or considered action will isolate a man from his fellow men, will disrupt the balance of Nature. Things must change slowly. They must grow in accordance with long-established natural patterns – like the olive trees on his father's estate at Cagnes. Like his father, Renoir seems to believe that 'anything that is slow is probably good'.[36]

In Renoir's earlier films, art would seem to be a marginally compensational activity, although still associated with a tendency to retreat from life. After the war, however, the emphasis shifted a little. In *French Cancan* and *The Golden Coach*, art becomes an alternative mode of existence, a superior mode that might transcend the turmoil and unpredictability of everyday life. In *French Cancan*, Danglar explains that 'the show' is more important than any individual woman's claim on him; and characteristically, during the final cancan number, we see him sitting in the wings, looking very much alone and by now very old. Yet the show lives on, young and alive. In *The Golden Coach*, Camilla is torn between her love for the Viceroy, with his aristocratic privilege, Ramon, the bullfighter, with his direct physical action, and Fillipe, with his desire for his idealized retreat back to a world of Rousseauistic simplicity among his noble savages, who, he has discovered, 'are better than we are'. Torn by these kind of choices, she of course chooses the stage and her own idealized persona of Columbine, guaranteed by centuries of tradition within the *commedia dell'arte*. Even so, the last image we have in the film is one of Camilla alone on the stage. Again, the moment of choice is accompanied by the feeling of isolation.

The qualities that most endure, that are most worth living for in the world of Jean Renoir, would seem to be the qualities of simple friendship. This, his films imply, constitutes the natural order of things. With characteristic paradox, there are no films more dedicated to this ideal than his two war films, *La Grande*

Illusion and *Le Caporal épinglé*. *La Grande Illusion* has been universally acknowledged to be the finer work, to represent along with *La Règle du jeu* the consummation of Renoir's art. I suppose it does and I certainly agree that it is a film of immense warmth and humanity. But it also seems to me to be a film that requires very little comment.[37] That war the destructive force can also unite the races (Maréchal and Rosenthal) and the classes (Maréchal and de Boildieu) is everywhere explicit. Similarly, the two warmest moments in it – the aristocrats' talk over the one surviving geranium, and the beautiful Christmas romance between Maréchal and Elsa, the German farmer's wife – are quite self-explanatory. Human love of the gentlest kind can unite people who cannot even speak to one another because of the barriers of language.

The most intimate comments between Maréchal and Elsa are exchanged obliquely, through Maréchal's response to Elsa's daughter. '*Lotte hat blaue Augen.*' This is all he can say at the end, for he cannot say good-bye. Nor can he say anything more intimate in the German language. Certainly, *La Grande Illusion* is a magnificent film. If we are concerned with formal perfection, along with *Monsieur Lange* it is the most completely successful film in the Renoir canon. It is the most successfully balanced between the prison sequences of confinement and the farm sequences of liberation. Even the setting of the First World War seems now sufficiently distant in time for Renoir's characteristically gentle treatment of the war to work successfully and not to offend. Quite different from *La Règle du jeu* in this, *La Grande Illusion* has virtually no moments of intense personal feeling that exist, so to speak, to one side of the plot. Yet to my mind these characteristic moments are so much a part of the manner of Renoir that I have always felt in *La Grande Illusion* an element of thinness, as if everything is too neatly resolved by the end.

With *Le Caporal épinglé*, however, the situation is different. First of all, except for William Pechter,[38] I know of no one who has hailed it as a masterpiece. Yet it seems to me to provide, in its quiet, episodic way, a summing up of the main moral themes in Renoir. Beneath its grey surface are the characteristic concerns with friendship versus action, with the need to take a stand in this difficult world even at the risk of destroying yourself, or at least of alienating yourself from your friends. We must act, this film seems to say, even though we cannot discover the reasons for action. It is in this way one of the most personal films that Renoir has ever made.[39]

*

Apart from external, technical matters – the apparently effortless manner in which Renoir's films seem to have been executed, their freedom from big-studio trickeries – *the* modern quality in his work seems to revolve around paradox and uncertainty. Although his films contain some of the gayest moments in the history of the cinema (like Chaplin again in this), over them all hangs an atmosphere of sadness. *Une Partie de campagne* is a film that everyone remembers with affection. Everyone remembers the girlish gaiety of Sylvia Bataille on the swings or the randy ribaldry of Jacques Brunius's dance of Pan. Yet the film depicts the failure of youthful promise to find fulfilment in life, to find any means of sustaining the exquisite Oneness with all living creatures that the young Henriette shares with her mother in the opening sequences of this film.

With greater complexity, there is the same feeling in *Toni*. In that particular film, there is such a strong feeling for the natural landscapes and for the immigrant communities – a sense that some sort of happy collective life *should* have been possible. But the passion motif intervenes again and separates the individuals. Toni's desperate run across that long bridge is yet another peak moment in the history of the cinema. Again with immense simplicity, virtually in a continuous take, Renoir executes this penultimate scene of his film. The scene could almost stand as the metaphoric embodiment of a recurrent theme in Renoir – the futility of isolated action, doomed to come to nothing at the end.

Apart from his colour films, Renoir's natural world is curiously without sun. In the passage already quoted, Roger Leenhardt has referred to the '*gris-noir profond qui baignait sa photo*'; and indeed, everywhere in Renoir, in films as different in story-line as *Madame Bovary* and *La Règle du jeu*, there is a strong feeling for *la grisaille* of a wintry landscape, for the present bleakness of a countryside *potentially* green and alive. Nowhere more so than in *Le Caporal épinglé*. The film begins with Nazi planes dropping bombs – destructive newsreel footage that Renoir employs most skilfully to punctuate this film – and then with Nature dropping rain. Not a productive, fertilizing rain, but the depressive, wintry rain of a world that has lost its sun. *'Mais, mes vaches, mes vaches!'*, exclaims Émile, the simple-minded farmer, in the rain, anxious to return to his cows. After all, an amistice has been signed. But the problems posed by the war have not yet been solved, even if the war itself remains very much in the margins of this particular film.

The central problem within *Le Caporal épinglé* seems less the concern with the freedom and confinement than the search for a basis for constructive action, action which in turn might set a man free. The Corporal, nameless throughout the film, is the least personalized character that Renoir has ever created. In the penultimate sequence, when he explains that he has a family waiting for him at home, that there is a *domestic* reason for his continual efforts to escape from the camps, we might be tempted *not* to believe him. For we really know nothing about him at all.

Some people have considered this thinness of characterization one of the faults in the film. They have contrasted Jean-Pierre Cassel's deliberately distant and dead-pan performance with the more conventionally humanized role that Jean Gabin created for *La Grande Illusion*. Yet this same quality of psychological superficiality intensifies the film's philosophical air. To my mind, Cassel is perfect for the enigmatic Corporal, as his deliberate superficiality can suggest so many things. There is not much in common between Renoir's Corporal and Antonioni's photographer-hero of the dazzlingly fashionable *Blow Up*. But they both remain nameless[40] and essentially inscrutable. They deny us the privilege of psychological response. With both the Corporal and the photographer, we can never know for certain *why* they act. We simply see that they do. In this way too, Renoir's film is more modern than it may seem.

Le Caporal épinglé is a more personal statement by Jean Renoir than has generally been recognized.[41] In his apparent impersonality, it is almost as if the Corporal *stands for* some obscure principle of action which Renoir now recognizes but cannot really personalize in a conventional way. The Corporal *must* go on escaping. Simply that. We never really know why. Of course, we may *think* we know, because we *think* we know about the war. Our common sense makes us assume that the Corporal has patriotic motives, that he shares our assumed ideals about truth and freedom and all the other abstractions that govern our thinking in times of war. Perhaps he does. But nowhere *in the film itself* does Renoir make this clear. It is as if Renoir has come to realize that in such a situation, one *must* take a stand, one *must* attempt to swim against the current, although Renoir himself cannot really explain why.

'I love a man who's not a slave,' the little German dental assistant explains to the Corporal one time, after he has been encouraged by Ballochet to adjust to life in the camp, to take things easy. And all of a sudden, he is off again – as if reminded of something that he was beginning to forget. From this context, we would have to assume it was from some notion of personal heroism. Yet even here we cannot be too sure.

The Corporal's motives for escaping are further complicated by Renoir's treatment of the war. Except for the newsreel cut-ins, there is really no violence in the film at all. There are, of course, the fatigues that the Corporal must endure each time he is recaptured. But even here, the fatigues might seem less like a realistic depiction of punishment by the Nazis than a more generalized depiction of the result of a man attempting to disrupt the Balance of Nature by swimming against the current. On a subconscious level, they could seem more like a kind of psychological hubris than a realistic presentation of the sufferings of war. In this film, typically, paradoxically, perversely (if you will), the moment of greatest pain for the Corporal occurs when he is in the dentist's chair!

The violence of the war is euphemized throughout. In fact, its advantages are continually dwelt upon. Like *La Grande Illusion*, *Le Caporal épinglé* presents the war as an experience capable

of uniting people who would remain separated in normal life.⁴²
So strong is this feeling that, for the third escape, Pater has a
last-minute change of mind. He chooses *not* to accompany the
Corporal because, as he explains, he doesn't want to lose the
comradeship and the social equality of the prison camp, qualities in *his* life which are apparently more important than some
unspecified notion of freedom. Just before this escape, during
the 'laryngitis' episode, the 'crawler' Hippolyte, a Frenchman,
had been swapping stories with his German superior, Otto. They
were discussing the skiving characteristics of their men. Each
time Otto said something, Hippolyte agreed – '*Tout comme chez
nous.*' The German troops and the French, it would appear,
were very much the same – perhaps a striking aspect of any war
situation, of the essential Oneness of military personnel, though
not the one that most artists would dwell upon concerning the
1939–45 war.

Ballochet, the coward, becomes the chief spokesman for this
kind of accommodation. Not only is he able to carve out for
himself a soft situation within the prison camp – *partout ...
une planque* – but he actually gains more status than he ever
had in civilian life. He is in that sense more 'free' – until the
Corporal turns on him, throwing all his tinned delicacies to the
ground after he himself has been shaken up by the dentist's
assistant! But why? What, really, are the issues? We might feel
we know them from our assumptions about the war, but they
are never explained in the film.

When the Corporal is brought back yet again after another
escape and encounters Ballochet also subjected to fatigues, Ballochet explains that they are 'to punish me for quitting my ivory
tower'. This kind of comment, purely personal with no reference to political realities, reinforces the feeling already noted in
relation to the Corporal: for Ballochet too, the fatigues seem less
a punishment inflicted on misbehaving prisoners than a kind of
moral retribution imposed by the gods. At times, this film would
seem very much to be working on a subliminal level, working
out problems that Renoir himself might be scarcely aware of.

The Ballochet episode ends with his curious latrine confession, followed by what can only be described as his suicide.

There has been a strong sense of dirt and rubble throughout the film, even of excrement. It is as if the film has chosen for its natural background the refuse of an errant civilization. Ballochet himself chooses this moment when he is sitting on a wooden privy to confess to the Corporal his pervasive sense of failure. Like Octave, Ballochet describes himself as *un raté* – a failure, a man who loved heroes but was himself a coward, a little man of no particular gifts. 'I'm a washout . . . so I retired into my pride.' His life, it appears, has been a constant self-deception.

The scene of his 'suicide' is the most theatrical in the film. Lit from below, as if by footlights, it even begins with the sharp three knocks that traditionally silence the audience for French classic theatre. Ballochet, too, it appears, is planning to escape. We cannot know why, in any realistic sense: simply, we assume, as an act of atonement for his own sense of failure, his previous inability to act. Yet his escape has been foreseen as doomed to fail. 'I've the best of plans – none,' he announces, holding up the key to the first set of gates which will only put him irretrievably in reach of the prison's machine guns. It is as if he feels that he can act only by rejecting the promptings of his intelligence, by design to no purpose. '*Un, deux, trois, quatre, cinq, six, sept, huit* . . .' His comrades all count as he marches forth, waiting until they hear the machine guns cutting him down. An extraordinary sequence of immense personal power through its feeling of intimacy; but meaningless, essentially, in any realistic way, by any reference to external standards of psychological plausibility as they might relate to the plot of this film. It gains its meaning, of course, by reference to other similarly implausible elements elsewhere in the film, but also, more profitably, by reference to other films by Renoir. In particular, we might think of Octave's confession of failure followed by his own self-banishment from the world he has known.

In a similar way, the last two scenes provide a summing up, not only of this film but virtually of the whole of Renoir. After another powerfully irrational moment involving the drunken German traveller, offering self-destructive comments about the

Twilight of the Gods as the bombs fall around him, the Corporal and Pater escape over the fields. We see them approaching a farmer, whom they recognize as a French prisoner-of-war. At first they think that they must be far from the border or he would have tried to escape. But no – they discover he is happy there. After the war, he plans to marry his buxom *Bauerin* beside him in the fields. Why should he try to escape?

The Corporal mutters something about the Land of our Fathers, shrugging off responsibility. 'My fathers had no land,' he replies. He had always worked for others. The war and his confinement had actually given him his freedom. The Corporal and Pater remain confused and apologetic. The Corporal explains that he has a family in Paris, and Pater that he always goes with the Corporal – something which we *know* is not true from the third escape. There is again in this scene a feeling of great intimacy, of shared friendship among the four of them, a friendship independent of any notions of race or frontiers, existing *as if* apart from the war. *'Gib ihnen unser Frühstück!'*, the farmer tells his German wife-to-be, so their friends won't be hungry. The momentary change of language has a most powerful effect, recalling Maréchal's leave-taking of Elsa in *La Grande Illusion*; but in the precision of its domestic detail, it might recall other moments in classic tragedy as well.[43] This sequence ends with the woman moving over to a haystack and clutching some hay to her breast. Friendship and Nature – the qualities that most endure in Renoir's world, even in the midst of war.

The film ends in the early morning in Paris. Pater and the Corporal are approaching one of the bridges. It is again a scene of considerable intimacy, yet of great tentativeness as well. It is also a scene of considerable ambiguity. The Corporal breathes in the early-morning air coming up from the Seine. 'One can breathe freely here,' he explains, even though the river smells of petrol, as Pater insists. There is a hesitancy between them, a kind of sadness. The Corporal seems withdrawn and distant, Pater anxious in some kind of way. They take their leave and Pater skips out of frame with a characteristically Renoirish movement, a bit clumsy and self-conscious. But he returns immediately. 'After you've seen whoever it is that's waiting for you and made up for lost time ...' Again he hesitates. He is wondering whether they might meet again, whether their life in Paris might now overcome the class barriers as had the prison camps. 'Swastikas still depress me,' the Corporal explains obliquely. (This is his first comment of this kind in the film!) Pater is excited. 'I know what you mean: the struggle is not over. We'll meet again.' This time he is eagerly enthusiastic as he shakes the Corporal's hand and then skips away again. Then, like the ending of so many Renoir films, like *La Chienne, Le Crime de Monsieur Lange, Les Bas Fonds,* even like *La Grande Illusion* with Maréchal and Rosenthal becoming tiny specks in the snow, we have a shot of the Corporal walking away from us up the street. A river whistle hoots on the misty-grey morning as the Corporal, all alone, walks away to an unspecified future, away from his friend, to see we don't know whom. Again, our assumptions about the Resistance and other historical matters might allow us to *assume* that we know what he and Pater have been talking about. But Renoir keeps it unclear in the film itself. We do not *really know* what is happening at the end, *where* the Corporal is going to, *what* he is going to do. Characteristically, within an atmosphere of considerable warmth – the warmth of Pater's friendship – while we *see* that the Corporal is free, there is the feeling not of celebration but of forlornness at the end.

If children habitually fall from heaven to end the majority of Fellini's films on a note of hope, Renoir repeatedly gives us the feeling of his characters walking into a world without a future, a world where one must indeed feel *mal à l'aise*. Along with the habitual greyness, this recurring note of melancholy provides the dialectic tug necessary to counterbalance Renoir's irrepressible need to believe in the essential goodness of existence, the beauty of nature and the reassurances of friendship. The greatness of Renoir's films and their astonishing modernity lie in this ability to contain their own confusion, to find a form that, while apparently saying one thing, encourages us to feel another.

'His nudes and roses declared to the men of this century, already deep in their task of destruction, the stability of the eternal balance of Nature.'[44] Thus Renoir, speaking about his father. Yet, whatever the simplistic implications of Renoir *the man's* view of life as he describes it to us, his films create for us an experience of uncertainty and confusion that enables us to realize that, no matter how attractive his philosophy might appear as he inherited it from his father, the violence and uncertainties of the modern world made it impossible for Renoir *the artist* fully to believe it himself.

LUIS BUÑUEL:

Spaniard and surrealist

As a view of life, surrealism begins with the acceptance of the disruptive violence at the centre of man and with the recognition of his essential isolation within the civilized conventions of polite society – conventions apparently designed to frustrate his instinctual needs. It thrives upon sharp contrasts and unexpected juxtapositions, upon images that acknowledge the unalterable irrationalities of human life. Like Freud, whose investigations of the unconscious lent to the movement a scientific authority, surrealism is essentially pessimistic. It holds out gloomy prospects for the social development of man.

As an organized movement, it really began in Zürich during the First World War. Though not yet called surrealism, the philosophical and artistic movement that formed itself around Hugo Ball and Emile Hennings at the Café Voltaire in 1917 was made up of refugees from all the countries of Europe, people exiled from their homelands by the violence of the war. In the midst of the destruction, there flickered the tiny hope that all this turbulence might help to bring about a better world. As the old world crumbled, man could begin again, and this time might be true to both his individual and social needs. And, of course, Lenin himself was in Zürich at the time.

After the war, when it moved to Paris, the Dada movement – as this prelude to surrealism was called – underwent a change.[1] Tristan Tzara, the Rumanian poet who had become the spokesman for the movement while in Zürich, now became less prominent than André Breton; and it was Breton who, borrowing the term itself from a play by Apollinaire, first began talking about a philosophy of 'surrealism':

I believe in the future resolution of two states (in appearance so contradictory), dream and reality, into a sort of absolute reality: a *surréalité*.[2]

It was under Breton's leadership that the surrealist movement began to consolidate itself into something like an organized system of thought. Central to its philosophy was the determination to honour the claims of the subconscious and to accept the validity of the confusion of our dreams. From this concern, which recommended less a methodology than a state of heightened awareness, certain tendencies followed. To begin with, the more rational, more formal elements of a work of art were thought to be inimical to the kind of intuitive associations at which the surrealists were aiming. The art product itself, then, might appear less important than the insights it recorded. Speaking of the comparative poverty of French surrealist verse, Anthony Hartley has written:

> The result of artistic activity, the poem or the painting, is seen as merely incidental to the inner regeneration of man brought about by the *ascesis* involved in its production.[3]

This is similar to the way in which Harold Rosenberg has talked about action painting. It also describes the aesthetic that has led to the current fashion of disposable art.

Secondly, in their concern with encouraging a state of heightened awareness (itself leading now quite naturally into psychedelic art), the surrealists could easily become obsessed with the pathological, with the sadistic or masochistic recesses of the mind. The writings of de Sade had been enthusiastically rediscovered, and many of the surrealist anecdotes that appeared in Breton's *Littérature* from 1919 to 1924 showed the same concern with gratuitous violence that, back in the 1790s, had characterized de Sade. Perhaps most relevant are Dali's anecdotes scattered thr-ugh his *Secret Life*:

> I was five years old, and it was springtime in the village of Cambrils, near Barcelona. I was walking in the country with a boy smaller than I, who had very blond curly hair and whom I had known only a short time. I was on foot, and he was riding a tricycle. With my hand on his back, I helped to push him along. We got to a bridge under construction which had as yet no railings of any kind. Suddenly, as most of my ideas occur, I looked behind to make sure

that no one was watching us and gave the child a quick push off the bridge. He landed on some rocks fifteen feet below. I ran home to announce the news.

During the whole afternoon, bloodstained basins were brought down from the room where the child, with a badly injured head, was going to have to remain in bed for a week. The continual coming and going and the general turmoil into which the house was thrown put me into a delightful hallucinatory mood. In the small parlour, on a rocking chair trimmed with crocheted lace that covered the back, I sat eating cherries. The parlour looked out on the hall, so that I could observe everything that went on, and it was almost completely dark for the shutters had been drawn to ward off the stifling heat. The sun beating down on them lit up knots in the wood, turning them to a fiery red like cars lighted from behind. I don't recall having experienced the slightest feeling of guilt over the incident. That evening, while taking my usual solitary walk, I remember having savoured the beauty of each blade of grass.[4]

Partly true, partly fictional (our common sense makes us assume), such an anecdote is nevertheless extraordinary in its combination of sadistic violence with a minutely detailed registration of the senses, as well as in its implicit flouting of the conventional sentimentalities about the innocence of childhood. It is not irrelevant to bear such an experience in mind when we come to contemplate the moral complexities of Joseph in Buñuel's *Diary of a Chambermaid*. To be appreciated, such an anecdote demands from us an analyst's patience and suspension of a moral point of view. We are asked not to applaud or to condemn, but simply to understand.

However, if this aspect of surrealism could slip into the excess of moral nihilism, it could also lead to an apparently opposite state of mind. It could equally be concerned with spiritual regeneration, with the perfection of the self. This had been the pattern for many of the Dadaists. As far back as 1921, Marcel Duchamp had withdrawn from the scene, apparently giving up the imperfections of life and art for the perfection of chess (we've seen him playing chess, of course, with Man Ray in René Clair's *Entr'acte*); and before that, Hugo Ball, losing his faith in the possibility of any external change, had given up his life as an artist, concerned to find in private 'the most direct way to self-help: to renounce works and make energetic attempts to re-animate one's own life.'[5]

In this way, the philosophy of surrealism could be seen as a discipline. In one of Breton's more self-questioning statements, he seems to acknowledge this: 'Dear imagination, what I like about you is that you do not forgive.'[6] On this level, surrealism comes to represent an obligation to onself, a determination not to cheat one's own feelings, not to deny the necessity of the 'dark gods' within us (to borrow Lawrence's appropriate phrase). Certainly for Buñuel the ethic of surrealism was both a liberation and a chore:

> Surrealism taught me that life has a moral meaning that man cannot ignore. Through surrealism I discovered for the first time that man is not free. I used to believe man's freedom was unlimited, but in surrealism I saw a discipline to be followed. It was one of the great lessons of my life, a marvellous poetic step forward.[7]

Yet this path too has its excesses. In its social passivity, it could lead to the extremes of personal isolation that can drive a man to suicide, as in its pursuit of inner perfection, it could encourage a narcissistic involvement with the self that could make a person not only socially ineffectual but positively destructive in his relationships with other people. In the world of Buñuel, this is undoubtedly part of the problem of both Viridiana and Nazarin.

Finally – to complete this abbreviated survey – the surrealist view of life never totally renounced its belief in the possibility of a better world which had characterized it since Dada. From the very beginning, in spite of its irrationalism, it had maintained a curious flirtation with the rationalities of communism. After all, both the surrealists and the communists believed in revolution as a means of achieving this better world. In the thirties, when the Spanish Civil War actually split the surrealist movement, André Breton and his followers remained uninvolved, while men like Paul Éluard underwent a gradual change. By 1936, not only could Éluard talk in terms of his life being 'deeply involved in the lives of other men', but his verse as well moved outwards from the exquisite intimacies of *La*

Capitale de la douleur (1926) to the more politically *engagé* verse of his later collections. And yet, as we'll have occasion to note again further on, the defeat of the Republicans at the end of the Spanish war, which was felt by many people to be the defeat of humanity, must have been accepted by some of the surrealists as the final justification of their socially passive view of life. For Buñuel, a Spaniard, it is impossible to calculate the extent to which this defeat has been one of the major sources of his own recurring pessimism. The outbreak of the Second World War in 1939 could have offered small grounds for any renewal of hope.

*

Although polyglot in its origins and surrounded by violence, surrealism, by becoming French in both its literature and philosophy, tended to become more intellectual and more civilized. In fact, there is an inherent discrepancy between the issuing of manifestoes, as Breton was fond of doing, and the belief in the intuitive powers of the subconscious. Manifestoes are always cerebral and polemical, whereas the language of dreams that these manifestoes claimed to believe in is always more intuitive. Though I have scarcely the space here to argue out such a position in detail, it has always seemed to me that in surrealism *as a movement*, there is a kind of superficiality that could easily degenerate into the futile pleasures of striving simply to shock the bourgeoisie. At the heart of surrealism *as a view of life*, on the other hand, there remains the recognition of the irreconcilable claims both of the individual and of society upon which our civilization has been insecurely based.

During the last few years, there has been a tremendous interest shown in the 'D-S Expedition', as Roger Shattuck has called it – an interest accompanied by reprints and translations of many of the original Dada and Surrealistic documents.[8] However, the movement was a complex one and has yet to find its definitive historian. An interpreter like J. H. Matthews, while helpful through the background information he provides, is completely uncritical of the assumptions behind the movement; and when he comes to Buñuel, he is unwilling to make any distinctions of quality between the films.[9] What we most need now, as Shattuck has argued, is a thorough attempt to *place* surrealism within its proper historical context and, most important, to measure the gap between its many manifestoes, with all their inconsistencies, and what finally, as a movement, it was able to achieve.

All I am attempting to do here is to give some idea of the intellectual and artistic atmosphere that obviously played such a formative part in the life of Buñuel. But there were other forces too, forces connected with his early life in Spain. In fact, while surrealism *as a movement* was at the outset very much a literary movement and, because of this, very French, the artists that we tend now to remember are, with the fine exception of Éluard, largely the painters, many of whom were Spanish. Indeed, it may be as much their Spanishness as their allegiance to surrealism that unites artists like Dali, Miró, and Picasso, as it might be their Spanishness that has kept them true to the most intuitive elements in the surrealist view of life. For in many ways Spain is instrinsically a surrealist country, maintaining side by side the medieval extremes of elegance and cruelty, as in many ways Luis Buñuel is the most probing surrealist of them all.

A land of extremes both in climate and in culture, a huge dustbowl surrounded by the sea, combining courtly dignity with animal brutality, Spain does seem to embody the sharp contrasts which lie at the heart of surrealism. Its national sport – the bull-fight – is emblematic: a ballet of elegance and blood. Like Sweden, culturally Spain is outside Europe; yet unlike Sweden, Spain's feeling of isolation from the history of Europe is not the result of a cunning neutrality. Spain has had its own war that has cut across the historically greater wars of Europe. For the Spaniards, Europe's problems may well have seemed provincial. The people of Spain failed to win *their* war.

Luis Buñuel, born on 22 February 1900 in Calanda in the province of Saragossa, is first and foremost a Spaniard and after that a surrealist. His view of life has developed from this primary fact. His inheritance has been Spanish, as his response to life seems largely to have been intuitive. It is only in his more playful moods that he sometimes seems cerebral, content to mock his pet hates from merely the surface of his mind.

A crucial part of this Spanish inheritance was his Jesuit education.[10] Spanish Catholicism, perhaps more extremely than that of any other country, must have brought home to the young Buñuel the surrealist antagonism between the ideals of the spirit and the exigencies of the flesh, as it would undoubtedly have brought home to him the terrifying gap between the rich security of the church and the destitute, precarious state of whole sections of the Spanish people. Yet it is a mistake, I've always felt, to see this influence as negative in any simple way. Not only has Buñuel returned to religious considerations in his films with such regularity that they must be taken as one of the mainsprings of his art, but it seems to me that a large part of what is most positive in his films could have come from this early training as well.

For instance, at the centre of Buñuel's vision is what the surrealists were to call the destructive forces of man, what Freud has categorized as the unmanageable 'id', but what Buñuel would have known from way back as the problem of evil. Related to any form of pessimism, there is always a belief in evil as an abstraction, or at least as an unalterable characteristic of the nature of man. If one simply believes that social injustice is the source of man's problems (as so many fans seem to think Buñuel does), then one can combat this injustice by constructive social action; but if one believes that evil is inherent to the nature of man, then constructive action becomes that much more difficult and one's belief in improvement that much more tenuous. If evil is intrinsic, if the impulse towards destruction is deeply planted in man's nature – as Christianity has always taught and as the Parisian surrealists were excited to reaffirm, as if making a new discovery – then the problem for any civilization is to find some way of containing it. Here too, the church may have helped.

While rejecting the metaphysical consolations of Christianity, Buñuel nevertheless seemed to gain from Spanish Catholicism an urgent recognition of the importance of ritual in combating our more unmanageable desires. Whether a violent ritual of expiation like the three-day drumming ceremony that still forms a part of the Easter celebrations at Calanda[11] – an interesting example, by the way, of the Catholic Church's quite remarkable ability to take over what I would imagine to be a pre-Christian ritual of exorcism and to make it a part of its own resurrection myth – or the more contemplative rituals of, for example, the celebration of High Mass, again and again in Buñuel references to such ceremonies appear. Often they are presented in a bizarre, even a facetious light – like the foot-washing sequence that opens the strange and magnificent *El* – and they are invariably tinged with the suggestion of a repressed sexuality; but sometimes, as in *Viridiana*, the sense of ceremony can lend to what might otherwise be a commonplace scene the feeling of intense personal involvement. Thus, hugely helped by the music, Don Jaime's premeditated seduction of his chaste and attractive niece achieves a kind of awe in the way it is presented to us, an awe intermixed with pathos at the realization that, finally, Don Jaime is too gentle and considerate to be able to express his most compulsive needs.

Intertwined with this feeling for ritual, there is also in Buñuel a concern with the peculiarly symbolic associations inherent to inanimate objects, a concern that also must have been encouraged by the iconography of the church. Whether, as in *L'Âge d'or*, it is Modot being distracted from his love-making by the foot of a statue or Francisco's valet in *El*, who polishes his bicycle in his bed, in Buñuel these actions take on an additional force from the symbolic role the objects play in the characters' lives.

Finally, when speculating in this way about the relationship of his early environment to his mature view of life, we might be tempted to relate Buñuel's continual concern with human solitude to the fact of his own exile. Almost all his life, in order to work, he has had to live away from Spain; for large sections of it, in order to live, he has had to perform menial roles within the film industry. Although in his private life apparently the gentlest of men,[12] in his films Buñuel has insistently returned to the problems of violence and evil and to the recognition that these passions seem often the result of a man being isolated and made to feel alone. From Modot's fury in *L'Âge d'or* to Joseph's rapacious fascism in *Diary of a Chambermaid*, their destructive urges could be related to their solitary lives.

This feeling of isolation in Buñuel's own life has obviously increased with his growing deafness and, as I've suggested, it may well have been aggravated by his life away from Spain. But in his films, it would seem to be part of a recognition that, finally, the individual *is* an isolated phenomenon, with only a limited ability to react profitably with another person or to act constructively upon the outside world. Though there is always great gentleness in the films of Buñuel, there is also great destructiveness; and the destructiveness seems, socially, to be the greater force. Power is much more easily organized than gentleness; and in any case, even within any individual manifestation of gentleness, there is also a dammed-up force of destructiveness threatening to break free or to turn in upon itself. So Don Jaime, who is so gentle he takes pains to save the life of a bee and who, with all his Bach and Mozart, is ultimately too civilized to enact his private ritual upon the body of his sleeping niece, in his frustration and despair hangs himself.

But if Buñuel is in essence both a Spaniard and a surrealist, he is interesting to us today not only for the persuasive power of his view of life but for the intricacy of its development in his individual films. He is interesting because, above all, he is an artist. The sharp contrasts and conflicting points of view of his troubled world are already present in all their force in his first three films, *Un Chien andalou, L'Âge d'or* and *Land Without Bread (Las Hurdes)*.

*

I should like to make even the most ordinary spectator feel that he is not living in the best of all possible worlds.[13]

I have dwelt at some length both on the origins of surrealism and on what I have called the naturally surrealist aspects of Spanish culture because it seems to me that Buñuel is an artist who has frequently been most misunderstood by those who claim most to admire him. The genuinely surrealist elements in his work, the more troubled, more involved, more intuitive elements, have often been misinterpreted as simply the zany pseudo-surrealist's love of the anti-bourgeois gag. The profundities of his work, as I understand them, have been much less elucidated than his pervasive sense of fun.[14]

In my urge to set things right, I don't want to appear too solemn about the troubled master; for there certainly is in Buñuel a strong iconoclastic impulse and, as in all great artists, a wry sense of the absurd. But, as I hope I'll be able to illustrate in the argument that follows, even Buñuel's humour is edged in black despair. More often than not, it is the self-protective humour of a deeply pessimistic person, the humour of a man distressed by his own vision of the universe but who has also a keen eye for the multitude of self deceptions that, for many of us, make life bearable.

Buñuel has, of course, his more facile side – the impulse to mock without self-involvement, the kind of comic spirit that is too much of our times. In Buñuel's early works, it would be convenient to attribute the levity to Dali while reserving the profundity for the more serious Buñuel. But this would be an oversimplification. Not only would it be an injustice to what is genuine in Dali, but it would also ignore the fact that Buñuel is quite capable of simply playing with his material in a facile manner when the script he is working with and the production conditions encourage him to do so.

The Exterminating Angel, Simon of the Desert, Belle de jour, and The Milky Way are all examples, in my view, of Buñuel working in this way. But whatever the ultimate explanation, and however the responsibility was shared between himself and Dali in Buñuel's first two films, both Un Chien andalou and L'Âge d'or seem to alternate between what we might call gags that encourage smugness and gags that disturb.

Un Chien andalou (1928) is clearly the less satisfactory of the two. The crucial question to ask about such a film, as about any kind of satire, is whether we ourselves feel implicated or comfortably left outside? Do we feel imaginatively involved in a way that might lead us to some kind of increased understanding, or do we simply feel smug? It is in the light of this kind of question, so rarely asked by Buñuel commentators, that recent films like *Simon of the Desert* and *The Milky Way* appear to be, while perhaps very funny, comparatively inferior works. If we bring the same question to bear on Buñuel's earliest films, what do we find? What kind of experience, finally, can we take away from *Un Chien andalou*?

Because of its wilful obscurity, it cannot help but appeal chiefly to our minds – the very reverse of the surrealists' intentions. John Russell Taylor is on to this when he complains that the film only works on the level of scandal[15]; but Frédéric Grange is the most perceptive in clarifying the gap between the film's intentions and its achievement.[16] Because of the inescapably real nature of the cinematic image, its sculptural physicality, the form of the film is less like a dream than like a *memory* of a dream, like a dream recalled. Similarly, the film is less concerned with insistent sexuality than with erotic gestures, self-consciously executed scenes, which, while often funny in a superficial way (the angry woman beating off sex with a tennis racket, or the distressed man dragging the dead remnants of his culture behind him), seem chiefly like an illustration to Freud. A cut from a man's face in apparent rapture to breasts and back to his face bleeding with self-inflicted martyrdom makes primarily a *mental* appeal. Direct emotional involvement is debarred by the editorial process.

Similarly, the final image of the couple buried in the sand only works as an illustration to a preconceived thesis (again vaguely Freudian); and the asserted disruption of time in the titles that occur at various points in the film – 'Eight Years Later'; 'Fourteen Years Before' – these editorial devices, gags if you will, are very unlike the direct and inescapably physical way a dream works upon us, genuinely disrupting our sense of time, which then invites a tentative interpretation by the mind.

The images in *Un Chien andalou* have all been pre-selected for us according to an idea about the workings of the subconscious and they appeal chiefly, I should have thought, to that slightly superior sense in most of us that we are above being shocked or moved. Years after the making of the film, Buñuel himself has referred to 'those foolish people who have been able to find the film beautiful or poetic when at bottom it is really a desperate and passionate call to murder'.[17] Yet it is doubtful if anyone has *ever* seen the film in this way.

Un Chien andalou was the prototype for that kind of 'experimental' film which really, by its very nature, fails in its best intentions. If we took the film scene by scene, and with psycho-analytical ingenuity offered to explain it all,[18] the explanation would probably seem more meaningful than the experience of watching the film. This too is unlike the experience of a genuine dream, which can create a feeling too complex to be conveyed in the telling of it (which is why it is often so boring listening to descriptions of other people's dreams).

L'Âge d'or (1930) exhibits some of the same problems but a greater physical power and complexity as well. As with all of Buñuel, it is less a complexity of effect than a potential complexity of response – an elusive, subjective matter. Images – many of them unavoidably real – are thrust before our eyes in a way which may disturb or arrest us but which eludes easy interpretation. Speaking of Buñuel, John Russell Taylor has referred to a 'sort of imagist poetry which comes from an intense heightening of individual sense impressions, so that certain selected objects take on the quality of a fetish, an instrument of ritual significance in the re-enactment of some private myth'.[19]

Even the opening images of the scorpions fighting is both compelling to watch in its unfamiliarity and ambiguous in intention. First of all, it declares a documentary veracity that has a relationship to the rest of the film which is not wholly ironic. This opening sequence contains an apparently objective statement of the theme of the film and of Buñuel's entire world – a recognition that life is founded upon aggression. Insects fight with one another and then are swallowed up by animals larger than themselves. Such, too, it would seem to be implied, is the nature of man.

From this opening follow all the discrepancies and ambiguities of Buñuel's personal world. On the one hand, we have the bandits (led by Max Ernst), in revolt amongst themselves and against the world, but disorganized, purposeless; on the other, there are the archbishops, organized and self-contained, chanting their litanies, but also self-petrifying, already ossified by the time they have become the basis of Western civilization. Hence the basic paradox of society: it is based on a system of order devised to repress the instinctual life, and so must rely upon a police state to hold in check the instincts that it sets out to deny. Hence, too, the ceremony of the Majorcans – absurdly pictured as the dignitaries arrive in all their unsuitable regalia and scramble over the craggy earth – this ceremony of state is based upon self-deception. It denies the force of sexuality (and its excremental regressions) and the even greater force of anger that such denial brings.

So Modot, torn from his woman, sees sex in everything he looks at but has to content himself with kicking a lap-dog, crushing a cockroach, or pushing a blind man into the path of an oncoming car. Even the class system springs from this deception and from the imagined necessity of maintaining it. The menials in their garbage-cart can carry away the shit and submit to the destructiveness of their passions (the waitress and the flames; the gamekeeper and his son) while the nobs carry on with their cocktails and polite conversation.

Gaston Modot most compellingly plays the role of the angrily instinctive man. His life (he imagines, like Monteil in *Chambermaid*) is dedicated to the pursuit of *l'amour fou*. Everything he sees in life reminds him of his sexual insistences and hence provokes his rage; while Lya Lys, on the other hand, tries to deny to herself the essentially physical nature of her needs (she chases the cow from her bed) and tries to escape into imaginative reverie which Buñuel presents as essentially narcissistic – the clouds in the mirror as she assiduously polishes her nails. Meanwhile, the cow's bell continues to ring.

For the critics who like to think of Buñuel as simply having fun at the expense of the bourgeoisie, interpretation of the film usually stops at this point.[20] But the essential fact about Modot is that he is defeated by the conventions of the society he is in rebellion against. Like Don Jaime in *Viridiana*, he is trapped within the society that has both formed and denied him. While inside it and driven on by his desire, he rebels against it (the slap over the spilt wine); but once he is free from it and alone at last with his woman, the social forms inhibit him (the chairs), infantile memories confuse him (his mother's voice), the artefacts of culture and religion distract him (the Wagner, of course, but most insistently the statue), and finally the business world with its own kind of violence interferes: 'The Minister of the Interior wants you on the telephone.' By the end of the sequence, he has lost his woman and is alone, impotent and self-martyred, tearing the feathers from his pillow as the drums beat furiously, striving to free himself from the devils that torment him and to rid himself of all the fetishes that have got in his way.

The orgy sequence that ends the film would seem to imply that these many discrepancies must lead to the perversion of even the finest elements within our civilization, where Christ himself plays the role of the Marquis de Sade. In some ways, it is not too satisfactory an ending for this basically probing work – tacked on as an *envoi* like the final image of *Un Chien andalou*, as if to summarize the preconceived moral. Like the final jump-cuts in *Chambermaid*, the *pasa doble* as an accompaniment to the tufts of hair on the cross strives to end the film with a laugh, as if finally our despair is essentially comic. Perhaps it is, but not really. Perhaps we have to pretend it is to carry on living with this dilemma without solution.

Land Without Bread (visuals 1932; sound 1937) could represent a continuation of the scorpions, a documentary glance at an essential aspect of man. It is an investigation of the total helplessness to be found within an arid recess of the same stream of Western culture that is symbolically present throughout the film in the heroic strains of the Brahms. Like the music in *L'Âge d'or* – bits of Mendelssohn, Beethoven, Schubert, and Wagner, made further bizarre by being rescored for chamber orchestra – the Brahms makes an ironic comment on the situation that we are exposed to. Like the spoken commentary, it reinforces the essential irrelevance of our civilized point of view, certainly of our pity, and of all the romantic aspirations of our culture.

The basic fact about this community is that it *has* no culture, no real way of life. Even the trappings of the church have mostly faded away, leaving chiefly a few hermits in decaying surroundings. What the children are taught in school bears no relation to the realities of life around them; yet the images of sickness and unhappiness all come from the natural surroundings of these people as part of nature's gift to them, an aspect of God's goodness.

The commentary doesn't plead. It simply states: the situation, a possible source of improvement, then the inapplicability of this source for these people. This progression of three continues throughout; and, visually, each sequence ends on an image of violence or misery so extreme that they are missing from most of the prints in circulation in Great Britain – a mountain goat plunging to his death, a donkey being devoured by bees, a sick man trembling with fever, an idiot's leer. Generally in Buñuel, it is the falseness of society that interferes with the fulfilment of man; in *Land Without Bread*, it would appear to be nature itself: 'On the surface, the film attacks the existence of misery: more deeply, it denounces the misery of existence . . .'[21] Yet finally, once we have got over the effect of the film and paid tribute to the power of its steady passion, a disquieting question might suggest itself to us. For what is our relation to all this? Indeed, what is Buñuel's? Is *Land Without Bread* the kind of film that invites social action or does it seem more like an expression of social despair? These questions are perhaps most easily answered by reference to some further films.

*

For eighteen years, from 1932 to 1950, Buñuel virtually disappeared from view. He worked in Hollywood for a bit, supposedly on the script of *The Beast With Five Fingers*, and at the Museum of Modern Art in New York. After the war, he went to Mexico, where he was taken up by Oscar Dancigers for reputed pot-boilers like *Gran Casino* (1947) and *El Gran Calavera* (1949).[22] After these, Dancigers allowed him almost total freedom with *Los Olvidados*, which won him the director's prize at Cannes in 1950. It was, Buñuel said, 'the only film I am responsible for since *Land Without Bread*'.[23]

There can be no finer account of this film than that offered by

Alan Lovell in his little-known pamphlet, *Anarchist Cinema*.[24] The one new moral factor in *Los Olvidados* that was not present in Buñuel's first three films in the same structural way is the factor of innocence. In fact, we could almost establish a hierarchy of innocence and vulnerability in the film, moving towards cruelty and violence, motivated by the urge to destroy. The quality that shifts along this spectrum is, of course, the quality of love – not quite the Christian *agape* but more like the simple physical tenderness, the habit of affection, that characterizes Bergman's early films and provides such a strong element of affirmation in them. In Buñuel, however (and here I disagree somewhat with Alan Lovell's refutation of the pessimism of the film), things are not quite that simple, not so schematic.

Ochitos, Meche, Pedro, Pedro's mother, Jaibo, the Blind Man these characters represent a crescendo of violence in the film, of the destructive forces of society. Yet, as with the Hurdanos, they are all seen as part of the same insistently physical world. It is a barren, shelterless place of poverty and hardship where the people are driven into violence by the insistent need to survive. The cocks and chickens, the gentler farmyard animals, the innumerable stray dogs that litter the film – these are all part of the same mendicant, animal world, a confirmation of its physicality. The characters are seen as wholesome in proportion to the degree that they share the gentleness of the more domesticated animals.

Thus, we have the comparative haven of the stable, with whatever associations you will. All the characters find shelter there. It is Meche's natural home and the place in which Ochitas can drink spontaneously from the teat of a donkey. Yet it is not just a place of shelter. Meche's grandfather gets angry there, and of course her brother is as much of the place as she is. Finally, while seeking the expected shelter, Pedro is brutally killed there and then disposed of as rubbish. Even this gentler atmosphere is not inviolate.

In a casual way, without formal emphasis, the characters tend to be associated with different kinds of animals. While still young in violence and attempting to resist it, Pedro is associated with young chickens – unlike the Blind Man, who is most frequently associated with the hostile and vindictive cock. Yet here too there are no simple contrasts. The Blind Man is also the one who handles the curative dove. In this superstitious society, he is received as a healer, grotesquely ironic though this may seem. In his admiration for the dictator Porfirio Díaz, in his home among the steel girders – 'an exact symbol of the violence and anonymity of life in a large modern city'[25] – even in his blindness and hence his isolation from the physical appearance of things, the Blind Man represents all that is most reactionary in contemporary society. Looking forward to both the Captain and Joseph in *Diary of a Chambermaid*, he believes in violence as a creed. 'One less,' he cries out in enraged delight as Jaibo is shot down. 'They should all be killed at birth.' This is followed by a desperate sequence that depicts the fruits of such a philosophy: the gentle Meche dumping the slaughtered Pedro on to the rubbish heap, shunning involvement.

In *Los Olvidados*, the characters are disturbingly interdependent, good and evil distributed in varying proportions throughout them all. Meche, although gentle, is also provocative (like Pedro's mother with her legs) and she is prepared to sell her kisses. Even Ochitos is tempted to rise to violence, both with Jaibo and then with the Blind Man, and may well have to if he is going to survive. All the clubbings in the film, whether of Julian, the chickens, or Pedro, are shot in the same way. The violence is directly recorded without editorial insistence but with a documentary matter-of-factness. Thus the title – *The Lost Ones* – refers to them all.

Structurally, however, there are some problems in the film, problems acutely analysed by Alan Lovell. First of all, we have the breakdown of causality in the Pedro/Jaibo relationship, the intrusion of coincidence that gives this part of the film an Oliver Twist kind of sentimentality, an added charge of pathos which is the very feeling that Buñuel supposedly is most against. Secondly, there is the corrective-farm sequence with its moralizing quality and all that it implies.

It would be convenient to assume that this farm sequence was imposed upon the film, but I'm not too sure. The clearest point about it is its isolation and its irrelevance to the world outside. Once away from its protection (implausibly or not), Pedro is lost. Like Buñuel's islands in both *Robinson Crusoe* and *The Young One*, as Frédéric Grange has said, the farm 'represents a utopia with regards to a reality that it is incapable of changing'. Finally, as we scrutinize the film and admire the delicacy of its interwoven network of shared responsibilities – even the association of Ochitos (= Big Eyes) and the Blind Man is troubling in the extreme: finally, we might ask, as with *Land Without Bread*, what is our relation to all this? What are the qualities in life that might help us to endure? Still not an easy question to answer.

*

In spite of the artistic success of *Los Olvidados*, for the next eight years Buñuel's career was not easy. Whether in Mexico or in France, it appears he had little control over the projects he was offered. My own memory of all the films made during this period is of seriously marred films of considerable interest. Whether they are marred by thundering implausibilities (*Susana, Archibaldo*), crabbed plots (*El*, and nearly all of the French stuff) or indifferent acting (especially *The Young One*), they seem to be films that are less interesting in themselves, each one separately, than they are either as interesting facets of the complete Buñuel or for the inescapable power of individual moments – their *raison d'être*, I've always felt, and the real source of their strength. Whatever we think of the entire films, after we've seen *El* we will remember Francisco alone on the stairs in his despair or preparing his needle and thread to enter his wife's room; and after *Archibaldo*, we will remember Archibaldo's fascination with the manikin's face melting and recall that when he first saw Lavinia, she was surrounded by flames.

Nevertheless, I should say that each time I've re-seen (for example) *The Young One*, I've become less conscious of the stilted way that many of the lines are delivered and more aware of the essential delicacy of presentation of the film's view of life. Phenomenologically, it is really as if the 'faults' become absorbed by the qualities, so intermingled they both seem to be.

At this stage, therefore, anything said about these films must be both tentative and provisional. The films will have to be made more available before we'll be sure about the elusive question of their quality.*

As I think about them, however, the ones I most remember seem to go in pairs. Both *Susana* (1950) and *El Bruto* (1952) explore the disruptive effect that sexual passion can have upon a controlled community. In fact, in a way that carries on from *Los Olvidados*, *El Bruto* really dramatizes the conflict between gentle love and erotic passion, with the brutal defeat of the former. In a way that anticipates *Belle de jour* (1966), *El* and *The Criminal Life of Archibaldo de la Cruz* (*Ensayo de un Crimen*, 1955) both deal with the inner plight of men locked within themselves.[26] Both Francisco and Archibaldo are imprisoned within their own fantasies. They are both essentially impotent and so are reduced to private rituals of a surrealist absurdity. By the end of the films, Francisco is confined to a kind of religious madness, zigzagging his life away in a monastery; but Archibaldo (however implausibly) has been set free from himself. Nevertheless, it is interesting to observe how, once Archibaldo has destroyed the symbol of his mother's hold over him (and as the music box sinks into the river, the water bubbles up over it as if it were human!), he is pleased to let a praying mantis live that he finds on the trunk of a tree on his way to meet his girl. Unlike poor Modot in *L'Âge d'or* he is now at peace with nature and with the world.[27]

But the most interesting of these films are the two in English, *The Adventures of Robinson Crusoe* (1952) and *The Young One* (1960). Not only are they both set on islands – like the farm in *Los Olvidados*, isolated worlds away from the corruptions of organized society – but also they really do appear to be Buñuel's most positive films. By the end of both of them, more plausibly than in *Archibaldo*, something has been achieved, some human qualities have prevailed.

*Since this chapter has been written, I've had the opportunity of re-seeing *El*. This too now seems to me a much finer film, far more successful, than I give it credit for here; it is certainly as 'interesting' as *Robinson Crusoe* and *The Young One*.

'I've never liked the novel but I love the character,' Buñuel has said of *Robinson Crusoe*[28]; and by the end of his film, through Friday, Crusoe has succeeded in coming to a greater understanding of the physical realities of life. He has broken away from his inherited concepts of a master/servant relationship into an awareness of what human contact might entail. Similarly in *The Young One*, through his contact with little Evie, Miller has come to re-examine not only his own racial prejudices but his whole way of thinking about life, about the supposedly clear-cut categories of good and evil. If *The Young One* must still be considered a 'bad' film by conventional standards, then it is one of the most subtle, most challenging, and most distinguished bad films ever made.[29]

Discussing all the French films made at this time – *Cela s'appelle l'aurore* (1955), *La Mort en ce jardin* (1956), and *La Fièvre monte à El Pao* (1959) – Frédéric Grange suggests that their greater social quality, their greater involvement with political corruption, is accompanied by an increasing degree of abstraction from physical reality that robs these films of their potentially most Buñuelian quality.[30] It is as if Buñuel, on the political level, simply couldn't care, or found that he was unable to believe. The perfunctory quality of these films seems to suggest a kind of artistic fatigue.

*

I love *Nazarin* because it is a film that allowed me to express certain things I care about. But I don't believe I denied or abjured anything ... I am still an atheist, thank God.[31]

I am very much attached to Nazarin. He is a priest. He could as well be a hairdresser or a waiter. What interests me about him is that he stands by his ideas, that these ideas are unacceptable to society at large, and that after his adventures with prostitutes, thieves, and so forth, they lead him to being irrevocably damned by the prevailing social order...[32]

Nazarin (1958) was an exception and, in artistic terms, marked yet a new beginning. Like so much of Buñuel, the film would repay a close analysis, a minute examination of its individual effects; but more briefly here we could perhaps best define its moral structure by looking at the characterization of three different men.

First of all, there is Pinto, the *caballero*. With his spurs and whip, he is obviously a development of the Jesus figure in *Susana*, but he is related to other Buñuel characters as well. In this harsh Mexico of poverty and authority, the Mexico of Porfirio Díaz that was recalled with such enthusiasm by the Blind Man in *Los Olvidados*, Pinto is obviously strong. Like Bergman's Squire in *The Seventh Seal*, Pinto accepts the physicality of life for what it is, and acts accordingly. He knows about horses and, as the scene by the fountain would imply, he knows how to subdue the devils that are tormenting Beatrix. He moves deliberately and noisily from place to place, the sound of his spurs always accompanying his movements. He is obviously a positive force in the film, an aspect of whatever social stability there might have been at such a time; but to what extent he actually endorses the values of that world, a rigid feudal world held in place by force, and thus looks forward to both Joseph and the Captain in *Diary of a Chambermaid*, is something that we'll have to decide.

On the other hand, we have Ujo, the dwarf. A physically grotesque and absurdly vulnerable creature, when we first see him strung up in a tree, we realize that he is dependent on the Pintos of this society to keep him alive. It is a *caballero* who sets him free. Yet, grotesquely, paradoxically, surrealistically, Ujo is the most affirmative figure in all of Buñuel, the most complete incarnation of *agape*, of Christian love. His acceptance of the world, of its physical reality, obviously forced upon him by the hapless shape of his own body, is total and untinged by self-deception. 'You're ugly, you're a whore, but I love you,' he says to Andara. 'What a kick! Were you angry!' he later exclaims at her cell window quite spontaneously, as he comes to re-accept her. There is scarcely any question here of forgiveness in the formally Christian sense of the word, of turning the other cheek – which, finally, Nazarin finds it hard to do when he too is kicked about in his cell. Ujo simply *accepts* the event as he accepts the violence and physicality of existence.

Whenever we see Ujo, he is helping people – offering fruit

to the female prisoners and the child, physical projections of his 'love', of his intensely real human concern. So too his final offering of the peach to Andara, his arm fully extended in his effort to reach up to her, his look of extreme pleasure and then his embarrassed turning away. The language of criticism always falters with such a moment in the cinema, for the richness of possible feeling (both in Ujo and in ourselves) is impossible to describe. But it is a most affirmative gesture, made disturbingly pathetic as he then hobbles after her, unable to keep up.

Just as the surrealists at their most engaged set out to challenge the nature of matter and the meaning of art and life, so Ujo challenges our sentimental notions of virtue and charity, of moral goodness in an authoritarian world. Although with our conscious selves we claim to know better, we still tend to equate virtue with beauty of some kind. The Keatsian fallacy persists in its attractiveness. Through Ujo, Buñuel will not let us do this; and I have found it extraordinary how few critics have even *noticed* the presence of Ujo in the film, let alone paid tribute to the moral role he plays.[33]

Between the two extremes of Pinto and Ujo walks Nazarin – we could really say, looking neither to the left nor right. Until the end of the film, Nazarin notices nothing about the world he inhabits, certainly nothing of its violence and its physicality. If he is a man who stands by his ideas (as Buñuel has said), these ideas have not been derived from an observation of the real world. In this sense, he is as much a prisoner of his own self-delusions as Francisco in *El* or the hero of *Archibaldo*. If he is a Christian striving to live a thoroughly good life of self-denial and of spiritual ideals, he is a text-book Christian about whom, constantly, we sense there is something wrong.

Obviously he is self-denying (we scarcely ever see him eat), and he does try to reject the accusations of sainthood that superstitious people keep thrusting upon him; yet nothing in his life works out as he might wish. Something seems odd. Is it really the society that will not accept him (again as Buñuel has claimed), or is there something in himself that brings about rejection? Not only is he ineffectual in everything he tries to do – indeed, often destructive, unleashing passions in others – but there is the sense of some discrepancy in the man himself (like the window that serves as a door for his room – just a tinge of the old surrealist absurdity, of the cow in the bed).

Most simply, most conventionally, it could be seen as a matter of spiritual pride. He sees himself as above the petty trivialities of the rest of the world and is determined to stay there. He rejects the world of the flesh with such insistent thoroughness that he is unable to know what it is all about. So he is useless to everyone.

Like *Los Olvidados*, *Nazarín*'s world is an intensely physical one, punctuated throughout by animal sights and sounds; and this world remains unaffected by anything that Nazarín can do. The woman dying of the plague wants not heaven but Juan; Beatrix's devils are her sexual and emotional needs; and Andara remains unrepentant and without 'charity' to the end. 'May all your children be still-born and may you choke on your own pus!' These are the last words we hear from her, directed against the fat thief. It is an intensely physical curse.

It is the thin thief who, while contriving to rob Nazarín, begins to bring about his inner regeneration. 'Your life is wholly good and mine is wholly bad but what has either of us accomplished?' When this question is put to him, Nazarín – here looking most deliberately like a classic Rembrandt Christ – is for the first time in the film directly affected by something outside himself. Up to this point in the film, he has always had an appropriate homily ready as an answer, but this question brings about his silence.

The final stage is achieved when he is alone on the road. It has always seemed to me that it is less the offer of the pineapple that moves him so deeply than the fact that the woman blesses him. It is the blessing, I feel, from a simple peasant woman that he really cannot accept and which he three times refuses. With the drums referring back to Modot's defeated rage in *L'Âge d'or* and beyond that to the Easter ceremonies at Calanda, the ending is affirmative in a way, as if Nazarín has at last come to accept his own frail humanity, his own need to be blessed. But he passes out of frame. Where will that road lead? Even if he has been brought to some point of self-awareness, what will now be his role in the world? Again we have the question, what does Buñuel believe?

*

If I have dealt in some detail with the problems of *Nazarin*, it is because I feel that it is the film that most successfully holds in balance these problems of personal belief, belief not in any kind of metaphysical benevolent Patron but in the relationship between good and evil in the world. What qualities in life does Buñuel believe will survive? This is again the question asked implicitly by *Viridiana*.[34]

When *Viridiana* first burst upon the world in 1961, if it had been seen in the light of the more reticent *Nazarin*, the response to its apparent extravagances might well have been more subdued. While stylistically very different – *Viridiana* is so much more exuberant, more exciting technically, and displays a denser observation of the variety of human life – thematically the films are very much the same. Whether it's Don Jaime in his stately home surrounded by the artefacts of a culture somewhat at odds with the urgency of his private needs, or Viridiana in her convent, *Viridiana* depicts the intrusion into these too private and self-deceiving worlds of the brute facts of reality.

In some ways Viridiana is a more positive figure than Nazarin – certainly Buñuel constantly associates her with images of great beauty – yet finally she is not much more successful. The ending of *Viridiana* is just as tentative and just as disturbing as the ending of *Nazarin*. Certainly, in an inward way, with her crown of thorns burnt and her hair now let loose, Viridiana has achieved some acceptance of the physicalities of her own life. Yet what is the world she is moving into? With this increase in self-knowledge, what role now will she be able to play?

Always the same question to which there can be no cheerful answer, although Buñuel takes pains to give us the feeling of something open at the end. Yet the more I contemplate his work, especially with the unambiguous defeat of all decent impulses represented by *Diary of a Chambermaid* and the vindictive cruelty so much a part of *Tristana*, the more I feel that there is really no ambiguity about the end of these earlier films.

Buñuel simply shows us that there are certainly manifestations of individual tenderness and through these some measure of individual salvation still possible in the world; but outside the individual, the forces of darkness await us, for there is nothing we can do. His supposed ambiguity is more frequently his unwillingness to draw this bleak conclusion. Surrealist to the core of himself, he simply presents the situation and lets us make of it what we may, deceiving ourselves if we will.

At the end of *Viridiana*, what in fact have we? She has moved on in the direction of reality, and there is something radiant and affirmative even about her timidity at the end. After her rape, like Nazarin, she is silent and unsure of herself and so, we might feel, more ready to receive life. And yet what kind of life is there for her to receive? A *ménage à trois* with Jorge and the long-suffering Ramona? What will she be able to achieve with that?

Jorge represents a positive spirit in the film. A bastard heir to this great estate, he feels no obligation to respect any of the past, unlike Ramona who keeps him from merely diddling with his father's cherished organ. Though no great philanthropist, he is nevertheless capable of isolated acts of kindness when a problem is brought to his attention. He sets one dog free that is tied to a cart, without much worrying about all the other dogs.

His attitude to love-making is probably much the same – casual and efficient; but before he pounces on her, he inspects Ramona's teeth in a way that makes us remember Pinto and his horse. He believes in the future and has big plans for the great estate; yet, while we see many scenes of energetic activity, intercut with Viridiana and her beggars serene beneath the almond trees, we see nothing that is built. Nor, for all the talk about points and plugs, do we have any electricity by the end. The Bach and Mozart and the *Hallelujah Chorus* have been replaced by *Shake your cares away*, an undistinguished pop song which may have, in comparison, 'a certain humanity' as Alan Lovell has argued, but is not very encouraging. As the camera pulls back from Viridiana playing cards with Jorge and Ramona, seeming more and more imprisoned in that little room, we do indeed see that order has been restored after the beggars' orgy but the clutter of the place is no different than in Don Jaime's day. Though no conclusions are drawn, the implication would seem to be very black indeed – and almost indistinguishable from the ending of *L'Âge d'or*.

At the centre of the finest aspirations of our culture (this film would seem to be saying), with all our Bach and Mozart, there is a suicidal sexual repression that struggles to get free. If we liberate ourselves from this repression, then the culture seems to go as well and we're left with the feeble suggestion that we should shake our cares away. Meanwhile, outside these disturbingly personal matters, these insistent questions of personal salvation, there is the church in its solidity, organized and impenetrable, and its opposite pole, the poor beggars – like the bandits in *L'Âge d'or*, in revolt against the world and amongst themselves but without a purpose. It is not an encouraging view of the world.

*

With the exception of *Diary of a Chambermaid*, which I'll talk about later, the films that have followed *Viridiana* have disappointed me slightly. I have also been disappointed by the way they have been received. Perhaps I *am* too solemn in my response to Buñuel. Yet I don't think so. I really need to return to the distinction made at the opening of this chapter, a distinction between gags that encourage smugness and gags that disturb. There is certainly room for both in the world, as there is obviously much to enjoy in films like *The Exterminating Angel* and *The Milky Way* – especially if one has been brought up within the hagiography of the Roman Catholic church. Nevertheless, I would like to argue that films like *Los Olvidados* and *Nazarin* represent achievements of a much finer kind. If I dwell on them unduly at the expense of Buñuel's more playful, more popular works, it is partly in opposition to the uncritical enthusiasm with which these comparatively superficial films have been received.

For instance, even as thoughtful and original a critic as Raymond Durgnat gives three times the space to disentangling the playful perplexities of *Belle de jour* than he gives to *Viridiana*.

Yet Durgnat himself has been most lucid in explaining the 'dramatic logic' that Buñuel's films possess:

Dramatic logic is suggestive rather than exclusive, divergent rather than convergent. It's not 'this must follow from that ...' but 'had you realized that these apparently distinct factors could be related?' The value of dramatic logic lies not in its irrefutability, but in the insights which it offers, and the lived experience of those insights. By sharing certain experiences with the screen characters, the spectator explores himself and others simultaneously. What he had cursorily dismissed now becomes, not only a theoretical possibility, but in the fullest sense, comprehensible.[35]

This is the very quality, I would argue, that the more playful of Buñuel's creations lack. Yet critics as diverse from one another as William S. Pechter and Tom Milne make no distinctions of value between the different modes of Buñuel's films.[36]

Of his most recent work, *Tristana* (1970) marks a return to his more serious mode, a mode which, as Durgnat has said, invites us to share certain experiences with the screen characters, the better to understand. Derived, like *Nazarin*, from a novel by Benito Pérez Galdós, *Tristana* contains one of the most disturbing and sympathetic portraits in all of Buñuel, the portrait of Tristana's 'guardian', Don Lope.

Like Don Jaime in *Viridiana*, a character also created for us by Fernando Rey, Don Lope is an old-fashioned man of principle. Or so he likes to believe. His sense of self-respect is based upon his strongly-held principles of freedom in personal relationships and on an aristocratic dignity. Yet his own need to be pampered forces him to deny both freedom and dignity to others. While he stops Tristana from wiping up some cleaning fluid that she has spilled – servants are for that, he explains – he immediately asks her to fetch his slippers and to take off his shoes. Later on in the film, we see that he has come to take this servitude for granted, as throughout his life he seems to have assumed that every attractive woman exists to satisfy his sexual needs.

A large part of the compassion that this film creates in us springs from the fact that we witness, bit by bit, the destruction of everything that Don Lope has believed in – his complete humiliation, in fact. The opposite of Nazarin in this, Don Lope is a man who, one by one, gives up his ideas for the sake of a woman, a woman that he began by abusing but found that he loved, and a woman for whom every act of kindness is answered by contempt. Like the Modot figure in *L'Âge d'or*, in the course of *Tristana*, Don Lope meets with complete defeat.

If *Tristana*, splendid though it is, does not quite equal the achievement of Buñuel's finest work, it is not because of any recurring facetiousness but because of certain ruptures in its form. A lot that seems crucial happens off-screen. As Tristana's relationship with her lover, Horacio, is merely a sketch, her return to Don Lope's household is really inexplicable. Similarly, while the loss of her leg is obviously central to it, the intensity of her anger is hard to understand. Even before her flight away from Lope, she was becoming hostile – as if her sexual awakening were accompanied by an impatience that Lope was too old to appease.

Or might this portrait of an awakened yet angry woman represent a reversal of what other Buñuel films have seemed to imply? In past films, there was always the sense that such violence as existed in Buñuel's characters was at least partly the result of their bottled-up sexual instincts. In Tristana's case, however, the more sexually aware she apparently is, the more defiant she becomes. Might Viridiana have lived on, *Tristana* now encourages us to speculate, to become a shrew who torments the complacent and self-deceiving Jorge? That is not the feeling that I get from the end of *Viridiana*; but now, with *Tristana* before me, I am no longer sure.

Finally, in *Tristana*, while there are sympathetic portraits of a number of minor characters in the best Buñuelian fashion, there is not the same interweaving of their relationships, one with the other, that is such a persuasive part of the structure of *Los Olvidados*, *Viridiana*, and *Diary of a Chambermaid*. Tristana's servant, Saturna, while beautifully observed in her defeated passivity, as is her deaf-mute son Saturno, nevertheless seems somewhat of a prop in this film if we compare her with Ramona in *Viridiana*, who, in different ways, was linked with Don Jaime, with Jorge, and with Viridiana.

For some time now, Buñuel has been telling us about each film that he makes that it is definitely his last. As the films keep pouring forth, it is hard to believe him. However, as the final moments of even his most serious films seem to entail little jokes, so perhaps the final films of his recent prolific period will continue to possess a playful air. For me personally, Buñuel's last *great* film was made almost a decade ago. In keeping with my desire to end these chapters on an affirmative note, I'd like now to conclude this account by looking at *Diary of a Chambermaid*.

*

After the light relief of *The Exterminating Angel* (*El Angel Exterminador*, 1962), Buñuel returned to France with all the resources of his late maturity to make what is in many ways the most astonishing film of his career. In the early days, perhaps because of limited finances and primitive production conditions, Buñuel never seemed very much interested in the techniques of the cinema. True to his surrealist inheritance, he has been less concerned with the formal perfection of his presentation than with the interiority of what is being said. In both *Los Olvidados* and *Nazarin*, for example, Buñuel employs the simplest of technical means, making us all the more aware of what Raymond Durgnat has nicely called 'the sardonic restraint of his style'.[37] But with the exception of the Mexican-made *Simon of the Desert* (*Simon del Desierto*, 1965), Buñuel's films since *Viridiana* have possessed a more prosperous air; and perhaps to compensate for the indifference of his French films in the 1950s, Buñuel contrived to make *Diary of a Chambermaid* (*Le Journal d'une femme de chambre*, 1964) one of his most expertly executed films.

So much do I admire every detail of this film, and so appropriate is each detail to the significance of the whole, that it is difficult for me not to launch into a full-scale analysis which, for the sake of space, I must resist. So once again, perhaps too schematically, we must look at certain details, the most telling features of the form. When Célestine (Jeanne Moreau) first arrives at the railway station and asks the coachman Joseph if it is far to the priory, he replies: 'You'll find out – *Vous le verrez bien.*' This is what she finds.[38]

First of all, within the wintry seclusion of the place, there is the master, Monteil, who always goes out shooting. Denied by his wife (except for 'certain caresses'), he is reduced to seducing chambermaids and with his gun destroying things, inflicting upon the outside world his anger and frustrations. There is also Madame Monteil, whose private life centres around a locked-up ritual of flasks and tubes of the most hygienic kind, an aspect (we assume) of her compulsive need to stay clean. Intercourse with her husband causes her too much pain, and the first question she asks Célestine is concerned with her cleanliness. Unlike her husband, Madame Monteil preserves things. She wants every detail in the house to remain exactly as it is. In collusion with her father, she demands that no shoes ever be worn in the salon except by her father, 'For he is always spotless.'

When we first see the father, old Rabour, he is taking pains to blow clean little Claire's nose, and complains about his son-in-law's unshaven state. His entire life is lived at one remove from reality. For the most part, we see him locked up in his room with his postcards of young women and his cabinet of women's shoes. He is a gentleman of the old sort, Marianne says; and so he is. He is urbane and civilized and extremely courteous to Célestine, though he calls her Marie since to him all the chambermaids are the same. Célestine is his one contact with the physical world. She models his boots, lets her calf be gently fondled, and reads to him passages of his favourite author, Huysmans (from whom Buñuel has selected the most telling bits – *'il n'existe plus de substance saine . . .'*). In the old-world style he maintains a real gentleness; for, like Don Jaime before him, his dissatisfactions are inflicted upon himself. And like Don Jaime, this inward-turning quality leads to a troubled death.

Next door, there is Captain Mauger, Félicien Mauger, a professional man of force whose career as a soldier gives him status in the society no matter how he actually behaves. (We might remember Modot in *L'Âge d'or* who, once he has presented his credentials to the men who are restraining him, is allowed to attack a blind man with apparent impunity.) Mauger's life·is filled with a petty war he is privately waging on his neighbour, with no apparent reason since it is made up by the end. He lives in a common-law alliance with his housekeeper, Rose; after twelve years he decides to send her packing so that he can be free to approach Célestine. With the exception of Célestine, who is obviously his match, he thinks of women as creatures who serve him, as creatures to clean his boots. In the Buñuel galaxy, this unites him with Jorge and Don Lope and contrasts him with Rabour who takes a strange delight in reversing this man/servant relationship.

Close by, there is 'la petite Claire' – a watery-eyed, full-lipped little creature who is so provocative that Joseph cannot look at her. To his sadistic mind, she must seem as moistly physical as the snails she is so fond of. And, of course, most central in this household is Joseph, a man too complex for any cameo.

Into this world comes Célestine, creating desire in every man she meets but holding out for what she thinks will be the safest bet. As the film ends, we can see she has made a mistake. She sits on her bed, impatient with Mauger's unctuousness (even though he talks of money), biting her little finger as she recognizes her fate. It might seem like punishment of a kind, having made such a choice. But there is no sense of divine retribution. The dice have simply rolled the wrong way.

Although a thoroughgoing opportunist of the most unscrupulous kind, Célestine has some redeeming features. In this world of moral sickness that Buñuel presents to us, she is comparatively well. In this way, like Joseph, her cynicism makes her strong. She accepts things that happen to her, even the kinky insistences of old Rabour. She is respectful of kindness (for she is harsh with Monteil) and discreet in her verbal fidelity to her friends (she defends Rose to Mauger). Her most decent impulse springs from her response to little Claire, whose brutal murder she would have done anything to avenge. But even here, decency is flouted and Joseph is set free. *Diary of a Chambermaid* is a film that celebrates the triumph of evil over the world of good intentions. It is Buñuel's most unambiguous film, and thus seems the answer to all the questions that have been raised before.

Because of the presence of Ochitos and to a lesser extent Meche, one could feel in *Los Olvidados* that gentleness and goodness might stand a chance.[39] But in the grim light of *Chambermaid*, even this faint glimmer of hope seems to be a self-deception. If Pedro's mother washes her legs in a way that recalls Meche, then we might from this parallel feel that Meche's course in life is not too promising. Similarly, though Ochitos in his considerateness is nicely contrasted with the fascist violence of the Blind Man, we have seen that twice in the film he has been ready to rise to violence himself – as he will probably have to do if he is to survive. Thus by this declension there is the feeling that Ochitos might have to be less wide-eyed in relation to existence if he is going to stay alive. For the Blind Man has stumbled through.

In *Chambermaid*, the only ambiguity is the uncertainty of what Buñuel might feel for his two principal characters – especially for Joseph. The killing of Claire is immediately followed by a brief autumnal evening scene, with Joseph wheeling a wheelbarrow. Then a scene in the kitchen where the maids are asking Célestine why she has returned to the house, to which she gives the evasive answer 'Because . . .'[40] Then the scene by the bonfire at night with Joseph raking the leaves. 'You are like me . . . way down deep,' he says to her, and we know that this is true; just as we know that the '*salaud*' she scribbles on the table after she has turned Joseph over to the police applies both to herself and to him. It is the old story of the thief to catch the thief, of combating evil with more evil; except that in this case it doesn't work and Joseph is set free.

The ambiguity of attitude springs from the scenes of sensual softness that surround Claire's murder and that give the whole film a troubling aesthetic lift. We are back to the Dali anecdote again, with its psychopathic sensibility. There is no moral judgement made in this film about the central characters because Buñuel must recognize that in such a world such characters are strong. If Célestine and Joseph genuinely admire one another, Buñuel would seem to a certain degree also to admire them.

The film ends with a gag, as if, like *L'Âge d'or*, in the effort to set us free. Joseph has realized his desire and taken that café in Cherbourg with a woman to whore for him. He has allied himself with the most reactionary forces of the Action Française; and, of course, the film would seem to imply, the future is on his side. As the demonstrators march past the café with its Picon advertisement, the last syllable of which remains on the screen throughout the sequence, Joseph starts shouting '*Vive Chiappe*', which the others then take up.[41] With its absurd jump-cuts and the tilt upwards to the thunder and lightning, this sequence is totally out of style with the rest of the film; yet the very unrelatedness of this intensely personal joke makes the film's pervasive grimness seem that much more grim.

Perhaps it was the defeat of the Republicans in the Spanish Civil War; perhaps it has been Buñuel's hard and (one assumes) lonely life[42]; perhaps it is just the way he sees things that makes his world so without a hope for the eventual triumph of the gentlest impulses in mankind. And even though we might strive to see things differently, Buñuel's vision is not an easy one to disagree with. Whatever films Buñuel might still have in store for us, it is doubtful if they will offer a more positive view of the world.

Often in Buñuel we experience great tenderness; but almost constantly in his films it meets with defeat. As an emblem of his world, we might remember the deformed Ujo, as if even genuine goodness must be achieved at a terrible price; or we might remember Don Jaime as he writes out his will, the resigned smile on his face as he makes the final dadaist surrender to the powers of darkness, as if his attempt to achieve goodness has been the biggest joke of all.

The Troubled Pilgrimage of
INGMAR BERGMAN

I've never been able to keep myself from believing that I'm in charge of so sensitive an instrument that it should be possible to use it to illuminate the human soul with an infinitely more penetrating light. *Ingmar Bergman*, 1954[1]

More than any other film artist, Bergman's work is rooted in the past. His early films grew out of the culture that surrounded them and they were invariably concerned with traditional themes. *Prison (Fängelse)*, *Thirst (Törst)* and *To Joy (Till Glädje)*, all released in 1949, were each in its own way a kind of allegory, a journey through defeat and despair towards some kind of hopefulness at the end. The first film that Bergman was associated with, *Frenzy (Hets)*, directed by Alf Sjöberg in 1944, had the same kind of form. The allegorical mode seemed the very cradle for Bergman's own imagination, a mode that was common to virtually all the serious film-makers working in Sweden at that time.

In fact, in the early 1960s, when Bergman's films first came flooding into the English-speaking world, what seemed so striking about them was the homogeneity of cultural background that they seemed to imply. For those of us who knew something about other Swedish film-makers – about directors like Arne Mattsson, Alf Sjöberg, Gustaf Molander, and Anders Henrikson – this feeling of cultural homogeneity was all the more striking. Furthermore, it seemed to have been going on for ages!

The silent films of Mauritz Stiller and Victor Sjöström had been largely cast in the same mode. Moreover, both Stiller and Sjöström had been enormously influenced by the novels of Selma Lagerlöf, which were also basically allegorical in format. *Gösta Berling's Saga* (not to probe back any further) could be taken as the prototype for so much Swedish art; and of course as part of Bergman's theatrical background, there were as well the plays of Strindberg, and, from Norway, of Ibsen.

Another striking characteristic of Bergman's early films is that, through these traditional and hence old-fashioned qualities, they seemed so distant from us in time. This sense of distance, of historical isolation, is also very much a part of the history of Scandinavian art, especially in Sweden. Selma Lagerlöf was writing at the same time as Proust and James, yet her novels have more in common with *Pilgrim's Progress* than with any novel then being written in the French- or English-speaking world.

Similarly, one might look at the wood carvings of Axel Petersson. His work consists of sculptures of rural life which show the same obsession with the traditional preoccupations of so much of Scandinavian art, with life and love and sin and death, usually in that order! Occasionally there is hope of salvation at the end, although in the best Christian puritan tradition one cannot really look to it in this life on earth. In the novels of Selma Lagerlöf and the carvings of Axel Petersson we find a curious phenomenon within the history of European art: two local artists, essentially folk artists, who were at the same time *the* national artists acclaimed by their country.

What this means in terms of cinema is that Bergman, from Selma Lagerlöf, through Stiller and Sjöström, literally inherited a folk tradition that he transferred to the screen. Of course, the situation is not that simple. If on the one hand Bergman inherited a folk tradition, on the other he inherited a dramatic tradition of greater sophistication and complexity, a tradition not quite so isolated from the salons of London and Paris. Nevertheless, even here, Strindberg and Ibsen work in what is often basically an allegorical mode. Strindberg's *The Road to Damascus* is as much an allegory as *Gösta Berling's Saga* and is the acknowledged inspiration for *Wild Strawberries*; and *Wild Strawberries* has many motifs in common with the late plays of Ibsen, with *John Gabriel Borkman* and *When We Dead Awaken*.

As part of this allegorical inheritance, Bergman also received what we might call a tradition of metaphoric density in relation to his art. In fact, there is room here not only for aesthetic analysis but also for a good deal of sociological speculation: because another striking characteristic of Sweden as a country is that nothing is simply as it seems. At least from a visitor's point of view, there appears to be a deliberateness and self-consciousness about so many characteristics of Sweden's day-to-day life.

From the heraldic blue-and-yellow of their national flag to the tailored bleakness of their northern countryside, a bleakness that seems to lead naturally into the ascetic beauty of Scandinavian furniture design, so many elements in Swedish life seem so deliberately and so consciously thought out, as if to imply a meaning beyond the simple fact that they are there. They seem to acquire, that is, some kind of metaphoric resonance. At any rate, whatever the ultimate validity of such impressionistic responses as have been made by visitors as diverse as Desmond Fennell and Kathleen Nott,[1] the chief point about them is that many people *do* respond to Sweden in this way and that there is certainly an additional invitation to do so in Scandinavian art.

It is almost as if the contemporary modes of psychological realism that characterized the novel in the nineteenth century never quite found their way through to Sweden. Isolated geographically and cut off historically and emotionally from the twentieth century by contriving to stay out of two world wars, as late as the sixties, Sweden still in many ways seemed a country apart, locked up in its own past, obsessed with its indigenous traditions. The international discovery of Bergman, the founding of the Swedish Film Institute, and the emergence on the Swedish film scene of figures more contemporary in feeling, like Bo Widerberg and Jörn Donner – all these factors have helped to change this. Nevertheless, a sense of isolation was very much a part of the atmosphere in the early films of Ingmar Bergman.

Were there space to do so, I would really like to investigate Bergman's cultural background in more detail, for with so traditional an artist it is important to sort out his inheritance from his individual contribution.* Furthermore, with the change of

*Readers who wish to explore more fully the cultural back-

style that we discover in Bergman's work after *The Virgin Spring*, we have the additional problem of deciding what happens to an artist like Bergman when he comes face-to-face with world acclaim, what happens to his sense of self in relation to his work when he no longer feels that his inheritance is valid.

However, briefly here: if I were to isolate one single factor as characteristic of Scandinavian cinema, I would refer to the desire to achieve a metaphoric concentration within a cinema of the open air. At the time when it was neither so easy nor so fashionable to do so, the Swedes constantly filmed their stories against a natural landscape yet in such a way that it seemed *more* than a natural landscape. The mountain retreat at the end of Sjöström's *The Outlaw and his Wife* is both convincingly real and yet as 'symbolic' as the mountainous perch at the end of Ibsen's *John Gabriel Borkman*. At their best, both Stiller and Sjöström were highly sensitive to what I would call the symbolic potentiality of any given landscape. Even in Sjöström's (= Seastrom's) American films, we find evidence of a similar sensitivity.

In *The Wind*, for example, as in his Swedish films, there is the same concern to present his characters as part of the land that is constantly moulding and threatening them and at the same time to project some sort of poetry on to the screen, to liberate his films from the merely representational. At various points throughout this film we have the ghost-like image of a white stallion – a creature of Indian legend that is supposed to haunt the West when the north winds blow – superimposed upon the scenes of howling sand and wind which are threatening the sanity of its heroine. This ghostly image of the white horse adds an eerie touch of the unreal to what might otherwise have been a conventional twenties melodrama of a girl's struggle to adapt to a hostile world that she does not understand. But more than this, the image of the horse comes to stand for the forces within herself that are part of her own sexual fear. At the end

---

ground to Bergman's work might want to consult *Cinema Borealis: Ingmar Bergman and the Swedish Ethos* by Vernon Young (New York, David Lewis, 1971).

of the film, through her terror, she has learned to accept not only the landscape but herself, these two elements intertangled in a most Scandinavian way. Technically, of course, this device of the superimposition is reminiscent of Sjöström's *The Phantom Carriage*, a film which (with Bergman in mind) is even more prophetic, dealing as it does so deliberately with the theme of sin and atonement and presenting on the screen a personified image of Death.

No doubt encouraged by the language difficulties of exporting their films, but also inspired by the fine traditions of the early silent films, the Swedes have endeavoured to convey their meaning as much as possible in purely visual terms. However, nowhere in the Swedish cinema can we find an Eisensteinian concern with the potentialities of editing or an Ophülsian concern with the choreography of camera movement. Technically, Swedish films have always been simple, their editing and camera movement utilitarian. Their achievement has been to concentrate on creating a density of imagery on the screen, a landscape of natural objects which at the same time has a metaphoric force.

*

About the way a film grows in his mind, Bergman himself has written:

> It often begins with an image; a face, suddenly and strongly illuminated; a rising hand; a village square at daybreak where some old women are sitting on a bench and are separated by a bag of apples. Or else, sometimes it's just a few words exchanged by two people, but in a completely personal tone of voice ... All these images are caught up like sparkling fish in my net; or, more exactly, I'm caught myself in a net of which, fortunately, I don't yet know the texture.[3]

Indeed, in his early work, one was struck especially by Bergman's imagery, by a recurring pattern of images that seemed to have for him a special force. It would be simplistic, however, to attribute to these recurring images a fixed symbolic significance. While it is true that in his early films Bergman was fond of mirrors, of human hands, certainly of wild strawberries, of the sun and the endless stretch of long summer days, and that dolls, bears, and cannons appear in several of his films, these images by no means always acquire the force and stature of symbols. To generalize about their 'meaning', as some of the French critics have done,[4] is to a large extent to destroy the delicacy of implication that they acquire in his most successful films. At their simplest, Bergman's images are employed to enforce or clarify a given mood or feeling, or sometimes to suggest an idea that in the film is left unsaid.

In *Waiting Women* (*Kvinnors väntan*, 1952), for example, one of the most moving moments is a verbally silent one. When young Marta learns that she is pregnant, both her happiness and her fears are presented in purely visual terms. We see her sitting on a bench by the Seine in the warm Paris sun, being delighted by the ebullient happiness of a small baby in its mother's arms and feeling content at the young life stirring inside her. Then she notices a cripple, an old man on crutches, also smiling at the baby. The realization of the precarious future of her child is thus forced upon her, and she suddenly becomes frightened and runs away.

Similarly in *Summer with Monika* (*Sommaren med Monika*, 1952) Bergman reinforces a narrative point by the simplest of visual devices. Near the beginning of the film, the difficulty that the boy has in striking a match for Monika's cigarette is not only charged with the awkwardness of the moment but it also suggests the difficulty he will encounter in his attempts to please her in the future. Nothing is *said* that could give us this feeling, but the image is vividly placed before us and later on in the film is answered by another image of a similar kind. After Monika has left the boy and their child, we have a rapid cut to a man's hand putting a coin in a jukebox. Then, with the blare of jazz, a striking close-up in profile of Monika's face, with her cigarette being easily and sinisterly lit for her – this time by a cigarette-lighter. In this way, through employing one of the most commonplace actions and certainly the most standard of film clichés – the lighting of a cigarette – Bergman succeeds in reminding us that Monika is a girl who is determined to go wherever life is easiest for her. Simple though these effects may seem to us now, especially in comparison with Bergman's later work, such patterning of images was very much a part of the form of these early films.

One of the most delicate and most perfectly balanced of what Peter Cowie, following Jacques Siclier, has called Bergman's 'rose-coloured films' is *Summer Interlude* (*Sommerlek*, 1950). Bergman himself has expressed his fondness for this particular film,[5] and it is the first Bergman film in which Robin Wood detects 'the presence of a great artist, not merely a gifted, or precocious, or ambitious one'.[6] Certainly, the film does possess a transparency and perfection which are exceptional. On the surface, especially when compared with his later and frequently more opaque productions, it might seem a slight film; yet it achieves an emotional depth and impact largely through the use of a significantly suggestive pattern of imagery.

Summer Interlude tells the story of young love, of disaster, of disillusionment, and, finally, of a curious kind of resignation and acceptance. 'I'm not so fussy nowadays,' Marie is made to remark; and at the end of the film, she is ready to accept the somewhat slovenly journalist, David Nyström – who, we might have noticed, cleans his nails as he talks to her – and thus to relinquish her memory of Henrik, who had 'such kind and beautiful hands'. The slight emphasis given to the hands of these two men links them, at least in Marie's mind, and by emphasizing the contrast between them, it intensifies the tragedy of the girl's loss. Similarly, the diabolical Uncle Erland's hands are seen by Marie as both beautiful *and* terrifying; and we remember that he was able to play Chopin on the piano, but while drunk with alcohol and lust.

The fleeting joy of summer is suggested by the call of the cuckoo which opens the film and (as so often in Bergman's early work) by the patch of wild strawberries that the young lovers share together. But when Marie returns to Pike Island for her afternoon reverie, the autumn leaves are blowing about, now crows are calling; and when we see her in her dressing-room at the theatre, we might be further moved to sympathize with her advancing age and vanished happiness if we notice that the pattern on her dressing-gown consists of medlars – an autumn fruit.

But the image, or symbol, most central to this film is that of the dance. When we first see Marie, she is twenty-eight years old and has become the prima ballerina of the Stockholm ballet. She has achieved her life-time ambition, we might imagine, but she appears tired and unhappy. As we are watching the dress rehearsal of a ballet we are given a kind of dumb-show of the dance of love that is to follow: suddenly, there is an accident – a short-circuit – and her dance is broken off just as it has begun. Similarly, we learn later in the long flashback which is the substance of the film, thirteen years before, she had had her short summer of love with Henrik, who, by an accident, had been killed, leaving her to return to the ballet to become a 'star' but not to escape from the weight of her unhappiness.

I stress the importance of the imagery in this film rather than offer a more 'psychological' analysis for a variety of reasons. Partly, the authority and detail of Robin Wood's monograph make all further interpretations seem somewhat redundant; but partly too, it is in this patterning of imagery that the achievement of these films most securely lies. At this stage of his career, Bergman was a most traditional, one might even say, a most classical artist. In many ways, his films were playing with conventional themes, themes already thoroughly explored by other Scandinavian artists. His distinction, as I understand it, lies chiefly in the quality of the play.

Bergman is, of course, a master in making us actually participate in the joys and sorrows of his characters. As we watch the film, we too are dazzled by the sun on the water and we feel the bleakness and hostility of Pike Island once the summer has gone. As a film-maker, however, Bergman is far from alone in this ability. One of the problems with the film medium is that we can all too easily become too uncomfortably involved in the action on the screen and so lose the distance necessary to respond to the film as a work of art. In these early Bergman films, I think it is largely the presence of some kind of form or pattern, of some perceptible sequence of imagery, that keeps us from being uncomfortably distressed by what we see.

Ingmar Bergman

By having crows answer cuckoos, and medlars follow strawberries, Bergman not only moves us by the strong emotional effect of these sounds and images but he thereby distances the action sufficiently from real life to enable us to be conscious of it as a work of art. To my mind, to complain that such effects are too deliberately done, with the implication that they are too cerebral, as many English-speaking critics did when these films first appeared, to complain in such a way reveals a complete incapacity to feel their force in the film, plus an unwillingness to accept the conventions upon which Bergman's art was based.

There is still, I suppose, the dry rational mind that cannot accept the conventions of Elizabethan blank verse and so cannot tolerate the fact that Macbeth, a soldier and a murderer, should sometimes speak like a poet; that he should be allowed to complain that life

> is a tale
> Told by an idiot, full of sound and fury,
> Signifying nothing.

In this passage, we are strongly presented with what Macbeth is feeling at the moment; but if the despair is Macbeth's, paradoxically the poetry is Shakespeare's. As spectators, we are saved from being depressed by what Macbeth is saying, for one thing by the realization that if Macbeth had acted differently, life might have signified a good deal more and, for another, by the quality of the verse with which he says it. I hope it doesn't sound far-fetched to suggest that Bergman's early films work in somewhat the same way. Inheriting as he did so many conventional themes and traditional forms, his artistic energies were occupied largely with the process of refinement rather than invention in the accepted European, post-Romantic way. His insights are invariably Christian-humanist; and even the 'romantic fatalism' that Robin Wood singles out as the one lingering immaturity in *Summer Interlude* might be seen to have traditional literary origins that Bergman, at this stage of his career, felt no great need to re-examine.

Bergman once expressed the wish that his work might have the impersonality of a medieval cathedral. I would argue that, in many ways, his early films do. Somewhat like the pre-Renaissance painters, it is as if Bergman could take his subject matter for granted while he strove to discover new methods of presentation. We are delighted as much with the manner as with the matter of these early films. In these films, we may indeed be at times unbearably moved by the convincingness of the action, but at the same time we experience an exhilaration because, among other things, we can feel the presence of the artist's controlling hand in all the situations that are moving us. By the symmetry, by the beautiful pattern of images, with often the suggestion of a controlling symbol, and by the frequently stylized characterization, we are continually reminded that what we are witnessing is not real life with its irrational muddle and chaos, but the creation of one man's individual mind, reshaping and refining traditional Christian-humanist insights with more than just a touch of Pauline romantic gloom.

*

This sense of the young Bergman playing with conventional material is probably what lies behind John Russell Taylor's complaint concerning the split between Bergman the writer and Bergman the director.[7] It is also no doubt related to his theatrical background and his reputed skill at discovering astonishing ways of presenting a variety of dramatic material. It may also account for the variety of film styles which, in the early days, Bergman could so effortlessly command. For instance, think of two films that are as different from each other as it is possible to be and which are as well completely different from the work of anyone else: *Sawdust and Tinsel* (*Gycklarnas afton*, 1953) and *Smiles of a Summer Night* (*Sommarnattens leende*, 1955). Like *Prison* before it and *The Seventh Seal* that follows, *Sawdust and Tinsel* is a 'dark' film, as the French say. Ostensibly it is the story of a circus, a circus which we are told has seen better days. 'Alberti', unable to resist the call of circus life, has left his wife and son to the settled life of a small town, which to him had been a kind of death, to her, fulfilment. Now the circus is returning to this small town; times are bad, Albert is older and is growing tired.

Since he has been away, Albert has acquired an attractive young mistress, Anne, with whom – we gradually discover – he is not entirely satisfied. She in turn is sick of the life on the road and longs to escape from her obligations both to the circus and to Albert. Furthermore, as they return to this particular town, she is seized by the fear that Albert will try to leave her and go back to his wife. They are both, thus, tired and somewhat mistrustful of one another.

In several of his films, Bergman includes a scene, generally in mime, which is in a way the epitome of the entire film. In *Summer Interlude*, not only is there the opening dance sequence and the 'accident', but the night before Henrik is killed there is a curious moment when the two lovers amuse each other by drawing pictures on a record sleeve. In Bergman's hands, these drawings come alive. They become, in fact, an animated cartoon which, in theme, is the rest of the film in miniature.

Rather similarly, just at the beginning of *Sawdust and Tinsel*, Bergman offers us the most extended of his 'dumb-show' prologues, as strange and terrifying in its way as the first dream sequence that serves a similar purpose in *Wild Strawberries*. Here we see Frost, the circus clown, being humiliated in his attempt to reclaim his wife, Alma, who in a fit of boredom has been swimming naked with some artillery officers stationed nearby. As he attempts to carry her back from the seashore, holding her awkwardly in front of him like a cross and stumbling on the sharp stones, we have a preview of what is to come, of what is to happen this time to Albert.

This prologue is most forcefully handled. The intense emotion of the characters is conveyed almost entirely in mime, as if in their extreme distress they had lost their sense of hearing (as apparently Albert does also just before his threatened suicide); and it is accompanied by irregular, sharply incisive music, punctuated by timpani and by the sound of cannon firing out over the sea. Of course, the cannon here are 'phallic', if you like[8]; but as so often with Bergman's imagery, any possibly Freudian implications are gratuitously felicitous, not essential to our understanding.

Here, the cannons help to deaden our ear-drums as they have

Frost's; they are, of course, extremely effective dramatically; and they also suggest the harsh theme of aggression, even of sadism, which is to follow. When watching this film for the first time, we scarcely know what to make of this scene; but on reseeing, we are able to feel not only its force but its significance as well.

But the film goes on: Albert tries to return to his wife, who is kind but rejects him. Anne gives herself to an actor in the hope of freeing herself from her present life, but is cheated and made use of. As they both are dissatisfied, they both attempt to escape; their attempts are unsuccessful, however, and they are forced back on one another. Albert's final humiliation occurs when he is defeated in the circus ring by the odiously complacent actor who had 'used' his Anne, a scene hard to take in entirely because of its brutality.

The ending avoids the theatrical climax of suicide or any attempt at restored self-esteem. Albert, unable actually to kill himself, smashes his image in a mirror – attempts to destroy, that is, the reflection of his weakness which, in his defeat, he has been forced to see and to acknowledge – and then kills instead the circus's mangy old bear, curiously associated in the film with Alma and with her personal failings and yet which, in many ways, is rather like Albert himself. He then collapses in sobs, apart from his companions, reduced to seeking comfort from his horse.

The circus moves on, out of town, away from the scene of humiliation and despair. Albert walking slowly behind his wagon is joined by Anne. There are tears in her eyes and there is a strained little smile that is shared between them. But nothing is said. They just walk slowly off together, into the prolongation of their life as they have come to know it.

Even though these early films are very much cast in the traditional allegorical mode, Bergman takes pains not to present his characters in too schematic a way. They all live in a tangle of responsibilities to one another, as in fact we do in life. The issues may seem simplified, but not (I would argue) falsified. Albert and Anne are shown to be fond of one another and capable of moods of tenderness, though each is prepared to desert the other if the occasion offers itself. There is also a kind of affection that we feel for even the most pathetic of Bergman's characters. Albert's march through town to ask the help of a travelling theatre director, with the absurd pride he takes in his own pomp and his gaudily provocative Anne, is one of the many touches that help to soften the harsh edges of this grimly conceived film. It also implies a kind of moral value in the processes of life itself.

For instance, not unlike Beckett's *Waiting for Godot*, *Sawdust and Tinsel* deals with two people who have somehow become dependent on each other 'in this hell together' and who keep waiting for something to happen, something that will free them from their present life and from each other. Of course, like Godot, it never comes. Yet far more than Beckett in his much applauded play, Bergman, even in this gloomy film, realizes that man is still not entirely incapable of compassion, and that from compassion there is hope. If Bergman is fully conscious of the horror and possible vacuity of life, at this stage of his life he is also conscious of its warmth and joy.

Smiles of a Summer Night seems completely different in every way. Here indeed themes and images can almost be abstracted from the characters that embody them, for the whole film moves with the formal, studied gestures of a ballet, or perhaps one should say an opera. In fact, Robin Wood has persuasively presented the film in terms of Mozart opera,[9] and the film does seem to combine 'artificiality' with 'complexity' in a way much closer to operatic than to novelistic or cinematic modes.

In this film, the psychological plausibility of the characters is not only stretched to breaking point, it is abandoned altogether. While ostensibly an erotic farce in the twenties manner of Mauritz Stiller, it is a film that grows in the mind as we contemplate it and, while remaining a farce, becomes something else as well. The element of farce is more the point of view from which the characters and action are observed; in themselves they are not entirely comic.

While playing with his theme, 'this farce of love', Bergman is also exploring the conditions that might make lasting love possible, a characteristic seriousness of purpose which relates the film, as again Robin Wood has suggested, to Renoir's *La Règle du jeu*. Yet far more than in Renoir, the potential destructiveness of the characters is everywhere present, a hint of something sinister that troubles the comic surface of the film so that sometimes – like Count Malcolm's wife – we don't know whether to laugh or scream.

This theme of the various attitudes towards love and of the difficulties of each is explicit in *Smiles of a Summer Night*, with the lustful flunkey, Frid, playfully acting as a kind of choric commentator. Real love, that of young lovers, says Frid, is both a gift and a punishment. It is very rare and, unless watched for carefully, is easily missed. Young Henrik Egerman and his as yet untouched loved-one, of course, embody this attitude; and though we may be charmed by the beauty and the stylized romance of Bergman's treatment of it, as we are by the petulant innocence portrayed by Ulla Jacobsson, we can see that such love has its dangers. Young Egerman is almost the stock student figure that we can find in the plays of Chekhov or Ibsen – an idealist whose ideals are hopelessly at odds with his self-consuming passions. He is horrified by the sexual intrigues of his father's friends; and the sight of Frid chasing the provocative Petra in the woods finally drives him to attempt suicide.

This attempted suicide is indeed an odd moment in this farce and creates on the screen an effect that is all but impossible to describe in words. The scene depends upon a series of gimmicks that results in a bed being ushered in from the adjacent room, the bed which contains his father's still-virgin bride, who seems to have been preserved in this sexually corrupt world just for him. And then, as if in some fairy-tale romance, a toy trumpet sounds to their future happiness in love.

The effect of the scene is both deeply moving and yet ridiculous. Nevertheless, however difficult we may find it adequately to describe our response to it, we do get the sense of the precariousness of the relationship, with its magic beauty and its once-upon-a-time atmosphere, as in the legend (told us by Frid) when the complicitous bed first brought the beautiful lady to take her pleasure with her future king.

Robin Wood has pointed out the parallels with Mozart's *The Magic Flute*, parallels 'at once too free to constitute a "borrowing" ... and too close to be coincidental.'[10] Through its combination of beauty and fragility, this love scene might also remind us of the meeting of Romeo and Juliet, sharing a sonnet together in a highly stylized way and seeming very fragile in the world of, on the one hand, the murderous Tybalt, on the other, the unreflective, licentious Mercutio. With Shakespeare in mind, Frid, in his animal high spirits, might even remind us of Mercutio, or at any rate of the boisterous Shakespearean figure whose attitude towards love is a wholly physical one. In *Smiles of a Summer Night*, Frid represents a kind of health in his uninhibited delight in the physical fun of rolling in the hay with a pretty chambermaid, who, for her part, insists upon marriage and is at times a little sad. She realizes that, with all their momentary pleasures, they won't experience the 'magic' of being young lovers.

The other characters in the film, incapable either of Frid's simple responses or of Henrik's tortured but here rewarded idealism, represent various kinds of failure in love, each one seeking satisfaction while failing to satisfy. 'Sincere love is a juggler's act,' says Désirée at the beginning of the film; and later the Countess Malcolm confesses that in her opinion 'love is a detestable business'. Advocate Egerman, simultaneously a cold but pathetic figure, suffers his degradation as a kind of atonement, the complete humiliation and loss of self-respect that we see so often in Bergman's work.

The film gains its force and strikes its notes of seriousness beneath its comic mask largely as a result of this intricate series of relationships and by the juxtaposition of contrasting moods and scenes. The climactic centre of the film, the banquet scene, enclosed by images of swans on still water and complete with wigged servants and a Mozartian gavotte, is a masterpiece of stylized filming. There is the suggestion here of some kind of ancient ritual in the drinking of the wine that contains a drop of a young mother's milk; while the lavish splendour of the piles of fruit, the swelling drops of melting wax clustered about the candlesticks, the baroque superfluity of the scene, all contribute to the effect of an abundance of some kind, of decadence perhaps, but also of rich resources for those who can seize them. In sharp contrast, we have Henrik Egerman alone in his self-denying torture at the piano, in a bare room lit by candles that show no sign of drip. Everything is still and cold, while Frid and Petra chase each other in merriment in the woods outside.

*

Smiles of a Summer Night was the first of Bergman's films to secure for him some degree of international acclaim. This acclaim was then consolidated by the two films which immediately followed, *The Seventh Seal* (*Det Sjunde Inseglet*, 1956) and *Wild Strawberries* (*Smultronstället*, 1957). The Bergman craze had begun.

I have never been a great admirer of *The Seventh Seal* myself. It is a highly rhetorical film, containing all kinds of extraordinary moments which seem more effective locally than intrinsic parts of the entire film. I have always preferred *Sawdust and Tinsel*, because I feel that the implied pilgrimage of the circus in the earlier film is more subtle and successful than the overtly symbolic crusade in *The Seventh Seal*.[11] Also, *Sawdust and Tinsel* is not weakened by unnecessarily abstract talk. Furthermore, the presentation of Albert and Anne's relationship does still seem representative of the lives of so many people today. But I have come to recognize that *The Seventh Seal* is striving to be a more complex film and, in spite of its weaknesses, it has too its characteristic strengths.

A Swedish film that would aid foreign audiences in understanding better the cultural context in which Bergman has worked is Alf Sjöberg's *The Road to Heaven* (*Himlaspelet*, 1942). While not exactly a masterpiece of achieved cinema, it is a film of interest. It too is an allegory, and the visual style of the film is directly derived from the Gourd painters of Dalarna. The Biblical characters who appear in the film are all garbed in what looks like eighteenth-century dress; and Mats, the tormented hero of the piece, in search of earthly justice, encounters God in a top hat and frock coat. These scenes indeed seem strange to an

English-speaking audience and probably a bit strange even to the Swedes! But three points are pertinent here: one, the artistic freedom granted to Swedish film-makers that allows experimentation of this kind; two, the concern with national legend and traditional modes; and three, the audacity of the film-makers to present Biblical characters in this way. Yet this audacity seems less extreme when we recognize that Mats sees his Biblical figures the way he does because this is the way, through the paintings, he has been encouraged to visualize them.

Similarly with Death in *The Seventh Seal*. He appears as he does, simultaneously grim and somewhat comical with his white face and black cloak, because this is the way Bergman (and so the Knight) has imagined him from a painting.[12] 'I've been a long time at your side,' says Death when he first appears; and we realize that he is not merely death in time, the end of our actual life, but he also represents the inner death that the Knight, Antonius Block, has been carrying with him ever since he first left his wife and home in search of the absolute, ever since he gave up singing songs to the beauty of his wife's eyes and began to pursue an abstraction. However much Bergman may make us sympathize with the Knight's pursuit, we see that in the film it has been meaningless. His sturdy squire, Jöns, is disgusted with the whole business: 'The crusade was so stupid', he says, 'it would have taken an idealist to have thought of it'.

The game of chess could be seen as the series of moves Block has taken throughout his life which has led him away from the warmth and potential happiness of life towards the cold abstraction of death. Block now confesses that his heart is empty and that – like Dr Borg in *Wild Strawberries* – he has always been rather indifferent to his fellow men. He has wasted his life in the pursuit of an ideal. 'I want knowledge,' he cries out; and in the film we see that what he means by knowledge is some kind of intellectual explanation of the suffering and emptiness of life as he has experienced it. He wants a *verbal* guarantee that his search has not been meaningless, that his high ideals will be rewarded.

The point of the film, it seems to me, is that, however much we may share the Knight's desire (and we certainly feel that

Bergman does), Bergman presents it as both presumptuous and futile. In *The Road to Heaven*, Mats too wanted some evidence of 'justice' after the witch-hunt burning of his wife; but it is only when he relinquishes this desire, when he relaxes the assertions of his conscious will, his merely mental self, that – like a child – he finds his 'heaven', and experiences once more the peace and happiness of his youth. In *The Seventh Seal*, this is what Block cannot or will not do.

Even at the end of the film, when Death comes to collect his victims, to claim all those who have stuck by the Knight and associated themselves with his pursuits, Block still clings to his abstraction of a God without feeling: 'Oh God, who *must* be somewhere, have mercy upon us.' Jöns, on the other hand, has long understood the futility of that kind of request or faith. He seems almost contemptuous of the Knight throughout the film. He is fed up with the 'fairy tales' of the church and is revolted by the sight of the flagellants mutilating one another in the name of Christianity. He recognizes that it would have been far better for the Knight had he been able to give himself to the 'triumph of being alive', instead of spending his life in the attempt to answer questions to which there are no *merely verbal* answers. Jöns is a source of strength in the film chiefly because, with all his earthly wisdom and highly practical turn of mind, he acknowledges the arrogance of our intellectual claims.

At this stage in Bergman's career, it seems a misunderstanding of his work to say that he is guilty of posing 'problems that he is clearly incapable of answering adequately'.[13] In *The Seventh Seal*, this surely, is the Knight's failing. It is the presumption of a man who wishes to understand everything with his mind alone and who allows himself to become indifferent to his fellow creatures in the process. The horror and despair in *The Seventh Seal* is seen to a large extent as a loss of faith in the church (which is presented as a deceiver and tormentor) but more in the essential qualities by which we must live, qualities of feeling, of sympathy, of compassion, and of love. In the film, the plague seems almost the result of this indifference. The flagellants torment themselves and each other, mutilating all that is good in themselves in a useless attempt at atonement for their inability to feel. They lacerate themselves so that at least, if not love, they will feel pain.

The priest who encourages this self-abuse is presented, much more than the Knight, as a life hater. He rails at what he calls the ugliness and pollution of the body and he appeals only to fear. He tries to shame a young woman who, from the joy of love, through pregnancy, is struggling to bring forth fresh life into this self-tormenting world.

Images of pregnancy and birth have always fascinated Bergman; and here, in this 'religious' setting, they clearly achieve a symbolic force. The travelling minstrels have a child whose naked body is unashamedly displayed and delighted in throughout the film. The minstrels are called Jof and Mia – Joseph and Mary perhaps a little obvious in terms of symbolism but nevertheless an effective way of underlining the suggestion that through such simple goodness, faith in mankind, and capacity for love as these two people reveal, a finer race of men might be born. Rather like the Knight, Jof too is an idealist, a seer of visions, and a wanderer over the face of the earth; but unlike the Knight's, Jof's visions are those of birth and love. He sees the Virgin Mary dressed up with a crown like a queen, teaching the young Jesus to walk. Jof's truth, such as it is, is within him. He makes no intellectual demands and shows no desire to 'have time to perform at least one significant action', as does Block. Jof is content to take pleasure in the beauty of the world and in his wife. He composes songs, and plays with his young child. The flagellants, the sadists, and the masochists are all living in a world that the Knight *thinks* he understands but which he cannot face squarely. The little witch girl is part of the same world, victimized and tormented by the church. Her eyes at the end disclose no knowledge of the devil, of any supernatural force, but simply terror and emptiness. Like the Knight, she too has been the victim of an abstraction.

That some part of us must die before we can truly live, that we must be 'as little children' before we can find real happiness, that the 'Kingdom of Heaven' is either within us or it is nowhere – all these insights form part of our Christian-humanist inheritance and, at this stage of his career, Bergman seemed to be accepting them uncritically. Those of us who admired these early films went to them, not for fresh insights about the nature of life, but to observe the individual working out of traditional themes and attitudes. Watching his films seemed rather like stepping back into a nineteenth-century world.

It is not my concern here to emphasize what could be interpreted as the more Christian elements in Bergman's work[14]; but as in the Book of Revelation, when the seventh seal is opened and life emerges from death, so throughout the film there are little rhetorical flourishes to reinforce this idea.

When Death saws down the tree containing the third minstrel, immediately the tree is down, a squirrel runs up on to the tree-stump and nibbles at a nut. After we have experienced the horror of watching a man die of the plague, the moon comes out from behind the clouds and fills the forest with light. But most striking of all, and an extraordinary example of Bergman's feeling for the cinema as a conjuring act, is the scene in Block's dark, cold, empty castle when Death comes at last. We have the face of Jöns's mute and kneeling concubine, radiant in some way at the thought of release from fear and suffering. Now with tears in her eyes, her voice is suddenly released as well: 'It's all over,' she says; and with these words, the image of her face is blended with that of Mia's, smiling with joy in the light of the warm morning sun.

*

Writing about Bergman's early films seems to dictate a different tone from the other chapters in this volume. One is less analysing the complexities of form in order to gain a deeper understanding of the implications of the content than simply analysing Bergman's extraordinary skill at finding new ways of presenting what, after all, are centuries-old insights. There is a sense in which his early work is a kind of embroidery around traditional themes – sometimes loosely woven in striking colours, as in *The Seventh Seal*, sometimes closely knit in quieter tones, as in *Summer Interlude* and *A Lesson in Love*, but most securely, in my view, in *Wild Strawberries*. *Wild Strawberries* represents the peak of his early achievement and a few words must be given to it before we move on to his later, certainly more original, yet in some ways less satisfactory work.

Very different in surface organization, thematically *Wild Strawberries* has a lot in common with *The Seventh Seal*. In *Wild Strawberries*, the aged and apparently genial Dr Isak Borg is presented, if not as an idealist, at least as a man of principle, a man who has governed his life according to certain preconceived notions of conduct. He is now travelling with his daughter-in-law, Marianne, to receive the official acknowledgement of a life-time of useful service in the form of an honorary degree. Dr Borg's is a more fully developed character than the single-minded Knight in *The Seventh Seal*. The subtleties of his relation to other people in the film are thus more difficult to perceive, especially at a first seeing.

Bergman takes care to present him as, in many ways, a well-meaning and considerate individual, and includes the scene with the petrol attendant chiefly to emphasize this aspect of his character. This gentle aspect, however, has been more apparent to people who have not been too close to him in life. In fact, Marianne criticizes him for having always tried to hide his selfishness and egotism behind a surface of old-world charm and, we see, even of philanthropy. There is an added irony in the fact that both old Borg and his son, Evald, are medical men – healers of mankind. Yet in private, they have both all but strangled any life they have come in touch with.

Along with Borg's actual journey to Lund in the car, giving it symbolic force and meaning, there is also Borg's private journey towards self-knowledge. The stages of this journey are revealed to us in a series of dreams and reminiscences during which Borg comes to a dim awareness of how his 'principles' have always been enforced at the expense of the natural warmth of human life. They have thus prevented him from tasting the perishable strawberries at their sweetest, when the time was ripe. Along with the sight of the old summer home and the patch of wild strawberries, the 'cheeky' young girl helps him to enter the vault of his past by reminding him of his first sweetheart, the first to have been turned away by the chill that envelops him.

Even more insistently and certainly more subtly than its per-

sonified presence in *The Seventh Seal*, here death is everywhere
Dr Borg's principles, we are told, while possibly gaining his son's
respect, have also gained his hatred. Borg's old mother, while
complaining that no one ever comes to visit her, complains as
well that she has always felt cold, and she wonders why. It is
Borg's son's fate to be stone dead, just as it is Marianne's fate to
oppose him by creating life. Thus, by a series of such scenes, we
come to feel the force and contagion of the emotional death
that inheres in the heart of the Borg family; and indirectly, we
have a series of probings into the problem of what for Dr Borg
might *really* have constituted a life-time of useful service.

Even Borg's apparent kindness, as the scene involving his wife
would imply, was adopted originally as a kind of principle. He
believes in forgiveness in the abstract. Yet, significantly, during
the dream of his first medical examination, he fails to remember
that a doctor's first duty is to ask to be forgiven. His principles,
we see, were not deeply rooted.

But if the chilling spirit of death thus pervades the film, so
also does the spirit of youth and happiness, of the ephemeral
magic of wild strawberries. There are, of course, the young
hitch-hikers, and also the scenes of laughter and high spirits in
the old summer house. These scenes reveal a simple,
unreflective, even superfluous joy, like the superfluity of the song
the twins wrote for their deaf old uncle's name-day and yet
which gave such delight to all. 'Isn't that just like the twins!'
Sara smiles at the thought of it. But even here the fun is disturbed
by the guilt she feels for wanting to be kissed in the strawberry
patch instead of just reading poetry, playing duets, and talking
about 'the next life' with the fine and noble Isak. 'He makes me
feel like a worm,' she cries out in her innocence and wishes
she were not attracted to his brother Sigfrid, who is 'so naughty
and exciting'.

With the help of the sensitive camera work of Gunnar Fischer,
Bergman floods these scenes with an almost dazzling white
light, which finds its foil, of course, in the darkened interior of
Borg's mother's home as well as in the darkened hall from
which old Borg watches the re-creation of this scene from his
past life. In Bergman's work at this time, the music too was

always an important, evocative element. In films like *Summer Interlude* or *Waiting Women*, an ascending harp arpeggio seems perfectly to evoke the expansive freedom of the long summer days. In *Wild Strawberries*, Eric Nordgren provides a wild strawberry motif (a perfect fifth ascending into a minor second) which impinges on Borg's consciousness, as on ours, whenever he is on the brink of a moment of increased self-knowledge. This theme haunts the film, nostalgically, plaintively, as if pleading for recognition. It also serves to underline the irony of certain moments in the film.

For instance, amid the pomp and ceremony of the scene in the cathedral, after the trumpets have sounded and the cannons been fired off, in the midst of the recital in Latin of all Borg's medical achievements, the appearance of this theme reminds us that at this moment supposedly so important in his life, Borg's mind is elsewhere. He realizes the irony of the honours he is receiving and recognizes that, for him at least, the celebrations are hollow.

Throughout this film, even more persuasively than in *The Seventh Seal*, the images of birth and death, of youth and old age, are curiously associated. During the opening dream sequence, when the carriage catches on the lamp-post and the coffin begins to sway and creak, the shrill sound of the creaking wood bears a hideous resemblance to a baby crying. During the second dream in the car, after young Sara has made Borg contemplate his prematurely old face in a mirror – has forced him to see himself, that is, as he has appeared to others – and has run away to attend to her sister's child, Borg advances slowly to the child's cot and stands, an old man, contemplating in turn the thought of young life. Above his head is a canopy of leaves; but as this moment in the film ends, the camera singles out one dead branch among them.

In a way that might take us back once more to Sjöberg's *The Road to Heaven*, Borg finds a measure of happiness by reliving a moment of his youth, a moment when he had felt the peace and happiness of seeing his mother and father sitting on the shore and fishing together. By the end of the film, he has attempted to atone for his failings – to his frozen son, Evald, and to Marianne.

He has been genuinely moved in the course of the day and has felt at last some real human contact. He has come to see how, as in the opening dream, he had lost his way in life. Like Mats in Sjöberg's film, Borg finds a kind of 'heaven' in the purer feelings of his boyhood, although, in any practical way, for him it is too late. For old Borg, 'there are no strawberries left'.

The ending of the film, like that of Borg's life, has no dramatic flourish. The image of his parents and the two contrasting images of his own face, one tired and restful in bed, the other straining at last towards some degree of warmth and love, are blended with one another while Eric Nordgren supplies a sequence of harp arpeggios that brings this film to its peaceful resolution.

When the film first appeared, there were some complaints about the strained facility of the dream sequences, about what British critics especially felt was a too facile appropriation of expressionistic techniques and Freudian symbols. Critically, it is difficult to establish what seems persuasive, or fails to, in any filmic dream sequence. However, in *Wild Strawberries* all the dream images are taken up elsewhere in the film and thereby gain their clarification. The terror of these dreams is necessary for us, as it was for Borg, to realize fully the horror and vacuity that can lurk beneath a life of surface smiles.

During his medical examination, the room is filled with indistinctly familiar faces who now appear dead to him as they have, in fact, in life. His examiner and the woman whose illness he must diagnose are the couple he picked up in his car who, like the flagellants in *The Seventh Seal*, take pleasure in tormenting each other quite openly without any pretence of tender feeling or love. This couple is presented as beyond hope of redemption, since absence of love has hardened into hate.

The opening dream sequence is but another of Bergman's dumb-shows of what is to come. In the course of the day's journey, old Borg comes to see how, like his corpse in the dream, he has been gradually strangling himself by driving away all those who might have been able to bring him some measure of lasting joy and love. And one needn't ferret through

Freud to see in the clock without hands the image of a life where time has been meaningless, where it has lacked its sense of purpose and fulfilment. Bergman frequently employs clocks in his work and he puts them to a variety of uses. Here the clock without hands is not only answered by his own watch and then by the watch his mother shows him later on in the film; but the dream sequence is broken abruptly by the sound of the alarm clock ticking insistently beside his bed. This both marks a return to reality and emphasizes the incessant passing of time.

In *Wild Strawberries*, as in *The Seventh Seal* and with a rather different effect in *Smiles of a Summer Night*, there is a kind of banquet scene, a scene of the pleasure of eating and relaxing together, one might almost say of communion. In *The Seventh Seal*, only when Block sits down to the simple feast of strawberries and milk does he forget his present troubles and remember how he too had once loved his young wife and had sung songs to her beautiful eyes. Jof is singing quietly in the background as the bowls of milk and strawberries are passed round among them. For the first and only time in the film, Block is moved to forget his self-created torments by the simplicity and goodness of the happy couple. 'When I'm with you, everything seems unreal,' he says ironically, with no apparent recognition that *here* is the reality he rejects when he walks off to continue his game of chess with Death.

Similarly, yet even more ritualistically, in *Wild Strawberries* the travellers all have lunch together. They eat and drink wine together, while Borg is moved to entertain them with stories about his days as a young doctor. Then, while strumming his guitar, the young theological student begins to recite a poem: 'When nature shows such beauty, how radiant must be its source.' When he stops, old Borg carries on: 'I see his traces everywhere, wherever flowers bloom.' When his memory falters, Marianne helps him out. Like the strawberries and milk in *The Seventh Seal*, this poem is passed round the table. They all seem to know it and to appreciate it, even if in different ways. To the theologue, it is a poem about God; to the young atheist, simply a love poem. But the two boys are united in a common feeling for this poem, as indeed they are in their appreciation of the high spirits of the girl. They are thus freed from their 'merely intellectual' disputes.

This scene is magnificent, and, considering the nature of the poem, the sharing of the food and wine together, and what could be called the spiritual theme of the film, it seems to have implications of the most far-reaching kind. If at this time of his life Bergman was still preoccupied with the validity of Christianity in the metaphysical sense of that word, he seems in *Wild Strawberries* to be re-creating in a most sensitive way some of the ritual that has held the church together. This luncheon sequence contrasts sharply in its warmth and affection with the actual communion he was to re-create some five years later for the opening sequence of *Winter Light*.

When discussing *Summer Interlude*, because its theme seemed so simple, I was more concerned with the form of the film, with the craft of its construction. Yet when it is placed beside *Wild Strawberries*, we can see that its insights are basically the same. In *Summer Interlude*, Marie, by accepting David Nyström at the end, is releasing herself from the hold that the memory of her dead Henrik has had upon her, inhibiting the development of her own life. After her reverie at the end of the film, when she is made to see herself clearly in the mirror, without make-up, she realizes that she is even happy in some way. At least she is still alive and is capable of forming new and living relationships, even though of a less ideal kind.

Similarly in *Wild Strawberries*, while the thematic concerns seem primary, there is the same careful construction, the same parallelisms, the same symmetry, that we found in *Summer Interlude*. It is only on the surface that the film might appear formless and episodic. The contrasting images of Borg's face at the end of the film relate to the two comparably contrasting images at the end of the opening dream sequence, when his corpse is attempting to pull him down into the coffin. Old Borg's relation to his son is suggested by, among other things, the dead tree by Evald's head during the scene in the rain with his wife, which reminds us, of course, of the dead bough we saw hanging over Borg's own head. Most tellingly of all, when the hitch-hikers have gathered flowers for Borg and have sung him a song and have given him three cheers for being 'a wise old man who knows all about life', not only do the words have an ironic reference to what in his dream the original Sara has just said – 'You know so much, yet you don't *really* know anything' – but the scene itself recalls the similar one when wild strawberries were gathered for Uncle Aron's name-day. Then too a song was sung followed by three cheers. So in this scene with Borg, there is the added ironic implication that, even more than Uncle Aron, Borg has been deaf to all such happy, superfluous, spontaneous appeals in life.

To my way of thinking, *Wild Strawberries* is a magnificent film, surely deserving its place in anyone's 'top ten' list. Yet it has failed to gain this kind of fashionable prestige. I wonder why. Perhaps Robin Wood is close to the problem when he writes about the film from the vantage-point of *Persona*[15]:

> In retrospect it looks on one level *too* complete, *too* self-contained in its jig-saw structure, to stand as an adequate response to the stresses of the contemporary world. Though far removed from Art for Art's Sake, it is perhaps more satisfying as a Work of Art than as a record of fully lived experience … one is so aware of the intellectual virtuosity of the working-out that one begins to ask whether it is not all *too* conscious? – whether Bergman was working from the whole of himself? – whether the deepest levels of his being were not still untapped?

These comments, of course, imply a notion of art that is highly romantic – a notion of art as personal exploration. Nevertheless, Wood is not alone in thinking of art in this way; and certainly, as I began this chapter by stressing, Bergman's early work, like so much of Scandinavian art, does seem to stand apart from time. Personally, I don't find the film too *intellectually* structured, but I can see that in its achievement it is comfortably old-fashioned. The moral sensibility that it contains could have existed any time within the last two hundred years. It is only the cinema that gives it the feeling of being of our era.

Yet this old-fashioned quality is what pleases me most about these early works by Bergman – the sense of a man working in isolation from the rest of Europe, sorting out the validity of his own cultural inheritance. The whole symbolic understructure that we find in Bergman's films seems to come from far away and thus to be much more profound than his merely personal preoccupations. The recurring symbols of the quest, of the forest of darkness, of the life-giving powers of the south and sun might, to the English-speaking world, recall Bunyan, but to the Scandinavians could suggest Ibsen.

In Ibsen's late plays, *John Gabriel Borkman* and *When We Dead Awaken*, there is the same feeling of the pervasive cold that attends the emotionless will; and there are the same life-giving symbols of laughter, music, dancing, and the sun. In *John Gabriel Borkman*, young Erhart, with a woman on either side, escapes from the dark and cold of his father's will to the freedom and warmth of the south; and in *Wild Strawberries* Sara, with a man on either side, is off to sunny Italy.

Old-fashioned as these preoccupations may be, they are not for this reason any the less true nor, indeed, any the less profound. But it is true, as Wood implies, that the patient working out which we find in Bergman's early work does assume a notion of social cohesion which is less and less a reality for most of us. Robin Wood implies that in his later work – in *The Silence, Persona,* and *Shame* – Bergman seems more aware of this and is therefore more 'mature'. The films are certainly exceptional. But it is this concept of maturity that I would like to focus on when we look at the later works by Ingmar Bergman.

*

Without coherent metaphysics, art is no more a comprehensible activity than travel without a sense of direction.   *Alex Comfort*

In 1957, Ingmar Bergman directed *Brink of Life (Nära Livet)*. At the time it seemed very much a marginal film. Appearing in the same year as *Wild Strawberries* and just before *The Face (Ansiktet,* 1958), it was so different from his work at that time.

To begin with, it was the first film in seven years *not* to be based on a scenario by Bergman himself. Secondly, it was shot by a cameraman that Bergman had never used before (and has never used again). Thirdly, there was no music at all. The harp arpeggios by Eric Nordgren and the glistening photography by

Gunnar Fischer had become so much a part of the traditional Bergman repertory that their absence struck us at the time as a distinct impoverishment.

True, the familiar faces were still there; but even here there was a difference. The clear-eyed, fair-haired matronly figure of Eva Dahlbeck which had provided such a point of rest in so many previous Bergman films at first appeared the confident female figure we had always seen her to be. But her confidence proved unfounded. After an excruciating labour, her baby was born dead. Her dreams of easy maternity were shattered, and our own expectations almost perversely played with.

Similarly, the other two women in the film resolved their situations in unexpected ways. Cecilia (Ingrid Thulin) hated her own maternity because her husband hated it. She was afraid that her child would send him away from her. This is in direct contrast to the role the same actress had played in *Wild Strawberries*. In that film, although the problem was similar, Marianne was determined to bring forth the new life within her, whether her husband wanted it or not. There was an affirmation in her pregnancy, an affirmation which formed part of the positive quality of that film.

Similarly, Bibi Andersson, who had played the radiant Saras in *Wild Strawberries* and the saintly Mia in *The Seventh Seal*, in *Brink if Life* played the indifferent Hjördis, a somewhat tarty teenager who got knocked up by a guy she didn't really care about and then did her best to abort. But without success. Again somewhat perversely, we might feel, the indifferent Hjördis is the one woman who easily and confidently brings forth her child.

Pregnancy has always provided Bergman with images of affirmation, and in many of his previous films he had dealt with the pain and loneliness of giving birth. But Ulla Isaksson's script from her own story for *Brink of Life* troubled the conventional imagery. Unlike *The Seventh Seal* or *Wild Strawberries* before it, the film no longer gave us a neatly symmetrical picture of forces that affirm opposing forces that deny.

Stylistically, the quality which at the time seemed most striking was its greyness and austerity. Taking place entirely within the maternity wing of a hospital, the film has little sense of any 'natural' life at all. Excluded are all the bird songs and flowers, the sense of wild strawberries that had provided a hopeful punctuation to so many of Bergman's previous films. Excluded too is any sense of season, of rebirth of nature that might be taking place outside.

When Harry brings some flowers to his happy expectant wife Stina, in contrast to previous Bergman films they provide a false symbol as her baby is born dead. In fact, the play with hands and mirrors, with dolls and teddy-bears, all the paraphernalia which had provided such a large part of the screen business in his earlier work, such a large part of their family, domesticated atmosphere, these elements are almost entirely absent. There are no sharp contrasts of any kind. The absence of any sun allowed in the film also means an absence of shadows. In photographic terms this means a comparative absence of blacks. The film is predominantly white upon grey. So it is in a moral way as well.

Within the context of Bergman's films at that time, indeed even within the context of the two films that were to follow – *The Face* and *The Virgin Spring (Jungfrukällan*, 1959) – *Brink of Life* really seemed a step to one side. Within the context of his later work, however, it provides an eerie premonition of what was to come. It is as if, at this time in his life, he sought out a subject not of his own creation which would allow him more freely to experiment with a new approach. It is as if, perhaps in the face of the international acclaim of the richness of his past work, Bergman wished to set himself an exercise in austerity. Whatever the explanation, *Brink of Life* seemed exceptional at the time – exceptional and rather unpleasant.

It may be merely fortuitous that this gradual change of emphasis began with the world's discovery of Bergman as an artist, with the beginning of the Bergman craze. Until *The Seventh Seal* created its big stir in New York, Bergman had been left very much alone. He had been allowed to direct at least sixteen films, script a few more, and work constantly in the theatre without the world press taking much notice or asking him what he was up to.

It may well be that this isolation, so much a recurring theme in

all Scandinavian art, was important to him as a film-maker. Certainly his cultural contact with his native Sweden has remained an essential element of his ability to work. In spite of repeated offers from Hollywood and elsewhere, he has refused to film outside his own country. Even *The Touch* (1971), though filmed in English, was shot in Sweden. In this sense, whatever the stylistic change in his films, he remains a traditional artist, drawing confidence and inspiration from the familiar world around him.

It might almost seem that *The Face* was made especially for the American press. It is not a film that I would normally want to spend much space analysing, but it does seem to make most sense as a kind of self-parody. All the visual rhetoric that formed an authentic part of the medieval dread in *The Seventh Seal*, in *The Face* is just the hocus-pocus of a traditional gothic thriller. Yet all the lines about death and the meaning of life, especially as asserted by Spegel, the drunken actor, might have been taken seriously in *The Seventh Seal*. I cannot believe they are intended to be.

However, unlike *Now About All These Women* (*Föratt inte tala om alla desse Kvinnor*, 1963), which is also best read as a playful dramatization of an artist's relationship to his critics and of the gap between his professional and private lives, there is a core of something splendid in *The Face* that lends substance to the gothic farce. Beneath the playful brouhaha, Bergman seems genuinely to be concerned about his powers as an artist, about how he might be expected to perform in the face of world acclaim. Bergman has talked about the artist as conjuror, as partly charlatan, working his marvellous spells for the delight of his fellow men. It is almost as if he mistrusts the power that, as an artist, he feels he has over his audience.

In *The Face*, Albert Emmanuel Vogler thinks of himself like this. He associates with charlatans who peddle love potions and magic spells and he dresses himself up as a saviour figure as if to disguise the poor creature he really is. And yet, in spite of his uncertainty, of the ability of reason to unmask him, he does possess a certain power, as he demonstrates to Dr Vergerus in the attic sequence towards the end.

Vogler's power, in his one moment of glory, rests in his ability, through a series of tricks, to make the rationalist doctor doubt his own powers of reason; and this, of course, is what Bergman does to us. In spite of Vogler's unmasking, his pathetic asking for alms, through the demonstration of his powers he earns his reward. The depressive rain suddenly turns to happy sunshine as he is swept off by the courtiers to perform before the king. A rather splendid film, in its way, as a kind of parodic divertissement; but only obliquely related to Bergman's finest work.

After *The Face* came *The Virgin Spring*, a film that would indeed repay close analysis. But the analysis has already been so expertly done by Robin Wood[16] that I will content myself here with pointing out one or two structural characteristics.

The most basic would seem to be the virtual change of style in the middle of the film, a change made more noticeable by the sudden transformation of the feeling of spring into the feeling of oncoming winter. The sections before the rape are all studded with natural effects in the traditional Bergman manner. Flowers abound everywhere, and there is a great sense of colour, of the clothes that Karin wears and of the sky and fields as a herdsman sings his ballad when she sets off with the candles. As Robin Wood has pointed out, the film is an immensely tactile one, with the touching power of hands everywhere in the foreground of the film.

After the rape and murder, however, all this changes. Snow begins to fall and the world becomes drab and cold. After the ritualistic slaughter of the three herdsmen, when the family set off to retrieve the body, all the domestic animals from the farmyard have gone, and the streams have dried up. It is not until Töre (the ubiquitous Max von Sydow) has expressed his own unworthiness, his own inability to understand, that the waters of life begin to flow again.

Although based on a medieval ballad with a traditionally miraculous close, and scripted by someone else, *The Virgin Spring* is central to Bergman's moral universe. As in *The Seventh Seal* or *Wild Strawberries*, the 'message' here is the conventionally humanist one: unless we relinquish our claims on life, our desire to

control it by the strength of our own will based on our own imperfect understanding, then we shall not enter the Kingdom of Heaven. Like so many of Bergman's films, *The Virgin Spring* ends with the sense of new life coming out of the sacrifice of the old. After all, Ingeri, the witch girl, is pregnant and she is the first to bathe her hands in the miraculous spring. Life will carry on.

These years immediately following *Brink of Life* seem to be ones of uncertainty, an uncertainty partly localized in the oblique confession of *The Face* but also represented, I would argue, by the fluctuation between films of an increasing austerity and strained little comedies. For some inexplicable reason, *The Devil's Eye* (*Djävulens Öga*, 1960) was presented to the English-speaking world as the first Bergman comedy. What it was, of course, was the first comic embellishment in a theatrically rhetorical manner that seemed, certainly in its diabolic episodes, very little re-created for the screen with very little at its centre. Like *All These Women*, the second 'comedy' that followed it, the basic impulse was facetious. It is as if Bergman was not really engaged by his material at all. It may even be that he was seeing how much he could get away with in the face of this new universal acclaim.

It was initially the existence of these two films, coming where they did within the Bergman œuvre, that created my own feeling of mistrust in the more serious Bergman that we were confronted with at that time. So diverse are the implications of, on the one hand, these two films and on the other, of *The Silence* that I found it difficult to be certain where Bergman stood in relation to his material. If he is simply playing with us and with the medium itself, as much of *All These Women* might suggest, mightn't he also be playing with us in a different way within the extremities of *The Silence*? If life is obviously not so farcical as it is presented in *All These Women*, perhaps it is not so grim as presented in *The Silence*? What is Bergman's relation to all this?

*

The 'new' Bergman really begins with *Through a Glass Darkly*

(*Såsom i en spegel*, 1961). This was the first of his so-called trilogy, a trilogy completed by *Winter Light* (*Nattvardsgästerna*, 1962) and *The Silence* (*Tystnaden*, 1963). His technique through this trilogy and into *Persona* (1966) has been to bring us closer and closer to fewer and fewer people, perhaps (as the epigraph of this chapter might suggest) with the deliberate ambition to 'illuminate the human soul'. One of his methods has been to let his characters speak directly to us, often with no editorial interference or recourse to flashbacks. One thinks immediately of Alma's beach orgy story in *Persona*, which Robin Wood has rightly applauded as a fine moment in that film.[17] But such a technique can lead to problems of response and interpretation of a most delicate kind.

For instance, in *Through a Glass Darkly* the sequence in the boat, where David gives Martin a long account of his attempted suicide in Switzerland and of his consequent discovery of the presence of God, raises a crucial critical question: we cannot *know for certain* whether David is telling the truth. He may be, of course; but then again he might simply be appealing to Martin for sympathy, immersed in the self-absorption which we see characterizes him at other moments in the film.

More serious still are the comments that close this disquieting work. This time David is talking to Minus after Martin has gone and the now insane Karin has been carried away. He is again talking about God and about how he knows that God is love. In the context of the film, this scene has a chilling air of self-deception about it. We have seen on the screen the disintegration of a family and the choice on Karin's part of a life in an asylum over the life she has known with her self-preoccupied father and husband. Except for the troubled Minus, we have seen no evidence of the compassion and understanding that, surely, must accompany love, even if of the most Christian kind, even if *agape* rather than *eros*. As he speaks, David is scarcely able to look at the boy, a sign of continued preoccupation made all the more evident by Minus's yearning towards his father, by his desperate need for reassurance of some kind. Like the ending of *Winter Light*, this last scene in *Through a Glass Darkly* conveys a most hopeless feeling, a hopelessness that springs from this suggestion of self-deception, a self-deception which is incomprehensible.

For whose self-deception is it? Bergman has failed to make it clear. Is David consciously trying to deceive the boy? I don't think so, though we cannot be *sure*. More plausibly, is he deceiving himself? The visual evidence of the film, its human implications, would seem to suggest that he is – like the useless, self-pitying priest in *Winter Light* who ends by offering sterile words into the empty air. But most serious of all, might Bergman be intending us to take those words literally? In other words, might the self-deception be only partly David's because partly Bergman's? From the evidence of the film, it is difficult to be sure. I have always been distressed, however, by the feeling in these films (and now again in *The Touch*) of something crucial left unresolved by the end.

This lack of certainty about the truthfulness of what the characters are saying plus our inability to be certain just where Bergman stands in relation to their words are the twin characteristics that give these films, for all their authority and stylistic asperity, a slightly hysterical, self-indulgent air. The dramatic context of the characters' remarks has often not been clearly enough defined for us to be certain whether we are watching the desperation of dramatically distanced characters (which would mean intellectually comprehended characters), or whether we are being subjected to Bergman's own undistanced and therefore uncomprehended despair.

Old-fashioned in form though they might have been, the inherited structure of his early films helped to contain such intellectual confusions as we might have detected in Bergman the man. In *Through a Glass Darkly*, however, and in all his subsequent films up to *A Passion*, there are immense confusions that accompany his formal experiments. In his recent films, there has been very little fresh observation of the surface realities of day-to-day life. In some ways, this is splendid, making for films of intense interiority. Yet at the same time one gets the feeling that Bergman, like his own characters, is totally locked within himself, imposing his view of the world upon the characters he creates.

Even *The Touch,* which does at least contain some fresh observation, is not free from this problem. It is too soon to know whether this film might represent a new start for Bergman or will simply appear, like *All These Women* before it, an uncharacteristic experiment. One can see encouraging signs in the film. It is good to see Bergman off that island and to realize that he can still produce a film which on the surface can seem so ordinary. Nevertheless, for all its sense of a greater surface normality, there is as well the same wilful obscurity which has characterized his late films – with the exception of *A Passion* – and which, quite unprofitably I feel, confuses the last scene of *The Touch.*

Has Karin's husband actually left her? The film implies that he has, but we cannot really know. Similarly, what is the precise nature of David's (played by Elliot Gould) relationship to his sister? Karin's interpretation of it would seem central to her decision at the end; but as this essential information is withheld from us, we cannot know for certain in that final scene which of the two characters is telling the truth, which is the more self-deceiving.

Throughout all the films which have followed *Through a Glass Darkly* there has been a crescendo of concern with humiliation. Peter Cowie has referred to 'the traces of bitter inferiority complex' that one can perceive in Bergman's films.[18] This could partly explain the over-emphases that have characterized Bergman's films, as it might explain as well his concern with humiliation. Central to all his films but most objectional in *The Ritual*, this determination of his characters to humiliate one another has been so extreme that it might almost seem that Bergman took a sadistic delight in striving to humiliate his audiences as well.

Since *The Virgin Spring*, up until the re-achieved balance in *A Passion*, it is rather as if the Knight had taken over the making of Bergman's films.[19] By isolating his characters so extremely, he has reduced his moral universe to the utterings of his most desperate characters. There is little sense of any kind of dialectical relationship with a less hopeless world outside, of any possible alternatives.

Ingmar Bergman

If I admire *The Silence* more than either *Through a Glass Darkly* or *Winter Light*, it is because the structure of this film does imply a tiny alternative. Three characters journey into this aggressive, destructive, unintelligible land and at least two of them journey out again. The boy even has a word or two from the foreign language scribbled for him to read, as if someday he might make sense of it all.

Were there space in this chapter, both *The Silence* and *Persona* would repay extensive analysis. They are the failed masterpieces of what we should by now be able to call Bergman's Baltic period. They are masterpieces because they courageously, astonishingly, break new ground – certainly for Bergman but also for the cinema itself. But they are failures, in my view, because the thinking behind them is simultaneously schematic yet unclear. It is as if Bergman the thinker has not kept pace with Bergman the artist, as if his new-found artistic authority, which has helped to free him from the allegorical modes of thought that held together his earlier work, has not been accompanied by fresh insights into the nature of human life.

Bergman at his best is a most inward director. Essentially, like Fellini's, all his films are about himself. The 'failure' occurs, in my view, when Bergman attempts to persuade us that his films are about more external matters – the validity of art, as in *Persona* or *Hour of the Wolf*; the ravages of war, as in *Shame*. In his earlier work, Bergman tended to pit good against bad, the life-affirming Saras against the life-denying Borgs. Technically this dualism was registered in the dazzling whites of all the exterior sequences in *Wild Strawberries* that contrasted with the dark interiors, say, of Borg's mother's home.

The dualism assumed a different form in *Through a Glass Darkly*, where there is an almost schizophrenic split between things seen and things said. In *The Silence* the dualism between the sisters is so exaggerated that one is tempted to explain them both as different aspects of one woman, as indeed one is forced really to interpret the dualistic structure of *Persona* as well. Interpreting the films this way means that the characters seem incomplete in some way *as characters*, that the dualism is too extreme for its implications to be psychologically convincing.

In *The Silence*, for instance, Anna lives entirely by her body,
Ester by her mind. Each would seem to need the other, although
Ester more than Anna. Yet Anna's physicality is a grim, tormented thing. Bergman no longer presents the body as a joyful
alternative to the troubled spirit, as the randy Frid and Petra
seemed to incarnate it in *Smiles of a Summer Night*. Anna seems
to hate her body as much as Ester hates hers. She feels perpetually unclean. There is no joy anywhere in this film. As in
Through a Glass Darkly and *Winter Light*, each character seems
locked within himself. In *The Silence*, any gesture outwards
leads one to the grotesque – whether it be Anna's ventures out
into that hot, masculine town or Johan's pathetic wanderings
along those corridors in the hotel.

The Silence leads us to the same kind of intersection that
Johan encounters after he has seen his mother keep her date
with her stud: a perfect circle, with corridors leading off in four
directions. But they all seem the same, no matter which we
choose. It is no wonder that Johan seems heavy with fatigue as
he trudges on his way.

Persona carries this dualism a step further, creating patterns
of such ambiguity that the final import of the film remains deliberately unclear, impossible fully to 'decode'.[20] However, it
seems an oversimplification of the structure of the film to
assume, as Robin Wood does, that Elizabeth 'knows more',[21]
and is therefore wiser in some way.

In one way, of course, she does. She recognizes that the total
silence which she imposes on her friend can virtually drive
her mad. It consumes Alma's self-confidence and destroys
almost totally her sense of social self – a sense which (as with
all of us) is dependent to a degree on some concept of social
utility.

There is thus something vampirish about Elizabeth in *Persona*, an element confirmed towards the end of the film in the
blood-sucking scene. Though she is handled very differently,
Elizabeth seems as absolute in her behaviour as was the Knight
in *The Seventh Seal* and she is equally destructive. In what sense
within the total scheme of things this can be taken as 'knowing
more' is not at all clear. She knows that she can destroy, that in

her absoluteness and her silence she gains a power. Whatever else she might know is difficult to say.

I have argued more extensively elsewhere how the Liv Ullmann character in *Hour of the Wolf* is not really so affirmative as Robin Wood feels that she is.[22] And the handling of her in *A Passion* should help to support my misgivings about her potentiality for affirmation in her other films. In *A Passion*, while Bergman once again presents her abundant beauty in all its fullness, immensely enriched by the colour on the screen, he creates for her a structure that quite unambiguously shows her to be the most destructive character in the film. Like the Knight in *The Seventh Seal* and Elizabeth in *Persona*, Anna is destructive because she has a passion for truth, for total honesty and commitment. Yet because reality denies her this, she builds up her life out of a fabric of lies, lies in which her inner needs force her to believe.

In the days of *The Seventh Seal*, Bergman made our acceptance of his moral world easy for us. He counterbalanced his negative characters with the child-like innocence embodied in the travelling minstrels, and further refined this balance by the partially affirmative scepticism of the Squire. But in *A Passion*, Bergman has presented his physically most attractive character as the one that causes the most damage. An insight this may be into the state of the world today, as Wood assumes it is. It certainly provides an insight into Bergman's own mind.

It is more in these personal, biographical terms that I have wanted to read his latest work. The Warsaw Ghetto photo or the Vietnam references in *Persona* or the unspecified civil war in *Shame* have always seemed to me extensions of an inner violence within himself for which, in Eliot's phrase, Bergman has been striving to find an 'objective correlative'. 'I've had this war going on inside of me for some time now' was Paul Klee's response to the outbreak of the First World War. I am sure that Bergman would have understood what he meant.

Largely because of Liv Ullmann, Robin Wood seems to find in these films a greater affirmation than he can in the equally desperate works of Godard or Buñuel. What Wood seems to interpret as lack of humanity, however, in films like *Weekend* or

Diary of a Chambermaid is the whole concept of *intellec-tual distance* between the life of an artist and the work of art he creates. Intellectual distance can release, I would argue, a kind of artistic energy. As in Swift, it can give to film-makers like Godard and Buñuel an element of wit which is itself a kind of affirmation. Furthermore, such a distance entails a recognition of historical perspective, of the violence and absurdity that have existed at all times since the world began.

To despair without humour is to surrender to self-pity, as Godard and Buñuel – again like Swift – seem to recognize. To despair without humour implies appropriating to oneself the role of prophet, assuming that one's personal grief and the viol-ence that one sees in the world around one are absolute and final in some way, that the world is about to end. Indeed, perhaps it is; but it seems a failure of nerve to give into this thought in the way that Bergman has recently been doing. It implies as well an absence of artistic humility. The lack of intellectual distance between Bergman's recent work and his private worries (which may be at least partly political) has always struck me as at least in part a failure in thought.

Bergman has always been mistrustful of intellectual sol-utions to the world's problems. In his films, it is partly his characters' *intellectual* preoccupations (all those games of chess!) that he has presented as inseparable from their *human* limitations. As far back as *Port of Call* (*Hamnstad*, 1948) we heard one character explain to his reading companion that 'Books are no solution'. Similarly in *A Passion*, we might have noticed that Andreas's study is lined with books, implying again that such failures as he embodies have been accompanied by at least some form of intellectual endeavour.

This mistrust of intellect has grown more serious in Berg-man's later work as the films have become more original and more ambitious in scope. It is particularly serious in *Shame*, I feel. The issues of such a war have a seriousness for us today and a reality independent of Bergman's use of them in the film which I would ask a serious artist to attempt to *understand*. '*Shame* is central to the experience I am living at this moment, and at most moments',[23] concludes Robin Wood, with as much courage and honesty as he attributes to Bergman. But if *thought* is what we want and if we would like better to be able to control these raging wars and to understand more intimately their political implications, we would be better off re-seeing *The Anderson Platoon* or reading Susan Sontag's most admirable and self-searching account of her own experiences of Vietnam.[24] Like Schoendoerffer's film, Miss Sontag presents her experiences in a personal and yet a *rigorously thinking* way – in such a way that might lead us to attempt constructive action.

Bergman's *Shame*, it seems to me, gives us less the feeling of the experience we are living at this moment than the experience of a sensitive artist who feels cut off from the violent issues in the world around him, who feels threatened by them, but whose temperament and training discourage him from struggling seriously to understand what is happening. It is easier for an artist like Bergman to poeticize images of war into images of total despair. This is the characteristic that gives these films, for all their surface astringency, a feeling of hysteria, a hysteria which is inseparable from a failure of thought.

This is what in *Shame* I feel Bergman is doing, distinguished in so many ways though that film obviously is. For Bergman, war is reduced to metaphor – an externalization of the violence that desperate people, in their inability to make contact, inflict upon one another, like Alma and Elizabeth in *Persona*, like Anna and Andreas in *A Passion*. In fact, in *Shame*, the war seems to play the same kind of role as the slaughtered animals in *A Passion*. It is an extended metaphor, once again a kind of objective correlative which will externalize for Bergman the latent violence that, in *A Passion*, all the characters in their different ways obviously feel.

The reason why *A Passion* is more successful than virtually every film Bergman has made since *Wild Strawberries* lies chiefly in this: the animal imagery in *A Passion* is handled with greater reticence and is a more impersonal though distressingly physical artistic device than the scenes of war in *Shame*. These scenes of war distress me as metaphor as they have their own reality in the political world outside the artistic world of the film, a political reality that urgently needs to be thought about and understood, not just responded to in a hopeless and emotional way. It is my own sense of the validity of this political reality and the need for clear-headedness that leads me to resent somewhat Bergman's reduction of this reality to convey to us the intensity of his own private fears and needs.

In discussing these issues, however, I don't mean to be positing a critical puritanism, adducing terms like balance, distance and success as the only ones relevant for contemporary art. For even if I am right in my feeling that Bergman's films since *Through a Glass Darkly* have frequently lacked these classic artistic qualities, I in no way mean to dismiss the films or to deny their immense power to disturb. The claim I would like to make for *A Passion*, however, is that it deals with the same problems that have troubled Bergman throughout his career, the problems of loneliness, humiliation, and of the essential isolation of the human spirit. Furthermore, it deals with these problems with all the authority and originality that have characterized his recent work (added to which is his immensely creative use of colour), but at the same time this film *is* balanced and distanced and successful in the most classical of ways. This means, for all its power, it also contains an element of restraint. This means as well, for all its hopelessness, there is an element of affirmation implicit within Bergman's ability to find an aesthetic resolution to all the difficulties posed by the film. *A Passion* is *complete* in a way that I don't feel his recent films have always been, complete and unpretentious in that the problems raised *in* the film are answered *by* the film as well.

*

A Passion opens with the sense of a slightly disabled, crippled, uncertain world, a world of diffused light, of burnt-out colour – a world in which we might feel strong moral certainties will prove to be impossible, where distinctions may be unclear. Behind the titles, we hear the sound of tiny bells, suggesting Chinese wind-chimes but blending imperceptibly into the sound of sheep bells that accompany the opening image of the film. It is an image of apparently serene animal life, a serenity, of course, that proves to be superficial.

Andreas Winkelman is attempting to repair his damaged house, his island retreat from the legal and emotional failures (the narrator explains to us) in the world outside. The first images we see of him suggest, through the continued close-ups of him tiling the roof and then hammering down below, a kind of physical energy which we will later see can erupt into a most destructive rage. But we also get the sense of a man suspended in time, as the twin dissolves of the sun might suggest. The sense of suspended time is carried on throughout the rest of the film in the alternation between snow-covered and snow-clear scenes, a device that both suggests an extended stretch of time and conveys a sense of uncertain seasons, part of the diffused quality that characterizes almost every element in the film.

Present in these first scenes is also the sense of Andreas Winkelman's tenderness in his concern with Johan Andersson. Andreas gets off his bicycle just to talk to him and to ask about his health. Yet this kind of concern is probably most active in situations where there is least demand. This might make us think of old Borg's relationship with the petrol attendant in *Wild Strawberries* where there was a similar sense of kindness offered to friends at a distance while emotional cruelty was inflicted on those close to home.

But in *A Passion*, the compassion is very real and a strong part of Andreas's withdrawn character, a hint perhaps of the kind of man he would like to be. As well as the scenes with the puppy and with Eva, I retain a vivid memory of the detailed attention that Bergman gave to Andreas's visit to the self-hanged Johan's house. Andreas lays his own live hand on the dead carter's folded hands. This gesture is not only affirmative in itself, an act of helpless compassion, but it also implies a recognition on Andreas's part of their sense of kinship. They have both been defeated by misfortune and driven back upon themselves. Through this gesture Andreas seems to recognize that he too might have been singled out as scapegoat for all the violence on the island, that he too shares such guilt as we all must share for the latent violence in us all – for the 'forces from underneath', as the narrator calls them at the beginning of Anna's *Shame*-ful dream.

Anna's first appearance in the film presents her on a crutch, reinforcing our sense, already gathered from Andreas's broken-down house and from Johan's bronchitis, of a diseased and crippled world. Her distress over the phone-call seems very real, and Andreas's eavesdropping somewhat ambiguous. Perhaps his simple curiosity is part of his tentative feeling outwards towards other people. It is certainly a necessary plot device, prompting him as it does to read his namesake's letter, a letter to which the film returns again and again as if in Andreas's memory, the remembered lines giving the lie to all Anna's assertions about the honesty and truthfulness of her past marriage. Yet her lies are not *just* lies. They represent as well an aspiration towards a truthfulness which, the film finally brings home to us, none of the characters can ever hope to attain.

Though it is difficult to convey in words the sensations received from the total aural and visual impact of a film as finely achieved as this, I'd like to draw attention to this eavesdropping moment as an indication of the delicacy of nuance that characterizes the entire film. As we hear Anna talking, we move in on Andreas and can hear a clock ticking – a sound heard in many Bergman films but insistently in this one, emphasizing the stretching out of time referred to a moment ago yet creating also a kind of suspense, as if of someone counting, measuring out the moments yet left to live. When Andreas realizes the extent of Anna's distress and slips out to leave her alone with her grief, we are left with a coloured pattern on the wall caused by the sun coming in through the stained-glass window. As I responded to it, I felt it was not just a 'pretty' effect: it conveyed in a purely visual and abstract way a sense of the delicacy that Andreas strives to bring to others in his relationship with them.

Somewhat similar is the moment after the silhouetted kiss between Andreas and Eva when they begin to make love. The camera focuses in on the window-pane, bringing to our attention the soft pink blur of a farm house, still out-of-focus, across the yard. Even more effective as a tiny visual detail is the orange lens flare just to the left of Andreas's face caused by the flasher on the police car that had come to announce Johan's suicide – a slight effect on the screen (possibly not even intended) that is in keeping with the sense the scene conveys of the fleeting precariousness of human life.

The central concern of *A Passion* seems to be with what I have already called the essential isolation of the human spirit. In this way the film is the summation of all of Bergman's work so far. Every detail in it contributes to this concern, even the magnificently staged dinner sequence at the Vergeruses' that shows the characters attempting to break through this isolation (like the ferry sequence in *Shame*). Even here, however, except for the closing four-shot and the moments when we hear them all chattering together, Bergman presents the bulk of the scene through single faces in close-up, separate from each other, each telling his own story. Similarly, the opening talk between Andreas and Johan is presented largely in action/reaction shots. At the very moment that we most feel Andreas's concern for the carter, through the editing Bergman emphasizes their essential separateness.

Related to this concern is the recognition of how unstable our sense of self is, our sense of who we really are. This is why the direct comments of the actors on the characters they are portraying work so well in the film. They not only distance us from the action slightly, in a Brechtian/Godardian way, reminding us that we are after all only watching a film, but they also give us the sense that even the actors cannot fully comprehend the characters they are portraying. This seems especially true of Bibi Andersson, who talks about her role in the same slightly over-sweet, over-sympathetic way that she, as Alma in *Persona*, talked about her life.

Sometimes this identity uncertainty is stated directly. Andreas wanders out into the wintry woodscape, screaming out his own name. But generally, it is more dramatically embodied within the discrepancies between what we see about the characters and what they say: *least* of all with Elis, whose cynical acceptance of his self and the meaninglessness of life gives him his kind of eerie power over the other characters in the film; *most* of all with Anna, whose problem seems the most serious in the film. After every scene with her when she talks about her marriage and her great need for commitment and truth, we return to that letter that Andreas has read, to Anna's husband's recognition of the failure of their marriage (at least from *his* point of view) and of his fear of the 'physical and psychical acts of violence' that they might inflict upon one another unless they part. Anna who in her talk can seem most certain is in fact most insecure; or, put another way, her assertions of certainty bring in their wake the very 'physical and psychical acts of violence' that her husband had feared. It would be too simple to say that, on a metaphorical level, it is Anna's passion for the certainty of truth that brings about the violence on the island, for in varying degrees it is brought about by them all. But as the film is presented to us, hers does seem to be the most destructive of the character dilemmas, and she has quite unambiguously been responsible for the death of her husband and her own son.

The violence on the island, inexplicable as it is in terms of plot, is clearly related to Bergman's concern with the theme of isolation. People who cannot reach one another and who are not certain who they themselves are flail out at one another. This psychological insight, implicit in this film, may also have political ramifications and be part of the cause of the persecution of the Jews or of the Vietnam war. But to utilize political references in the way Bergman has done in *Persona* and *Shame* (as I have already argued) seems to me simplistic and offensive, considering the political reality of these issues today, a reality that Bergman has nowhere shown he understands.

In *A Passion* Bergman seems to recognize this. Once again he shows Andreas and Anna watching atrocities on television. But the scene is immediately followed by the accident involving a little bird, which they then have to kill together, to put it out of its misery, and bury. Afterwards, they wash their hands together – he clean of the blood, she of the earth in which they have buried it. The juxtaposition of these two scenes seems to imply a recognition on Bergman's part that the real violence that we have to concern ourselves with is the violence closest to home, the violence that is directly a part of our own domestic lives. Certainly this is the only kind of violence that Bergman, the artist, as he once again seems to realize, intimately understands.

When I write about *A Passion* in this way, so much of what I most admire remains undescribed – the actual texture of the images and the meaningful juxtaposition of scene against scene. Andreas's scream on his bed after his night with Eva is immediately followed by the blood-red scenes of the gratuitously slaughtered sheep, suggesting that this act of destruction is in some way connected with the (would it have been?) violence towards Eva that, in his efforts to be kind to her, he has repressed within himself. Similarly, the red of the blood is most tellingly and sensitively recapitulated by Anna's bright red kerchief left in the snow after their angry fight together, the fluttering spot of red suggesting in this way the blood that might have flowed from her as well.

The final sequences form a most masterful conclusion for this most masterly of all Bergman's films. The burning horse that would not die might well stand as emblem for the desperate clinging to life of all the characters in the film, no matter how great their disease or pain. In this way even this image provides a kind of affirmation, the affirmation of blind animal energy within despair.

The drive back along the rainy road that Anna and Andreas take together, a drive punctuated at two key moments by flash shots from outside the car and the single stroke of timpani (the only non-naturalistic sound in this film), recalls similarly cloistered moments of truth in other Bergman films, especially Marianne and Evald's talk in the rain in *Wild Strawberries*. At the same time, the little key-chain dog dangling from the windshield recalls the hanging puppy which we saw towards the opening of the film. It thus prepares us for Anna's attempted violence to come.

Anna, who claims to believe in truth, when confronted by the *conflicting* truth about her marriage represented by that letter, is driven towards an act of destruction as she had been once before on a similarly rainy road. Yet she is not totally blind to her own part in the failure of their relationship, to her own way of provoking the violence that, a few scenes before, we saw Andreas inflicting upon her.

'Why did you come for me at the fire?' Andreas asks her, after he has prevented her from crashing the car. 'To ask for forgiveness,' she replies. This comment conveys her recognition of her own kind of failing and also recalls *Wild Strawberries* in the juxtaposition that we have in this scene of the need for forgiveness – a doctor's first duty, as it was put in that film – with the punishment of *ensamhet*, of loneliness. 'I want my solitude back,' as Andreas had previously said.

But this time, at this moment in *A Passion*, it is Andreas who seems unable to forgive. He gets out of the car and lets her drive away, leaving himself alone with his own uncertainty concerning who he is and what he can do. Even his name is presented through the narrator as if somewhat provisional: 'This time he was called Andreas Winkelman.' He could be somebody else in another situation. He could be any one of the characters portrayed in other Bergman films by Max von Sydow; or indeed, he could be all of us.

We believe that when we look more closely at something we see it more clearly, even when we look at another person's identity. The very form of Bergman's film gives the lie to this, certainly the form of the ending. In what is one of the most remarkable shots in the history of the cinema (if I may be allowed this enthusiasm), we move in on Andreas pacing back and forth and then falling to his knees, as the grain swells up and the light increases until the image literally disintegrates before our eyes. Then another stroke on the timpani provides the final punctuation to this most extraordinary film.

The Secret Life of

FEDERICO FELLINI

... I believe in prayers and miracles. *Federico Fellini, 1956*[1]

There is a sequence in *La Strada* (1954) that is crucial to our understanding of the films of Federico Fellini. It begins with a wedding celebration taking place in the open air. To one side of a long banquet table, really quite unnoticed by the wedding party, Zampano and Gelsomina are performing one of their tatty numbers, a raggle-taggle conga. Zampano is seated and is playing the drum, his huge form made awkward by the crumpled position necessary to hold the drum between his knees, while Gelsomina is performing her stiff little dance. Bowler hat on her head and clown's make-up on her face, she hops about in time to the music, thrusting her arms forward on every fourth beat. All about them is the litter that is always associated with any festivity in Fellini; and although Gelsomina is ignored by the wedding party, indeed scarcely noticed by the adult world, while she dances, a number of children in the background dance in unison with her. They respond in sympathy to what she is doing and imitate her movements. One of the guests offers Gelsomina some wine which, after a hurried sip, she passes on to Zampano. Then the lady of the house calls them to come and eat, and the sad little performance ends. On her way to the house, however, Gelsomina is led away by the children who have been so attentive to her dancing. There is apparently something that they want her to see.

She is led up a narrow flight of stairs by the side of the house and along a network of corridors where she almost loses her way. At one moment we see a little boy dressed in a black cloak gliding along. We've never seen him before in this film and we'll never see him again; but the fascination of his sudden appearance holds us for that moment and gives us the sense of something festive about to take place as well as perhaps of something that we can't quite understand. Who is this boy? What is he doing here? What is going on?

Gelsomina is then led into a large dark room, all the windows shuttered to keep out the sun, at the end of which crouches Osvaldo, a little boy in a big bed. There are two small mobiles suspended above him, little universes that rotate before his eyes. Indeed, his eyes stare out of his mis-shapen head, for he is apparently some kind of spastic, in the film regarded as a little idiot boy. The children ask Gelsomina to try and make him laugh, but her imitative bird flutterings only strike more terror into the boy's already terrified eyes. Finally, in a moment impossible to describe without limiting its implications, she draws close to him – he staring in confused terror at her, her own eyes opening wide to receive the full impact of this stare. Then abruptly, she and all the children are chased out of the room by a nun.

What is the meaning of this moment in *La Strada*? What is it that she receives from those wild staring eyes? Is it that in this misformed child she recognizes some affinity with her own gentle strangeness? *Un po' strana*, as her mother described her at the beginning of the film. Or is it that she senses in this blank unmovable face something beyond the powers of her simple goodness to affect in any way? And is it, then, a feeling of real terror that communicates itself to her, the result of a sudden recognition that at the end of long corridors hidden away in some sunless room there might lurk something terrible, something beyond our understanding, something deeply buried away and kept from conscious sight, but something terrifyingly real nevertheless?[2]

In the film, it is a moment of great power as Fellini creates it for us; and like the tatty party and the fleeting appearance of the bright-faced boy, it is a moment that can remind us of similar moments in other films by Fellini. Yet it is essentially dumb. It defies confident interpretation. Just as the idiot boy's eyes do not fully give up their meaning to the inquisitive Gelsomina, so the scene holds back its full significance from us. It is a moment when something deep and irrational passes between these two people; and if we are temperamentally attuned to Fellini's particular universe, then something equally deep and irrational passes through to us.

But the sequence continues. We cut to the kitchen where Zampano and the woman are stuffing themselves with food and talking about marriage. She is explaining how her first husband had been as big as he is and that no one subsequently has had any use for his clothes. Gelsomina appears and tries to tell Zampano about the sick boy she has seen; but she fails to communicate anything to him and is left alone with her meal and with the gradual realization of what is going on as Zampano and the woman go upstairs together 'to see about those clothes'.

Then a fade onto a typical Fellini post-festivity scene. The light of day has almost disappeared, making the foreground dark while the sky is still luminous beyond. Rags of streamers are hanging down from the house and posts nearby, and a single tree is isolated in mid-frame as one remaining couple carry on dancing to the sound of a lonely accordion player. Suddenly we notice a light-bulb dangling in the upper right-hand corner of the frame appearing comically out of place and apparently without function. But as we draw back a bit, we see that Gelsomina is in fact contemplating this scene from a barn window, and the light-bulb begins to make a little more sense.

Zampano is trying on his new clothes, absurdly self-involved in his new-found pin-striped elegance. Meanwhile, Gelsomina begins to hum her little tune and relates how she had first heard it one day in the rain while standing by an open window. She wonders what it is called and asks Zampano if he will teach her to play it on the trumpet. But as he continues to ignore her, she gets angry with him and stomps about the barn, finally falling down a hole where she decides to spend the night.

A cock crows as we dissolve into morning. Gelsomina is determined to take her stand. She is going to leave Zampano and return home, not because she doesn't like the work, but because she requires some human recognition. 'Io me ne vado', she keeps screaming to an unresponsive Zampano and later to the stillness of the morning; but then, after changing back into the togs she wore originally, taking care to return all of Zampano's property, she sets out on her way, waving in spite of herself at whomever she sees in a field nearby. There is no real sense of where she is going, simply the desire to get away.

After a bit (another dissolve), she sits down by the roadside, apparently in gloom. Then she notices a lady-bug or some such small creature and cannot help but become fascinated by it. She places it on her finger and blows it away. And immediately, without preparation, without a hint of plausibility in any social or psychological terms, a characteristic Fellini miracle occurs. Her sense of wonder is renewed. The impulse to live again surges up inside her as does her determination to continue her lonely journey in life. A little circus band of three musicians appears in the middle of a field, walking along by the side of the road; and in her turnabout way, she dances after them into town. Once in town she will come across another procession – a religious celebration – and, also in the rain as when she first heard her little tune, she will encounter Il Matto – the Fool – wearing an angel's wings and balancing precariously in the sky. Throughout the rest of the film, we will be aware of a strange affinity between Il Matto and Gelsomina, the stripes on his tights matching the stripes on her jersey as he also shares with her her little tune which he plays on a tiny violin.

*

I believe that everyone has to find truth by himself ... That is ... the reason why my pictures never end. They never have a simple solution. I think it is immoral (in the true sense of the word) to tell a story that has a conclusion. Because you cut out the audience the moment you present a solution on the screen. Because there are no 'solutions' in their lives. I think it is more moral – and more important – to show, let's say, the story of one man. Then everyone, with his own sensibility and on the basis of his own inner development, can try to find his own solution.[3]

In essence, the whole of Fellini can be found in this sequence from *La Strada*. His thematic centre is here. To begin with, reinforced by the title itself, there is the sense of life as a journey, as a constant tearing away from things known and a plunging into the unfamiliar. Unlike Bergman, however, whose allegoric wanderings are generally from place to place – in *Wild Straw-*

berries, the journey from Stockholm to Lund paralleling Borg's journey along the path of increased self-knowledge – in Fellini, there is seldom any sense of direction or eventual goal. The form of his films tends to be circular, the characters usually ending where they began.

This restlessness of movement can work in different ways. Occasionally, as with the nuns in *La Strada*, there is the feeling that we must give up things dear to us before we get too fond of them; but more frequently there is the feeling that only by moving on, by probing and searching, can we ever come to know the purpose of life. Fellini's fondness for processions is obviously related to this. Indeed, it sometimes seems as if the celebration of movement such as we witness in processions may by itself provide the purpose, as if in terrestrial terms there may be, in fact, no goal.

Of course, Fellini would reject such intellectual speculations. For Fellini is an intuitive in his response to life, a great muddle-headed irrationalist with very strong feelings and no clear thought. He lives life from the senses, yet his intelligence has informed him that the senses can deceive. Hence the intellectual indecisions, the apparently inexhaustible interviews with all their self-contradictions. Yet hence too all the passionate affirmations of his films up until their acme in 8½. It is as if Fellini recognizes that 'truth' must lie somewhere, though locked up in subjectivity, but he is unable to seize it with the merely rational surface of his mind. Hence all the turbulence, all the restless energy, the endless travelling along streets and long corridors.

Whether it is the Vitelloni wandering about the beach or the town at night or Moraldo setting off at the end on his own for we don't know where; whether it is the peasant families at the end of *Il Bidone* (the little children with ricks on their backs recalling the first shot of Gelsomina) that walk by beyond the reach of the dying Augusto; or whether it is the complete Fellini/Anselmi entourage descending that vast structure at the close of 8½ and dancing round and round the circus ring together in an infinity of perfect movement – whatever the context and whatever the film, this perpetual movement is central to Fellini. And it is also central to his irrational view of life that the movement should be without origin or goal.

But in this sequence from *La Strada*, there are also some examples of the twin experiences that, as Fellini understood it at this stage of his career, this directionless journey through life must entail – experiences of the freshness and unexpectedness of innocence which are immediately followed by the experience of something dreadful that in a world freed from the devil is now without a name. On the one hand, we have the presence of Gelsomina herself and of the somewhat querulous Il Matto who appears from on high; but more characteristically we have the fleeting image of that little boy in the cloak passing along the corridor that charms us so gratuitously. For it is also a part of Fellini's irrationality that childhood innocence should so often play such a formally gratuitous role in his films, that children should simply appear and then disappear – providing us with a momentary pleasure and perhaps renewing our faith in the wonder of existence but remaining essentially apart from the troubled business of life in Fellini's adult world.

In *La Dolce Vita* (1959), this goes a long way towards explaining the floating presence of Paola, the little Umbrian angel, who has so universally been disapproved of as a facile resolution to that troubling, too-long film.[4] Initially, Paola simply passes into a short bridging sequence and passes out again, like the boy in the cloak. We see her setting the table at a seaside restaurant, misunderstanding Marcello's difficulties yet attracted by some quality in him, while deriving simple enjoyment from the loud assertions of *Patricia* playing on the juke-box, a simplicity that is emphasized by the later degradation which we experience towards the end of the film when Nadia strips to the same tune. But Paola has been placed there so that, when she appears in the epilogue to the film as a kind of *diva ex machina*, she may suggest a quality in life that has been ignored in the compulsive distractions we have been witnessing. Dramatically, in any conventional way, she may leave much to be desired; but she is perfect for suggesting Fellini's sense of youthful trust that, although beautiful, is presented as ineffectual and so exists somewhat apart.

We may also remember in *I Vitelloni* (1953) Moraldo's child companion of the railways, with whom he discoursed about life and the stars, who is left to return to the hopelessness of the town, balancing precariously along the rails. Or we might remember the children towards the end of *La Strada* who (as if in gentle rehearsal for the end of $8\frac{1}{2}$) are dancing in a ring while their mother (we assume) is hanging out her washing and singing Gelsomina's tune. There are as well the young people who appear out of the woods at the end of *Le Notti di Cabiria* (1956): 'We have lost our way,' one of them says as they begin to circle round the disillusioned Cabiria, while another barks at her in a way that might remind us of the wild compère in the nightclub towards the beginning of the film. In spite of the hopelessness of her present position, the lack of 'solution' to any of her problems, she cannot help but return their smiles and their '*Buona sera*'. And of course in $8\frac{1}{2}$, when the lights dim and the ring of dancers vanish and even the circus performers disappear from the scene, it is the young Guido-Anselmi-cum-Federico-Fellini who is left alone in the spotlight and who moves with it to the side of the ring, leaving the screen in darkness. Although there's never a solution to any of the problems, up until the 'Toby Dammit' sequence in *Spirits of the Dead* (1967), there was always the sense of something young and fresh left to carry on. Yet, if on the one hand there are children, representing the possibility of new forms of life, on the other there is the recurring presence of this dreadful nameless thing, the presence of some form of evil, some kind of threat.

In all of Fellini's films, there are these disturbing images, moments of disillusion that serve to challenge simple faith. There is the sinister homosexual who so disappoints Leopoldo in *I Vitelloni*, as there had been the more-than-disappointing flesh-and-blood reality of the White Sheik before. But in *I Vitelloni* more powerfully and more like Osvaldo is the woman in the cinema who so easily tempts Fausto and who is again encountered one day on the beach. Within the subterranean depths of Fellini's imagination, she serves as a link between Osvaldo and La Saraghina and simply appears at odd moments as a threat to the flesh. Also in *I Vitelloni* there is the married man in

the dark glasses who tempts Olga away. He too is first encountered on the beach. But most ominous of all is the shot of
his dark car just before they drive away: it is almost hidden
by the early-morning shadows in the street while the light glares
out above it threateningly, like a scar. And if in *Cabiria* there is
of course the deceitful Oscar, more in keeping with the irrationality of these images of threat is the devil-dressed magician
who through hypnosis turns innocence towards evil ends.

Excluding for the moment La Saraghina, who is a more complex incarnation of this kind of nameless threat, simultaneously
described as evil yet *felt* to be beautiful, and excluding for the
moment the whole of *Satyricon*, which, on one level, seems a
surrender to this frightening aspect of life, in *La Dolce Vita* we
have a summary of this sort of effect in that strange blob of a
fish that pollutes the stretch of beach at the end of the film and
forms the imaginative counterpole to the young Paola waving
to Marcello across the protective inlet of the sea. It is as if something deep in Fellini recognizes that in childhood and childlike
responses to existence, there is beauty and affirmation of a frequently troubling kind, troubling because unconscious of the
terrible threats and temptations that can lurk in the un-
knowable depths of adult life; and in the way that so frequently
these polar elements seem more an accompaniment to the main
theme than a formally intrinsic part of his film, it is as if at this
stage of his development, Fellini cannot consciously work out
the exact relationship between these two extremes or even find
a settled place for them within the narrative structure of his
films. Constantly he creates situations for which he can find no
earthly solution, and his characters encounter difficulties
beyond their means to control. For the end of *La Dolce Vita*, it is
as if the gods themselves must be evoked to bring about the
closing affirmation. Failing to communicate anything helpful to
Marcello, the little Umbrian angel looks straight at the camera,
and at us. What do we make of it all? What do we feel about
innocence by the end?

*

Federico Fellini

All the formal philosophy you could possibly apply to my work is that there is no formal philosophy ... A man's film is like a naked man – nothing can be hidden. I must be truthful in my films.[5]

Among many film enthusiasts, especially in Great Britain Fellini has been undervalued and, I think, misunderstood. Before the appearance of 8½, *I Vitelloni* was often regarded as his most successful film. And so it is – on the social realist level. Along with *Il Bidone* (1955) in its somewhat grimmer way, *I Vitelloni* is the only Fellini film that truly works on the level of social observation, on the level of incident, as I call it in my Introduction. It is balanced in its narrative, minutely observant, beautifully paced, and very funny. Yet from a slightly deeper level, it can also make a more personal appeal. When looked at sympathetically, it is not essentially that different from Fellini's other films. Beneath its realist exterior, it too can make its more subliminal appeal.

One of the difficulties that Fellini's films pose for more rational minds – indeed, we could even say, one of the limitations of Fellini's particular kind of cinematic art – is that he has too often been too careless about the surface credibility of his films, confusing and alienating all but the most sympathetic of his viewers as the conventions of his films have seemed so strange. Yet at their best, in the early days, they are strange only to the expectations of literary narrative and of psychological realism. Fellini's conventions are not at all strange to the language of painting, which, beneath the narrative surface of his films, is the language that he used most frequently to employ.

There is in all real films – in all films that have the lasting interest that characterizes a work of art – what I have found it convenient to call a subliminal level, a level largely of images plus the complex associations of scarcely perceived sounds. Although we are often not really conscious of these vital ingredients, especially on a first viewing, we can nevertheless be immensely moved by their power to affect us. Indeed, it is generally these elements that give a film its atmosphere or mood.

If there are in Fellini certain constantly recurring themes or motifs, there are also certain constantly recurring images and effects that, when responded to, can make an extraordinary impression upon us and which are cumulative in their power. For these images to be discussed at all, criticism has to lean away from the comfortably confident tone of literary-cum-film analysis and draw upon the tentativeness of art appreciation. For the central fact about art criticism is the elusiveness of the total power of the image when talked about in words and of the greater subjectivity of the way paintings speak to us, moving towards music, which is the most subjectively elusive of all. Images and sounds cannot be argued with. They either affect us or they don't. When talking about a painting, there is always so much that we cannot know. The discursive element in painting is automatically much less than it can be in literature and the speculative element in interpretation correspondingly that much more. Once again, we might think of that moment between Osvaldo and Gelsomina, the inscrutability of which I've taken some pains to describe; but in Fellini's films, there are images of greater tentativeness than this.

If we look at a painting by Jean Carzou, for example *The Bay of Dreams*, there are many things that we might want to say about it, about the gentle flowing lines of the figure in the fore-ground moving through a variety of shapes and objects in ex-tended perspective to the sharply jagged quality of the mountains in the rear. But one of the most striking formal el-ements in the picture and part of what is for me the forlornness of its mood is the lateral shadow that cuts across its middle, intensifying its sense of space and further distancing these two contrasting worlds. If we next look at an image from *I Vitelloni*, just after the departure of Moraldo's pregnant sister on her shot-gun honeymoon, if we are responding to the impact of the images in the film and not just waiting for the next point of characterization or development of plot to emerge, we might be affected in much the same way. Similarly, if we contemplate the effect of the foreground shadow in Giorgio de Chirico's *The Rose Tower*,[6] and remember that the entire proposal scene be-tween Oscar and Cabiria is similarly played in shadow with the landscape and buildings luminous behind, we might feel that by the very light itself, both de Chirico and Fellini, working inde-pendently in their quite different ways, have employed these foreground shadows to lend a worried aspect to the scene and yet to suggest that there is something worthwhile in the distance, something worth achieving beyond.

In fact, de Chirico, perhaps because as an Italian he too has been particularly sensitive to Italian space and Italian light, can be used again and again to illuminate by analogy the images in Fellini. Along with images of the sea and of isolated trees,[7] the Italian town square with its fountain in the middle is a recurrent image in Fellini. It is generally seen at night or in the early morning, generally presented as a place of reckoning and is divorced from its more sociable associations of being a place where people meet.

In Fellini, the town square is never felt to be the social centre of a community. De Chirico too seemed to be sensitive to the empty feeling of such places at unused times of day – indeed, to the very irrelevance of such vast structures to the little intimacies of human life. And so in de Chirico, we find a number of such paintings that depict huge buildings and exaggerated shadows, where the tiny figures serve both to emphasize the hugeness of the structures (as do the miniature trains that we frequently see puffing away on the horizon) and to give a feeling that the little human things don't really belong in such a space. Sometimes this feeling is further emphasized by the presence of some stray object in the foreground, some object made bizarre by being torn from the context of its function – like that light-bulb in *La Strada* or the railway carriage that we see in de Chirico's *Anguish of Departure* in the middle of the square.

So in *I Vitelloni*, in the much-admired beach sequence – admired for its sensitive observation of these five men imprisoned in their own apathy and defeated by the feeling that there is nothing they can do – Fellini emphasizes their own feeling of irrelevance and functionlessness by the many apparently useless structures that we see sticking up out of the sand. Skeletons of summer changing-huts and odd inexplicable bits of wire frequently dominate the scene and create the feeling of something strange with an almost surrealist intensity. Everywhere throughout the film as throughout every Fellini film there is the recurring presence of the bizarre.

In fact, this recognition of the bizarre is at the centre of Fellini's world, the physical parallel of his response to the irrational, the source both of his humour and of his sense of dread. For if humour is uppermost in most films by Fellini, beneath the comic observation of the discrepancies of human life there is always this feeling of something beyond our control, something not fully known to our rational selves – like that grotesque fish at the end of *La Dolce Vita*, like Osvaldo in that guarded-over room, like the frightening labyrinthine journeys in *Satyricon*, or the grotesque distortions of *The Clowns*.

The first image we see in *Lo Sceicco bianco* (1952), the first film directed by Fellini himself, is an image of a structure sticking up out of the sand with a piece of cloth blowing in the wind. In front of this structure with his robes also blowing sits the White Sheik on his horse in all his phoney splendour – an opening image of immense absurdity, as indeed are so many of the images in this extraordinarily funny film.

But it is really in *Cabiria* that this purely visual absurdity acquires its most consistently surrealist force. Constantly surrounding Cabiria's box-like house is a litter of people and objects apparently devoid of function and deprived of any context of psychological plausibility. At one moment as we track along we see a post with a for-sale sign on top and a bicycle leaning against it, a baby in a push-chair a little beyond, and a woman squatting in the field further beyond that. At another moment as we see Cabiria stomping back from her unfortunate dunking in the river, wearing her characteristic horizontal stripes, we see the bulbous Wanda in the background, beside her some washing, a stray horse, and behind her quite inexplicably a little black creature with an umbrella in the field, and behind all that, above yet another box of a house, there is a kite sailing aimlessly in the sky.

But most absurd of all and most characteristically Fellinian is the strangely functionless structure that exists outside Cabiria's house. How did it come to be there and what purpose does it serve? Questions like that can have no answer on any rational plane, but the presence of this structure dominates a number of scenes in the film; and of course it is related both to the beach structures that we've seen more naturalistically in *The White Sheik* and *I Vitelloni* and to that structure to end all structures that looms over 8½.

As in 8½ where throngs of people are always walking up and down this unnecessary construction, so in *Cabiria* little boys are constantly clambering about these poles that exist outside her home. Like the circus itself so important in Fellini, like the apparently gratuitous accomplishments of the clown or aerialist, it is as if this kind of purposeless activity that nevertheless can give pleasure and even a kind of physical meaning to the absurdity of life should exist as an emblem of Fellini's view of the world – movement without direction, life essentially without a goal.

*

Visually, I've often made use of the theme of circus life which is a mixture of spectacle, risk, and reality. My characters are often a bit bizarre. I'm always talking to people in the street who seem rather unusual or out of place or who have some physical or mental affliction ... Since all these elements form a part of me, I don't see why I shouldn't introduce them into my films.[8]

So far in this account of Fellini, I have been concerned only with the thematic consistency of his work and with the peculiar force of his imagery. Taken all together, his films create a world that is uniquely and personally his own. Even the films that follow 8½, though less intimate, still manage to enact Fellini's vision of the universe. All this, although true, tends to ignore the great differences between his individual films, differences of surface characteristics but also finally of quality as well. For much as I respond with pleasure to nearly everything that he has produced, I recognize that if Fellini is a man of immense inventiveness, he is also a director of uncertain control over the many elements that his mind, with apparently so little effort, can with such energy invent. Also, if Fellini is a man who has created for us an immensely personal view of life on the screen, I recognize that it is just that – an immensely personal view of life which is frequently egotistic, self-indulgent, sentimental, and wilfully irrational, courting mystery at every corner and asking from us as much compassion for all these difficulties as he has bestowed upon them himself.[9]

So the critics who have preferred *I Vitelloni* to anything that Fellini has subsequently produced have probably done so because, of all his films, *I Vitelloni* least imprisons us in Fellini's private world. There is in the film such a wealth of surface detail that we can get a good deal from it without being too closely attuned to its more subjective elements, whereas *La Strada* presents Fellini's private world with a minimum of props.

In *La Strada* unless we are sensitive to the subliminal level on which the film is really operating and are sympathetic to Fellini's concern through his images to unite Gelsomina with Il Matto and the two of them with the sea, while at the same time he is enmeshing Zampano in his own chains of earth and fire and brute insensitivity, unless we are sensitive to the suggestive power of the imagery, the film will either make very little sense to us or it will seem terribly naïve. If by way of 'meaning' we carry away from *La Strada* only Il Matto's disquisition on the usefulness of pebbles, then we will come away with what we could rightly call a sentimental experience. But if we have been moved by the little children dancing round that tree and are aware that it is Gelsomina's beloved sea – both her natural home and her constant friend – that is washing up on the beach during that final image where Zampano lies crushed by a dumb and brutal grief, then the intellectually self-indulgent and sentimental elements will be buoyed up by some sort of aesthetic charge as well, by the sense of some depth of feeling and perception being communicated to us beyond what our merely rational selves can readily receive.

If it is true that there is nothing in Fellini's films that we can properly call thought, there is nevertheless evidence of an intelligence of a totally different kind. Everywhere in his films there is the presence of a mind that responds to life itself on a subliminal level, that is acutely conscious of the natural metaphors to be found in the trappings of day-to-day life and which struggles to find a structure both flexible and persuasive enough to contain them within his films. Even in a film as distended and episodic as *La Dolce Vita* (1959), there is an intricate interweaving of sounds and images that help to bind together this elongated experience.

When the lifeless statue of Christ is being flown to St Peter's at the opening of the film, only a handful of *ragazzi* follow its shadow through the streets of Rome; and at the injunction of the pneumatic Sylvia to 'Follow me everybody', this laughing, living goddess, this beatific creature who is more at home with little kittens than with the temptations of the flesh, gains an active and excited response as people follow her dance about the nightclub floor. I've already mentioned the ironic repetition of the *Patricia* tune which should help to give a slightly more settled place to the presence of Paola – if we're fully attentive to the soundtrack of the film, we should be remembering Paola while we're watching Nadia strip – but also at Steiner's party certain things occur that acquire a formal relevance by the end.

In fact, the portrait of Steiner offers a convenient example of how Fellini's compressed characterization works in this sprawling fresco of his own uneasy mind.[10] As his German name might suggest (and he is played by a French actor!), Steiner is the modern *déraciné* eclectic, a man with only intellectual allegiances. For him, all experience is filtered through the mind. He is a dilettante, as he himself says, 'too serious to be an amateur and not serious enough to be a professional'. He remains outside experience, unattached, and strives to bring to life the order and clarity of a work of art. In his self-created isolation, he draws what sustenance he can from the culture of all nations and epochs. When we first see him, he is carrying a Sanskrit grammar in a modern church and, after a few tentative chords of jazz, we hear him playing a Bach toccata on the organ.

For Steiner, life has meaning only if he can contemplate it as he can a work of art. Even natural sounds, the roar of the wind and the sea, are recorded on tape and listened to like music; and his delight in his daughter is largely the delight he takes in her fondness for words, in her own instinctive gifts as a poet. For Steiner, real life is apparently too much and he tries, through art, to find an escape. Of course, he fails; and through his failure Fellini would seem to be, too schematically, perhaps, insisting that there can be no path into the future through intellectual activity or through art. Yet, by the end of the film when we're confronted with the final beach scene and by our necessary Paola,[11] we should recognize that those very same sounds of the wind and the sea that Steiner had listened to as music are part of the disturbance that, along with the intrusive inlet of the sea, keeps Paola from communicating with Marcello. They are part of her 'natural' protection from his jaded world. And although I shouldn't want to make great claims for the power of such effects to hold together this too insistent film, nevertheless they do reveal the presence of an artistic intelligence of a rare intuitive kind.

*

Throughout this account of certain aspects of Fellini, as throughout all the chapters in this book, I am trying to do basically one thing: I am anxious to explain the form of each director's films in terms of the *view of life* that has necessitated it. With Fellini, as with Bergman and Buñuel, I tend thus to concentrate on the films where I feel the director has been most successful in resolving his artistic problems – in Fellini's case, most accessibly in *I Vitelloni*, most intimately in *La Strada*, and most inescapably in 8½. However, before looking at 8½, the film that I consider to be Fellini's most *complete* achievement, I'd like to glance at some of his less successful works and at the view of life that all his films embody; for with Fellini, as in another way with Renoir, any breakdown in the form of his films is inextricably tied to inadequacies within the view of life at the base of them.

In many ways, Fellini's view of life is that of a child – a simple creature of nature, a kind of self-regarding mystic. When we think of art in more social terms, Fellini's self-obsessions can be worrying. Yet surely society is still robust enough to be enriched by the products of its artistic egotists – Federico Fellini, Hector Berlioz, Benvenuto Cellini, a distinguished genealogy of men who have created in extravagantly personal ways. These men, with their insistence on the inner life of man, have made their own contribution to our increased self-understanding. At their best, they have pursued their self-bound concerns with such energy and completeness that their explorations of their purely private problems have managed to illuminate the problems of us all.

Nevertheless, on a more mundane and technical level, if we look closely at *Le Notti di Cabiria*, there are obvious formal difficulties. In spite of the surrealist effects that surround Cabiria in her box-like home and in her dealings with Oscar, the street sequences seem to be in a rather different style, as if from another film. Perhaps the substantial credit given to Pasolini in the making of this film has something to do with this disunity; and if we were concerned to offer an extensive critique of all Fellini's films, detail by detail, there would be a number of such discrepancies that we'd have to notice.

Yet, if we value him at all, a man like Fellini must be allowed to stumble. In the intuitive way that he approaches the screen, he is almost bound to run into difficulties and at times to fail to find the form adequate to his needs. What we ask for always is that he should be true to himself and that the film as a whole should be strong enough to sustain the difficulties – or at least that we can see in certain features valuable preparation for finer things to come.

Thus, while I can find little to admire in his sketch for *Boccaccio 70*, I can see in much of the poster-raising sequence, hilarious in its way and absurd in its chaos, a kind of rehearsal for the press conference in 8½, where both the hilarity and the chaos have a tougher context to contain them. But it is the essential tastelessness of the central conception of the Boccaccio episode that has always made me doubt that particular piece of film and wonder what it might presage.

In the image of the little puritan who has such grotesque fantasies, there is possibly something funny (though not to my taste) but there is also a contradiction between Fellini's most undeniable gift and his intentions in this film. Whether we like him or not, at his best Fellini has certainly succeeded in creating for us images that convey the innermost recesses of his own teeming mind. But what about the mind of another person essentially different from himself: could he explore that with the same kind of intimacy? I should never have thought so; and yet this is what he was offering to do in this film. He would appear to be trying to convey to us how another person thinks and feels, which is perhaps what makes the film so unsubtle in the effects that it achieves, so lacking in compassion, finally so lacking in taste.

This lack of subtlety seems everywhere a part of *Giulietta degli Spiriti* (1965).[12] Except for some of the garden sequences and the childhood scenes, its pace is so insistent, the harsh clash of its primary colours so dazzling, its editing so restless that the overall style of the film would seem to be working against the feeling of inwardness necessary if we are actually to feel very strongly for his heroine. Even when she is at home, away from the mad world that confines her, Nino Rota's music keeps up its nervous bounce, appropriate enough for the excited dance from scene to scene in *La Dolce Vita* or for the world of film production which provides the backdrop of 8½, but often irritatingly out of place here. As with so much of the extravagance of the decor and costumes, the music seems to belong more to some crazy world of Fellini's rather than to Giulietta. With the exception of the childhood scenes, all filtered through white gauze and softly evoked in diffused light, the style of the film seems so unvaried that we are exhausted by the final party near the end. There is too slight a sense of norm which might have provided a point of rest to which we could return. The barbaric Turks emerging from the depths of the sea might have been magnificent had they been placed within a more natural situation that could have represented the regular rhythms of Giulietta's day-to-day life – like the prolonged *ennui* of the Vitelloni that contained the momentary frenzy of the Mardi Gras. But in *Giulietta*, her friends that come to visit trussed up in Piero Gherardi's costumes are as fantastic as her fantasies; and the erotic Susy's mansion is even more fantastic still.

At the end of the film, where we can recognize that at last she is no longer afraid and so has been set free, it is difficult to relate this final feeling of release to her memories of childhood martyrdom even though this martyrdom sequence is one of the most delicately achieved scenes in the film. Our minds have been distracted by so many other things.

If *Giulietta* seems a failure, its failure lies in Fellini's inability to discover a form that would hold before us convincingly the intimacy of Giulietta's mind. So much like 8½ in so many of its effects, it is very unlike it in this: in *Giulietta* there is no inner structure of argument, no dialectical placing of effect within effect. And there is none of the self-criticism that distinguishes 8½ and which troubles and humanizes the close.

In *Giulietta*, although the Fellini-Giorgio character is certainly criticized – sleeping as he does with his ear-plugs and eyeshade, his senses blocked off against his wife – finally, as Guido had done with Luisa, Fellini seems to have imprisoned his wife within the inescapable fantasies of his own imagination. As with *Boccaccio* he has failed to make a film of any sustained sympathy about another person's life. If *Giulietta* is concerned with the infidelity of husband to wife, then, by a grim kind of irony, this film would seem to represent an infidelity indeed.

Fellini's view of life is intimately bound up with his sense of the prime importance of self, of the elements in his life that have formed his own imagination. Once he departs from this, he runs into trouble.* Thus, the opening twenty minutes and the closing

---

* With *Roma* (1972) now before us, I fear that this kind of explanation is increasingly insufficient to explain the imaginative emptiness of Fellini's latest films but especially of *Roma*. This film confronts us with a paradox: like *The Clowns*, it is a film again with Fellini himself supposedly at the centre of it; yet there is no feeling of intimacy at all. With the banishment from his work of the Gelsomina figure and of all his little children, Fellini's muse seems to have fled as well. In its place, in *Roma*, we have what appears to be the complete surrender to his position as superstar (as in *Alex in Wonderland*), where anything is possible as long as it bears the esteemed Fellini signature, no matter how tasteless and empty the film might be.

Perhaps the artist in Fellini is vaguely aware of this. If not, why include the moment with Anna Magnani where she rejects Fellini's attempt to interview her? 'I'm too tired,' she explains, 'and besides, I don't trust you.' Neither can we. If in *La Strada* Fellini seemed to be revealing his soul, in *Roma* he appears to be telling lies about the events in his life, as if to cover up the fact that, unlike 8½, this time he *really* has nothing to say.

five of *The Clowns* (1971) are archetypal Fellini. They mark a return to the sense of awe and fear which is so basic to his finest work and which, for Fellini, has always been associated with the circus. Yet, while there are many things to enjoy throughout *The Clowns*, in the middle sections which are simultaneously a television documentary *and* a parody of a television documentary, we learn less about the subject matter, the clowns themselves, than about Fellini.

There are two elements in this film, however, that require comment. In a film *supposedly* as autobiographical as this, a film in which Fellini himself appears, I was struck by the absence of any reference to the Gelsomina figure – the gentle creature of pure spirit that has been so central to his earlier work and which provides so much of the intimacy of these films.

What does this absence imply? Does it relate to something private in Fellini's life with Giulietta Masina? And does it relate as well to the evil child that helps to bring about Toby Dammit's death (for this evil child, with her eerie smile, bears an uncanny resemblance to Gelsomina in *La Strada*)? Whatever this omission might imply in terms of Fellini's personal life, in his public life, in the world of his art, it would seem to indicate a loss of faith. Fellini's latest films fail to mask a deep pessimism – a terrifying sense that there may, in fact, be no salvation, that even the purposeless movement that characterized his earlier work and which achieved a mystical authority in the final sequences of 8½ might prove hollow and unreal.

This recent sense of unredeeming purposelessness might help to explain the second observation that I'd like to make about *The Clowns*: it contains elements of self-parody of a most inescapable kind. There is one moment during which all the clowns are running round and round the circus ring in a frenzy of purposeless movement as if in deliberate mockery of the finest moments in *La Strada*, *Le Notti di Cabiria*, and 8½. 'Mr Fellini, what is the message of this sequence?' asks an onlooker (in words to that effect). Whereupon a pail is suddenly thrown over his inquiring head, as immediately afterwards over Fellini's. Obviously, Fellini is mocking both himself and his interpreters. We shouldn't even try to understand!

When an artist is driven to mock his own achievement, it may imply an artistic crisis. At the same time, such self-mockery may be merely a playful response to the role thrust upon Fellini of superstar; or, more seriously, it may be an attempt to exorcize once and for all his own clichés (as Bergman did in *The Face*), as if to prepare himself for new things to come. Moving backwards to *Satyricon*, perhaps that film could be seen as an exorcism of this kind – as an attempt at last to probe the fears that have haunted his earlier work but which have never been confronted head on.

As I've written elsewhere,[13] in *Satyricon* (1969) the fears seem largely sexual. Sexual love has always been somewhat oddly handled by Fellini, as if it were something that he himself didn't understand fully. 'You cannot tell a proper love story!' one of the 'nieces' associated with the production team giggled outrageously to the Guido/Fellini figure in *8½*, leaping up and down in the bed; and in all his films Fellini has been attracted to the androgynous figure of the clown. His wife and spiritual mentor (by Fellini's own confession), Giulietta Masina, has always been handled this way – principally in *La Strada* but also in *Le Notti di Cabiria*, where it is hard to match her impish antics with those of the prostitute she is supposedly playing. And, of course, in *Giulietta degli Spiriti*, Giulietta loses her husband largely because she cannot play her sexual role.

It is as if Fellini, in all his films, equates innocence of the body with purity of soul. He gives to all his children, his simpletons and clowns a sensitivity that seems lacking in his adult world. In the 'Toby Dammit' episode that he contributed to *Spirits of the Dead*, Fellini created for the first time an evil child, an eerie perverse creature that lured the central character to his death. In *Satyricon* however, with the exception of the children in the patrician's scene (and even here somewhat oddly, as I'll mention in a minute), there are no children in this film at all. As a result of this, given Fellini's private store of metaphor, there is little sense of hope. There is also little sense of any alternatives, little sense of a life that is not whole-heartedly opportunistic and grotesque. 'Friendship lasts as long as it is useful,' says Ascyltus in his opening soliloquy; 'at least that's what I think'.[14] And there is little in the film to give us the sense of characters behaving in any other way, especially as regards their sexual lives. With the exception of the patrician and his family, they are studs and whores all.

What does Fellini intend by this? The acceptance of so many of the homosexual elements obviously derives from Petronius himself; but one can never explain too much in films as personal as Fellini's by reference to his sources. Why did he pick this and not that? This remains the critical question. Similarly, he surely doesn't intend the film to be a realistic treatment of the mores of an ancient society, painstaking though much of his research into the authenticity of surface details in the film actually has been. Nor is it simply an allegory of our own times, as *La Dolce Vita* was erroneously assumed to be. The film is a mixture of all these things, and certainly not so obviously a personal statement by Fellini as his other films have been. Yet the perfunctory nature of the narrative and the paper-thinness of the characters, alongside the urgency with which some of the scenes are actually handled, would seem to be our clue for decoding the film, for locating Fellini's own centre of interest. Again and again he returns to scenes of banquets or arenas, and again and again these scenes become the settings for some kind of sexual humiliation.

Only Fellini could have turned the abundant Anita Ekberg into an airy goddess in *La Dolce Vita*, outstripping in her soutane all her pursuers up to the very top of St Peter's in Rome, at home with all the other angels there.[15] And only Fellini could have seen in Claudia Cardinale, as he presents her in $8\frac{1}{2}$, a kind of nurse and mother figure. In *Satyricon*, as in *Giulietta* and the 'Toby Dammit' episode before it, this ethereal element of love is almost totally absent, or if partly present, it has assumed a sinister air.

There is a slightly sinister Gioconda smile that Fellini's characters have assumed over the years. It was there in Gelsomina in *La Strada*, apparently harmless then, part of her slightly simpleton nature. Indeed, Fellini's simpletons have often assumed that smile, as have his homosexuals; but it wasn't until *Giulietta* that, both in the figure of the maid and more especially in the vision of Giulietta's young school friend who killed herself for love, this enigmatic smile began to seem menacing. And of course it is the same smile in the 'Toby Dammit' episode that lures the exhausted Toby to his alcoholic end.

In the *Satyricon*, this Gioconda smile is most evident on the face of the pathic Giton, but curiously, bafflingly, it is also painted on to the faces of the patrician's children as they prepare to take their leave. It also appears on the lean and sensual sphinx-like face of Tryphaena, both when Encolpius first spies her at Trimalchio's banquet, and most forcefully and most sinisterly when she sees her husband's head cut off and flung into the sea – a very strange moment in the film indeed and a most inexplicable and unexplained response. Yet it is a striking moment in the film, an image that stays with us, as does the preceding sequence when the crew on Lichas's ship hoist a dead whale (or something like it) up out of the sea – all in striking silhouette as if in early morning, after the male marriage between Encolpius and the brutal Lichas. Like that big blob of fish that is thrown up on the beach towards the end of *La Dolce Vita*, the whale, as inexplicable in terms of plot as Tryphaena's smile, gives us a strong sense of something revolting at the bottom of all this debauchery. It is as if Fellini feels, deep inside himself, that something disastrous will follow the surrender to physical love. So too, after Encolpius's and Giton's night of love together – another remarkably tender moment in the film – the entire building crumbles and stones its inhabitants to death.

In this surrealist world where, through the images, the tensions of sex seem related to pain and disorder, it seems right that the font of wisdom should lie in the hermaphrodite – a strange albino creature, with a small boy's penis and a young woman's breasts. Yet when the two protagonists steal their treasure away from the old man that guards him, the hermaphrodite cannot survive the full sunlight of the world outside. In yet another compelling sequence in the film, the screen itself is bleached to white and the hermaphrodite withers and dies. So compact a resolution to the sexual problem cannot exist in the outside world, this episode might seem to imply. We seem cursed and doomed to suffer the humiliations of desire, whether it be like the young wife whose hands have to be tied down so that her insatiable nymphomaniac rages will not harm the men who attempt to satisfy her; or whether it be like the regally demanding Ariadne, whose sexual demands render Encolpius impotent for a while; or whether it be like the negress witch, Oenothea, in yet another most extraordinary sequence in this film, whose curse has been that she must supply the entire community with light and warmth from the fire between her legs – a most meaningful digression in this film!

The most human (and hence most moral) moment occurs to one side of the central story – the gentle freeing of his slaves and the parting from his children of a noble patrician who then slits his wrists as he is having a farewell supper with his wife, a moment that I understand is based on the end of Petronius's own life. This scene stands out in the film for its quietness and for its single appeal to our old-fashioned natural human sympathies. In *Satyricon*, it is as if the little surrealist moments that troubled and deepened the surface narrative of Fellini's earlier films have assumed the centre of the stage while the more human elements have been pushed to one side.

While *Satyricon* is the film by Fellini that troubles me most, personally, I have been struck by the complete insensitivity with which the film has been received. If in his work since 8½ Fellini seems to be stumbling, even his stumbles seem full of interest and possess an undeniable authority. Besides, who knows where they may lead?

However, to tie together the various perceptions that seem to characterize Fellini's world, we have to backtrack and take a considered look at 8½ – the film that, in my view, most succeeds in resolving the dilemmas and balancing the paradoxes of Fellini's most personal, most fantastic universe. 8½ is the summation of Fellini's work to that date, and, for me personally, is one of the greatest films of all time.

*

I don't like the idea of 'understanding' a film. I don't believe that rational understanding is an essential element in the reception of any work of art. Either a film has something to say to you or it hasn't. If you are moved by it, you don't need to have it explained to you. If not, no explanation can make you moved by it.[16]

If 8½ (1962) is incomparably the finest film that Fellini has ever created, it is largely because, along with Fellini's characteristic sensitivity to sounds and images, the film contains within it a subtle dialectic. Beneath the astonishing technical virtuosity of the film and the sophisticated contributions of Gianni di Venanzo and Piero Gherardi (to mention only the most considerable), there is an inner argument at its centre that has a surprising toughness about it. The film shows itself as being very critical of the attitudes adopted by Guido Anselmi, who, we have a right to imagine, bears a strong resemblance to Fellini himself; except that – as Fellini has been quick to point out[17] – Guido was unable to make his film, while Fellini achieved 8½.

All the old ingredients are there in this film: the acutely accurate observation of surface behaviour which characterized *I Vitelloni* plus the response to both the semi-mystical and the bizarre that was so evident in *La Strada*. We still have the same sense of life as a quest, as endless movement with uncertain direction, as we still have the twin polarities in this film, principally of Claudia and La Saraghina, here seeming to imply a split between the subtler imaginations of the spirit and the coarser attractions of the flesh. But in this film things aren't quite that simple. Both figures in their different ways are presented as somewhat motherly and it is only the church that keeps insisting that La Saraghina is evil. Innocence and evil are no longer separate categories locked away on opposite sides in the wings of the film. But along with these familiar themes and effects, the film puts forward a structure of argument and self-criticism that recasts all these elements in a decidedly clearer light.

This structure can conveniently be examined by looking closely at the final reels. Guido is reaching the point of no return during the auditions while he watches with extreme discomfort the various imperfect approximations to the creatures who have meant so much to him in his private life. Daumier, his intellectual friend, scriptwriter, and adviser, is being particularly tiresome and unhelpful; so, in his imagination, Guido simply has him hanged. Luisa is growing increasingly impatient at the way that she, as his wife, is being made use of in this projected film and she stalks out of the theatre-studio. Then Claudia arrives.

We have seen her as part of Guido's fantasies several times before in the film – sometimes as nurse or mother, bringing him his elixir at the spa or turning down his bed, sometimes as the incarnation of his ideal mistress figure, freed from the physical vulgarities of his actual mistress, Carla. As his ideal mistress, Claudia has her black hair loose about her shoulders while she lies in bed stroking herself, smiling lovingly and talking about her desire to look after him and to create order – really less like a mistress than an ideal wife. But this is the first time in the film, twenty minutes before the end, that she actually appears on the level of present time as the possible star of this impossible film. They go off for a drive together, she at the wheel although she explains that she doesn't know the way.

Guido muses about his incapacities as a man and artist, about his inability to stick to any one thing, to select anything, to reject, to choose. And even here the structure is nicely balanced if we look closely. 'Could you choose one thing and be faithful to it?' he asks in some despair as the light in the darkened car narrows around him revealing only his eyes. While she simply smiles, as if reassuringly, and with a Fellini-like evasiveness replies: 'I don't know the road.'

They turn off into what looks like a deserted village square, the most de Chirico-like image in this film yet actually one of the few natural sets, close by some springs. (We never see the water although we hear it on the soundtrack.) There, in sudden silence, we now see the imagined Claudia as nurse-and-mother in an upstairs window, luminous in her white frock, at first holding a lamp in her hand and then descending the stairs to lay a table in this deserted village square. Then natural sound again as Claudia asks: 'What happens next?' Fellini/Anselmi is talking about the role of the woman-goddess in his film who must be both child and woman (as Sylvia was seen to be by Marcello in *La Dolce Vita*). They get out of the car, she expressing displeasure at the cold bareness of the place, he replying that he likes it enormously. Then he tries to explain that there will in fact be no role for her in the film because 'no woman can save a man' and because 'I don't want to film another lie'. Meanwhile she keeps intercutting her own interpretation of his difficulty. Three times she says 'because you don't know how to love . . . because you don't know how to love . . . because you don't know how to love.' But at his further announcement that there will also be no film, two cars tear into the square announcing a new idea to launch the film, and the swirling chaos of the press conference begins.

Partly here, but even more in the following episode, Fellini depicts the helpless quandary to which all his contradictory impulses seem to have led him. Everyone makes demands upon him and asks for explanations which he cannot give, while a harsh American face looms up into the screen taking obvious delight in the apparent fact that 'He has nothing to say.' Fleeting images of both Claudia and Luisa in her bridal gown appear, distracting him momentarily from the troubles around him; but when someone slips a revolver in his pocket, he climbs under the table and in a fashion that recalls the young Guido running away from the prospect of a bath, he crawls along the ground and shoots himself. 'What an incurable romantic!' he exclaims before the end. Then a glimpse of his mother standing by the sea; then the shot; and then silence except for the wind.

Here the epilogue to the film begins, the recapitulation of its argument, which is in essence a recapitulation of the complete works of Fellini. The huge rocket-launching apparatus is being dismantled, that useless structure which is the culmination of all the structures that we have seen throughout his films. It is apparently of no use. Daumier is talking incessantly about the wisdom of abandoning the picture: '. . . the world abounds in superfluity . . . it's better to destroy than to create what's inessential . . .' Throughout the film, it is as if Daumier stands for Fellini's more rational self, the self that has taken cognizance of all the critical attacks that have been made on his self-indulgent and irrational universe but which, like Steiner, Fellini feels to be destructive. At the same time, he recognizes that this rational analytical voice is not the only one in his life. At the very moment that Daumier is discoursing on the futility of unnecessary creation, the ring-master appears – that androgynous clown-like figure who has played such an important part in all of Fellini's work and seems to stand for something like creation for its own sake, for pure activity without thought or purpose. '*Aspetti,*' he smiles; 'wait a minute! We're ready to begin . . . All my best wishes . . .' It is as if Fellini cannot free himself from the conviction that in spite of all the reasonable criticisms that can justifiably be brought against him as against life itself, there is something deep within him that remains more affirmative and that exists beyond thought, that *must* go on creating simply for the sake of creation, as clowns or aerialists must continue to perform their intricate though meaningless routines.

Then another vision: first Claudia, then La Saraghina, then his parents appear before him – all dressed in white and all floating along noiselessly by the side of the sea accompanied only by the wind. And then most importantly, Luisa appears, her eyes slightly lowered as if in embarrassment or shame. If the critical voice of Daumier represents part of the toughness of the structure of this film, then the resentful, mistrustful, yet possibly forgiving presence of Luisa represents the other part that tugs against Fellini's natural tendency to make things a little too easy for himself. Guido is here experiencing a vision of love for all the creatures he has ever known and is trying to communicate the beauty and simplicity of this feeling to Luisa, even while recognizing his own unworthiness: 'Luisa, I do not know, I seek, I have not found . . . Only with this in mind can I look at you without shame . . . Accept me as I am.' And Luisa, while seeming to recognize the possible self-deception and self-dramatization of these remarks, nevertheless out of female kindness strives to accept him all the same: 'I don't know if that's true, but I can try.' So once again in Fellini, though in a far subtler form, we have salvation by grace. Man, although unworthy, can still be saved.

From this confession and acceptance, this exchange of imperfect terrestrial love, the characteristic Fellini miracle follows, the miracle of self-renewal that enables life to go on. Like the three circus musicians that appear at the comparable moment in *La Strada*, here a similar little troop come into view. With the characteristic horizontal stripes again very much in evidence, they march into the circus ring to receive instructions from Guido, the megaphone of authority having been thrust into his hands by the always smiling, always helpful magician/ring-master, this embodiment of the impulse towards life without demanding why. Then, from the top of this vast structure, itself miraculously reassembled, down the equally vast staircase – like the White Sheik from the sky – all the people we have seen in this film parade into the ring and join hands and dance in a circle about its rim.

Special attention is given to his mother and father and to the Cardinal and even to Carla, who gives us an overt clue (if we need one) for the interpretation of this scene: 'You're trying to say you can't do without us'; but he rushes her away with the rest of them into the magic circle of the dance around the ring as he prepares to receive his wife. Luisa, still a disturbing element in this final sequence, still with her eyes lowered as if not really wanting to be imprisoned in her husband's imaginative vision in this way, nevertheless allows herself to be led by his hand and with him to join the others as they dance around the ring. So we have this final image of the circus ring with the little band still playing at its centre, the circus that has meant so much to Fellini all his life and has played such a large part in his films. And so too we have the mystic circle of eternity, ancient symbol of the Christian church incorporated by Dante. And so too we have the final consummate image of movement without direction, dancing round and round for ever in an infinity of shared acceptance.

Night falls, the dancers disappear, and the little band is left. Then even they disappear, leaving young Guido with his flute and his white cloak alone at the end to take the final bow and to lead us off into darkness and to the end of the film. But even the final title tells us a little bit more: 'Fellini 8½. *Created* and directed by Federico Fellini.' The old ham must have realized that it is an astonishing movie!

GODARD LE FOU:

a glimpse of the struggle between love and politics in the work of Jean-Luc Godard

> What I want is to capture the definitive by chance.
>
> *Jean-Luc Godard*, 1970[1]

Within the limited space of an extended essay, how can one approach the compellingly tender, frequently repulsive, deliberately self-contradictory films of Jean-Luc Godard? It seems more than just an accident that, of the three studies of his work in English, two are anthologies. It is as if Godard's work appears too complex to be successfully organized by only one mind. Justifying his own anthology, Ian Cameron has explained that

> Godard invites such a wide range of interpretations that a single, personal view is unlikely to do him anything like complete justice. Indeed, one sometimes feels that almost anything one can say about Godard will be true.[2]

This gives us a lot of leeway; but I think that some of the things one might say will seem truer than others! Besides, establishing truth is not properly speaking the function of criticism. Its task is simultaneously more humble and more tentative. What it can best do is to suggest an approach or two, to put forward a hypothesis, to suggest a vantage point from which the work of a given artist might profitably be viewed.

With Godard, as his films flood upon us, it seems tempting to shift this vantage point from film to film. Their stylistic diversity might encourage this readjustment of perspective; but what I should like to do in my own account of his films is to try to discover within their diversity the recurrent preoccupations which run throughout them all, which make it possible for us to talk, in fact, about the *work* of Jean-Luc Godard. The task won't be easy, especially if we try to incorporate into this synthesis the scraps of films that have followed *Weekend* (1968); but I feel it worth attempting nevertheless. I am not concerned here with 'complete justice' any more than I have been in the other discussions in this book. Criticism is a collective activity and the purpose of these essays is simply, as Professor Gombrich has admirably put it, 'to keep the discussion of art in flux and to advance the subject'.[3] Critical 'justice', if it exists at all, can only be *post facto*. With someone so restlessly inventive and changeable as Godard, one can simply dive into the midst of the flux and see what one can find. For, as Cameron rightly implies, there is a great deal going on.

*

À Bout de souffle (1959) was an extraordinary beginning, old-fashioned as that film might appear to us now. With the wisdom of hindsight, we might well look at the film in some detail to see how much we can find that seems to prophesy greater complexities to come.

When it first appeared, *À Bout de souffle* seemed to many spectators as confusing as it was lively and funny; and it ended in the triumph of despair. By this I don't mean to be paradoxical so much as to evoke the paradoxical feeling that we derive from this film, centred as it is around the paradoxical character played by Jean-Paul Belmondo. For Michel Poiccard (Belmondo), alias Laszlo Kovacs, is a psychopathic killer. He feels no responsibility for his own actions and retains no apparent emotional relationship to his own past. Yet in the world that Godard created for him, he seemed at the time to be a new kind of hero – an embodiment of courage and fidelity to his own kind of life. 'Squealers squeal, burglars burgle, killers kill, lovers love,' he philosophically explains to his American girl-friend, Patricia Franchini (Jean Seberg) – a deterministic view of life which is at the centre of Godard's world and which provides a kind of moral reversal of the existentialist's universe. The Sartrian (or Aristotelian) precept that what we do determines what we are seems in *À Bout de souffle* to be reversed: what we are determines what we do. Yet not quite. Again paradoxically, Godard's characters always claim that they are free even though bound by necessity. '*Après tout, je suis con. Après tout, si, il le faut. Il faut.*' These words of Michel open the film: 'After all, I'm no good. If you've got to do it, you've got to do it.'

In this kind of assertive context, Michel's feeling of freedom would seem to come from the fullness of his acceptance of his own necessity. Patricia, on the other hand, is trying to have it both ways. She seems the archetypal American in Paris. She is taking courses at the Sorbonne, working for the *Herald Tribune*, flirting with the cultural world about her, while being cautiously promiscuous and working on her novel. She is felt to be the lesser person *not* because she turns Michel in (Michel would never judge her this way) but because she lacks real commitment to anything that she does, to any serious image of herself as a human being. At heart she is a square (as we used to say in those days) – a timid little phoney, a typical American *bourgeoise*, a little middle-class bitch.

The sense of Michel as a new kind of hero (as we saw it at that time) seemed to come from the courage with which he committed himself to the anarchy that engulfed him, to the meaninglessness of contemporary life. In terms of his own moral universe his fatal flaw is the one quality that might win approval from our own, more conventional, humanistic one – his declared 'love' for the girl: '*Elle est drôle. Je l'aime bien,*' as he laconically says. He chooses to die rather than to run away without her. By the end of the film, he says he is tired and no longer wants to run – at least, not without her. The 'triumph' of his chosen death comes from the fact that he does deliberately choose it. So we have his prolonged dance of death down the little street to the boulevard, having been shot with comic seriousness of aim by the police inspector Vital.

As Michel lies dying on the street, we witness once again his three characteristic grimaces that we have seen him make several times elsewhere in the film. Then after his final comment to Patricia – '*C'est vraiment dégueulasse*' – You really are a little bitch' – he closes his eyes with his own hand and dies.

The final image is one of perplexity: Jean Seberg's face in close-up with her thumb rubbing her lips uncertainly as we have also seen Michel do several times in the film (supposedly as a kind of homage to 'Bogey') – rubbing her lips and asking: '*Qu'est-ce que c'est, dégueulasse?*' What does it all mean?

Michel gains dignity from the world that surrounds him, a world that is simultaneously ludicrous and without sense. Everywhere there is restlessness and the sense of dispersal, a kind of polyglot fragmentation of many cultures and many values, none of them tied together except by the speed at which we race from one to the next. '*Ciao, amigo!*' says Michel (alias Laszlo) as he leaves his friend (another squealer) with the Polish name, Tolmatchoff, in his travel agency, using first a scrap of Italian then of Spanish for this international situation. A central sequence in the film takes place at Orly airport, with its own international atmosphere and the restless sense of planes coming in and taking off. The American Patricia with her Italian surname (who at one point in the film wishes she were called Ingrid) and the French (alias Hungarian) Michel/Laszlo confirm this sense of fragmented cultures and double identities. At the opening of the film, Michel races from Marseilles to Paris to collect his money and try to persuade Patricia to come away with him to Rome.

In fact, Patricia's foreignness and her incomprehension of Michel's slang serve Godard well in this film. They lend a naturalistic persuasiveness to the questions she asks him (and us) in this film. ' "*Gazer*" ... *Qu'est-ce que c'est?* ... *Qu'est que c'est l'horoscope?*' For Godard is less concerned with psychological verisimilitude (as an American, she'd know the meaning of horoscope) than he is with the questioning texture of the film. So too, Michel's Italian chorus-girl friend has '*pourquoi*' written across her wall. Why?

Whatever the unevenness, then, of *À Bout de souffle* (and Godard himself seems to have completely rejected it),[4] its distinction lay in its ability to embody in the texture of the film itself the uncertainties and fragmentariness that form the basic ingredients of its view of life and the view of life of many Godard films to follow. *À Bout de souffle* abounds in *non-*

sequiturs which become part of this meaninglessness. It also abounds in jump-cuts and restless tracking shots that deprive us of any sense of a logical transition from scene to scene as they deprive us as well of the sense of ever being still. Also in the movie as part of its gangster-film atmosphere, there is the feeling of persecution, a sense of the net closing in. The mechanics of the city seem to work against the protagonists.

Death in the streets by a traffic accident can be sudden and meaningless; pay phones don't function, or more frequently, the person telephoned never seems to be there. Even in the comparative safety of Patricia's bed, there is the recurrent sound outside of police cars at their work. The various narrative scenes in the film are bridged by shots of the tourists' Paris: Notre Dame, the Arc de Triomphe, the Eiffel Tower are all dwelt on for a moment and then we move away. They are as irrelevant to the main action of the film (we feel by implication) as they are to the values of contemporary life. And the police, although deadly, are simply ridiculous – like imitations of the fabulous Keystone Cops. Everywhere there is fragmentariness, dispersal, meaninglessness. What, in fact, holds together Godard's troubled world?

One of the most crucial elements that deepen Godard's fractured universe is his technique of allusion. The many allusions lend to all his films the irony of wit, yet sometimes with an indecipherable ambiguity. *À Bout de souffle* is obviously a *film policier* in its basic intentions; yet to what degree is it seriously drawing upon the conventions of the American detective thriller and to what extent is it a parody of the form? Where is Godard precisely in relation to his material? At the time it first appeared, it seemed impossible to know. We can now be pretty sure that Godard wasn't too clear about this matter either at the time, and we'll have to return to this question when we try to sort out the even more difficult and more serious issues concerning where Godard stands precisely in relation to the material of *La Chinoise* or *Weekend*.

Nevertheless, this technique of allusion as it appeared in the early films was a source of great richness. Not only was the mind kept alert to receive the impact of as many specific references as we could handle (a state of affairs both tiring and annoying for the less French-informed amongst us), but the allusions brought with them their own kind of values, often more traditional values that set up a dialogue with the more disruptive values that were so much a part of the texture of these films.[5] The ironic potential within such a technique can be baffling in the extreme. 'Sweet Thames, run softly till I end my song': this line from Spenser which T. S. Eliot incorporates in *The Waste Land* not only gains irony from the context in which it is found and from the implicit contrast between Spenser's Thames and Eliot's; but, paradoxically, the sensuousness of appeal of Spenser's line becomes part of the sensuousness of appeal of Eliot's poem, further troubling our response by the feeling that we should, in Eliot's context, no longer find it beautiful. Along with the Homeric references that run through *Le Mépris*, the most direct parallel to such an effect in Godard's work is found in *Une Femme mariée*, where the constant reshuffling of Beethoven quartets lends to that film a confusing richness which I'll attempt to talk about later. But even in *À Bout de souffle*, the unseizable fluctuation between imitation and parody of the American gangster mode becomes part of the texture of uncertainty that is created by that film. What do we really feel as we experience certain scenes?

*

It is important to insist upon the contribution that this texture of uncertainty in a Godard film makes towards the total impact it has upon us – towards its 'meaning', in fact – helping to underline as it does all the things we cannot know. For in a Godard film, even the most private allusions that are probably missed by us are cumulatively part of the feeling we get from him of a man terribly isolated and uncertain about his ability to make contact with more than a handful of people – evidently the way he lives and very much the way his films have progressed (or one might want to say declined). Even more than with Bergman or Fellini, who, at their strongest, have succeeded in finding magnificent forms to externalize their most private feelings, we get the recurring sense from Godard of a man talking very privately to us, indeed at times even whispering (as in *Deux ou Trois Choses que je sais d'elle*), wanting to say something to us but almost convinced at the outset that he will either not be heard or finally not understood.

Think of Paul's desperate attempts to propose to Madeleine in *Masculin-Féminin* (1966). He is constantly distracted by other scenes in the cafe. Furthermore, he is made even more uncertain and despondent by Madeleine's repeated avowals that she has no time, that she has her own life to lead. *Masculin-Féminin* is in this way one of the most personal films that Godard has ever made and is the last where this desperately personal quality has assumed so poignantly human a form. Paul is finally better able to express his love for Madeleine in a recording booth, all alone:

I want to live with you, tanned in a bikini. We'll play the slot machines. Ah, yes, look, the airport ... Hello, control tower here! Boeing 737 calling Caravelle! Paul calling Madeleine![6]

We see the same character (Jean-Pierre Léaud) in somewhat the same situation in *Weekend*, singing an intense song of love to someone or other while in a telephone booth!

These moments in Godard's films are simultaneously hopelessly tender and incongruously bizarre. But their recurrence throughout so many of his films might seem to tell us something about Godard's attitude to his own film-making. It is as if through a film like *Vivre sa vie* or later *Pierrot le fou* that Godard can best express his love for his wife-for-a-time, Anna Karina. In fact the whole structure of *Vivre sa vie* and parts too of *Alphaville*, or at least the feeling within them of something very private and personal, can perhaps best be approached with that scene in mind of Paul in his recording booth – cut off from any real contact with the person he most wants to reach, recording his most private passion through a mechanical device generally employed for the public at large – indeed, the one that Madeleine herself most covets in her ambition to become a pop singer.

We should remember too when recalling this scene from *Masculin-Féminin* that it is immediately followed by a scene of a man stabbing himself in the streets – gratuitously, inexplicably, absurdly in terms of the plot of the film. Yet most significantly in terms of the complete Godard. For in Godard, expressions of tenderness are always either accompanied or followed by scenes of violence, death, and despair. But there is no sense of causality in terms of the story of the film. The scenes simply follow one another or else, as in the bedroom sequence of *À Bout de souffle*, where Michel's attempts at tenderness are disrupted by the sounds of police sirens outside, they are intermixed. The causality, such as it is, seems the result of something very personal in the thinking of Jean-Luc Godard, the result of an increasing pessimism concerning the ability of personal relationships to survive in the modern world.

In fact, if we were systematically to enumerate in Godard's films the recurring motifs, this breakdown in causality would be prominent amongst them. I have already referred to the questioning texture of *À Bout de souffle*. The many *pourquois* are as often as not inadequately replied to or are answered simply by a *parce que* followed by a shrug. We can no longer know (Godard's films seem to imply) *why* things are happening to us or in any conceptual way hope to understand what they mean. We simply observe that they are there. So in *Alphaville*, 'why' becomes one of the forbidden questions; and in *Pierrot le fou*, while we are given ample time to see *that* Ferdinand is writing in his journal, attempting to order his experience conceptually, we scarcely have time enough to see *what* he is writing.

One of the great attractions of the cinema for many people today is that it allows us to present, often with playful persuasiveness, events and situations that our rational selves cannot fully understand. It is to this extent a superficial art in terms of thought and hence perhaps for this very reason *the* contemporary art in a world where cogent and purposive thought has become so difficult. The film-maker doesn't have to be able to analyse behaviour (as the novelist traditionally had to) in order to present to us its appearance and its ramifications, in order to make the physicality of an event seem plausible or fascinating for us on the screen. Though nothing *logically* follows from anything else, a film like *À Bout de souffle* is held together by the unity of its texture of uncertainty, by its troubling and frequently amusing technique of allusion, by its own rush forward, but most of all – we can now see this clearer in retrospect – by its hint of an obsession, an obsession to be taken up in more insistent ways in future Godard films.

'*Elle est drôle. Je l'aime bien.*' From these few words, delivered without passion, come Michel's destruction and yet his sense of purpose. The receipt of his money and his flight away to Rome are all contingent upon Patricia's acceptance of him; and the basic dialogue of the picture takes the form of his trying to persuade her to accept his view of life, to give up her social ambitions – her writing, her courses – and to come away with him. Although not uppermost in *À Bout de souffle*, this ingredient of male persuasion is basic to so much of Godard's work, certainly to all the films that are able to *move* us in any direct and emotional way. Thus it seems basic, or *seemed* basic, to something deep in Godard.

It is important to point out that its presence in *Charlotte et son Jules* (1958), a film prophetically narrated by Godard himself, precedes his meeting with Anna Karina, a relationship that on the surface might seem to have determined so much of this element in his films. This element of male persuasion, if fundamental to *Le Mépris*, to *Pierrot le fou* and to *Masculin-Féminin*, the most romantic films that Godard has ever made, is there as well in different forms in *Le Petit Soldat*, *Vivre sa vie*, *Bande à part*, *Une Femme mariée*, and *Alphaville*. Basically, this element of persuasion would seem to be related to a belief in salvation through love – love always as defined, of course, by Godard's particular males.

This belief in love provides the shallow optimism of the endings of both *Bande à part* (playfully) and *Alphaville* (portentously, with all its Orphic references so out-of-key with Eddie Constantine's immobile face). But more frequently, more compellingly, this belief in love which is the prime motivation of so many of Godard's characters seems to be enmeshed within a context of violence from which it cannot escape. It is as if Godard presents his characters as inescapably addicted to it but recognizes that it will destroy them by the end. It is in essence a belief in *l'amour fou*, a love that is instantaneous and inexplicable and, one must deduce, primarily aesthetic, not based upon a recognition of the character or personality of the loved one at al. No wonder it is doomed to fail! But to what extent the failure of love has largely personal or more broadly social-cum-political explanations is what I really want to examine in the rest of this chapter, as I'd like to consider what it is that Godard has left when he relinquishes this hopeless but meaningful obsession of his men for his women.

In an astute analysis of *Le Petit Soldat*, Richard Winkler has illuminated the dilemma experienced by Godard's men when they feel themselves in love. The love asserted by Michel in *À Bout de souffle*, by Bruno in *Le Petit Soldat*, by Ferdinand in *Pierrot le fou*, and by Paul in *Masculin Féminin* is invariably of a very abstract kind. It scarcely takes account of the diversity and human complexity of the loved one at all. It fails to allow her to live her own life. As Winkler puts it apropos of *Le Petit Soldat*: 'She loves Bruno: he loves her image'.[7] He loses a bet and falls in love with her uncontrollably when he sees her shake her hair about. Even then, he has to ask her to do it, as if to put her through some sort of test.

The moment of love for Godard, as I have said, is primarily aesthetic and is irreversible. It would also seem to be the kind of love that would make a developing human relationship impossible. The woman loved, so often Anna Karina, would seem to be trapped in her own icon, deprived of that very spontaneity that had made her lovable in the first place. She certainly would never be allowed to have children and grow old!

In Godard's films there is little sense of family. Even the child in *Une Femme mariée* seems to have little to do with the inward decisions that Charlotte is preoccupied with throughout her day; and Ferdinand in *Pierrot* thrusts the complexities of Élie Faure upon his little daughter, while he sends his maid to see *Johnny Guitar* and reads *Les Pieds nickélés* to Marianne! Similarly, with the gentle exception of *Masculin-Féminin*, there are no scenes in Godard's films where people sit down and have a meal together, where there is any sense of a group kind of gaiety, let alone any sense of family life. As in that seminal and virtually unknown first film by Jacques Rivette, *Paris nous appartient* (1958–60), for the most part Godard's characters inhabit the chill world of Paris hotels and cafés, the Paris not of La Belle Époque but of *Alphaville*. In this chill world where no one seems *organically* related to anyone else, each character carries about with him his own kind of identity problem, trying to define himself in something like existential terms, trying, like Bruno in *Le Petit Soldat*, to be faithful to his own image of himself and to find a purposive role in this increasingly dehumanized world.

This heroic stance assumed by so many of Godard's characters alternates with a longing for escape from it, as Michel in *À Bout de souffle* longed to get away to Rome and Ferdinand in *Pierrot le fou* away to the Mediterranean. This longing for escape is also part of Godard's characters' longing for love. Love provides them with a temporary relief from their lonely sense of isolation and offers release from the heroic responsibilities of defining one's own character when all alone in the world. As Nicholas Garnham has put it: '. . . love retains a particular value for Godard, because it is an escape from thought, almost a negation of thought'.[8] Furthermore, it seems to take place in suspended time, in a kind of stasis. Whether within the extended bedroom scene in *À Bout de souffle*, the even more extended apartment scene in *Le Mépris*, or the Mediterranean idyll in *Pierrot le fou*, the scenes of love in a Godard film always take place in little recesses apart from the main flow of the film. And in both *Vivre sa vie* and *Une Femme mariée*, the supposedly most tender moments in the film are so abstract and stylized that they deprive us as viewers of any *feeling* of love at all.

Le Petit Soldat (1960) took its hero out of the anarchic world of the American gangster movie and placed him within the political context of France at that time, the context of the Algerian struggles between left and right. Yet as Winkler and many others have pointed out, Bruno acts for personal *not* political reasons. His fidelity is to his own image of himself and to his own idealized love for Veronica. Basically, both images fail him and he is left, somewhat unconvincingly, with the resolution to learn not to be bitter.

In this most Bressonian of all Godard's films, it seemed difficult at the time to be sure to what extent the voice of Bruno represented the voice of Godard. In everything that he did and said, Bruno was so assertive, so dogmatic, so opinionated, that the film gave us the feeling that Godard possessed these unpleasing qualities as well. No doubt he does, among many others! Yet even with hindsight, much as I admire the film, I find it difficult to like. There is a sense, indeed, in many Godard films that they were designed specifically to irritate and annoy, that to *like* them would actually undercut their value.

Like Lemmy Caution in *Alphaville*, Bruno in *Le Petit Soldat* seems so drained of any living qualities that it is impossible to become absorbed in his talk, whether about politics or about love. Yet in its austerity, following the richness and excitement of *À Bout de souffle*, it presaged films to come. Certainly, without the exercise in austerity represented by *Le Petit Soldat*, it would be hard to imagine how the pleasing nonsense of *Une Femme est une femme* (1961) could have led on to the troublingly personal yet constrained masterpiece of *Vivre sa vie* (1962).

*

Nearly everyone who has written about *Vivre sa vie* has been struck by the fact that the film, as Victor Perkins has put it, 'upsets the notion of a correct balance between the word and the image'.[9] In her own masterly analysis, Susan Sontag notices a 'dissociation of word and image which runs through the entire film, permitting quite separate accumulations of intensity for both idea and feeling'.[10] This dissociation is part of a schizoid quality that runs throughout Godard's work. We can see its germs in the Michel/Laszlo, Patricia/Ingrid double names in *À Bout de souffle* and in the similar concern with '*l'homme double*' in the Ferdinand/Pierrot character in *Pierrot le fou*. This splitting in two is an element that seems to be threatening to break Godard's films apart, making them incomprehensible or at any rate unendurable to most of us as we sit trapped in the cinema. But more about this later. Just now I want to look at how its patterning affects our response to *Vivre sa vie*.

Bringing to the film her own creative interest in the problems of form, Miss Sontag tries to persuade us that in his rejection of causality and his preoccupation with form, Godard is offering a *demonstration* of something, not an *explanation*. 'He does not analyze. He proves.' Whatever this may mean exactly, most viewers will be struck by what I'd like to call the rhetorical nature of the film, its stylistically assertive characteristics. This goes hand-in-hand with what I also feel to be its didactic quality (perhaps what Miss Sontag means by 'proof'), the accumulative feeling that Godard has attempted to make valid and inevitable a certain way of life.

The rhetoric begins with the first images of the film, the shots behind the titles. A shot in profile of Nana's face; then a shot from the front (and we see her slowly lower her eyes and then raise them again); then another shot in profile, facing the other way. This film is to be about this woman, of that we can be sure; but we might be struck also by the manner in which she is posed and photographed and made to move, by what we might call the iconizing impulse behind the film. Godard may *think* he is presenting a woman with her own life to live, but rarely in the film does he allow her own natural movement. At the outset we are made aware of the fact that this is no psychological study of a particular human being; she will be one image among many others, the embodiment of a particular set of ideas, of an attitude teasingly asserted by the Montaigne quote that concludes the titles: 'One should lend oneself to others and give oneself to oneself'. Whatever can that mean? What in fact are we in for?

The first scene carries on this teasing, for many viewers, this infuriating mode. We see Nana and Paul, apparently her husband, sitting at a bar. Their backs are towards us as they discuss their separation, with references to their son. The din of the café about them threatens to drown out their words, and the camera moves slowly from right to left and back again, allowing us an occasional glimpse of either Nana's or Paul's face reflected in the mirror; but we are deprived of any direct involvement with these people, with their emotions or personalities. We are not allowed to look them in the eye.

Thus, we are simultaneously distanced yet drawn into the screen – drawn into Godard's personal world. We are distanced because we are kept apart from direct personal involvement with what is happening on the screen. At the same time we almost literally find ourselves leaning forward in our seats in the effort to catch what's being said, in the effort to see their faces in the mirror behind the bar, in the effort to respond more to these people, to get involved in their lives.

Similarly, this opening scene is simultaneously completely natural and highly stylized. It is completely natural, for this might well be the way we would overhear a conversation in a café, the voices almost swallowed up by the general din, the faces turned away from us because what they are saying is none of our concern. Yet in the deliberate way Godard creates this effect and in the calculated movement of his camera, we realize at the same time that Godard is intentionally (some people might claim aggressively) creating an anti-spectacular scene, creating a scene in which every element, although natural, has been consciously placed there and placed with such a deliberation that we tend to be less aware of its relevance to the story than we are of the fact that Godard is in charge. As with Eisenstein in the old days and with Resnais and Antonioni in their different ways now: the more stylized a given effect on the screen, the more we are made aware of the director behind the effect; the less involved we are in the characters and the story, the more involved we become in the world of the director, in his ideas and attitudes.

This invitation towards direct personal involvement in Godard himself at the same time as he seems to be distancing us from his characters is obliquely explicit in this film if we can pick up the clues. As Paul and Nana leave the counter to play at one of Godard's favourite pinball machines – superb emblem throughout his films of his mechanistic universe – Paul tells the story of a little eight-year-old girl who wrote a story about a chicken. Susan Sontag has explained the French pun here, making clear its direct relation to Nana; but even more important is the sudden change of voice as Paul tells his story: 'A chicken is an animal who is made up of an exterior and an interior. If you remove the exterior, you find the interior; and if you remove the interior, you see the soul . . .'

Like the epigraph from Montaigne, these words tease us with the hint of a profundity which (my Anglo-Saxon bias makes me feel) is typically French but which in any case is typically Godard: such little maxims as his films are full of are rarely fully assimilated into his text. Like the *Wild Palms* reference in *À Bout de souffle*, they are used opportunistically without any specific reference to the context from which they come. They are thus assertive and rhetorical in the way they are used – an essential part of the formal patterning of the films but rarely springing organically out of what we might feel to be the day-to-day life of the characters. They spring rather out of Godard's own mind, a characteristic made conclusive at this particular moment in *Vivre sa vie* by Godard's own voice that takes over these words from Paul. He whispers them at us urgently, almost embarrassedly, as the picture slowly fades from us on the screen.

Susan Sontag has suggested that 'the rhythm of *Vivre sa vie* is stopping-starting'. This is true not only of its total structure, its division into a series of tableaux, but also of the way that such a scene as the opening can physically work upon us. While Nana and Paul are sitting at the counter, we as spectators are strained in many ways. We are straining to hear, straining to see, straining to know more and to understand – as I have said. But when they leave the counter and go to the pinball machine, we might feel an enormous relief. Suddenly we are allowed to observe what might now appear as the natural movement of the characters. The sound itself seems freer as we now observe the characters as they talk and so are able to hear them more easily. For a moment, there is a tremendous sense of energies set free. Yet almost immediately Godard the director takes over again, snatching away Paul's voice and introducing his own, making us once more aware of his own presence in the film, an awareness which, like the stopping-and-starting rhythm, pulls us in contradictory ways – pushing us back because preventing us from direct involvement with his characters, yet pulling us forward towards the structure of the film, towards the mind of the director.

This stopping-and-starting rhythm characterizes a good many of Godard's films, most notably, after *Vivre sa vie*, *Une Femme mariée*, which seems in many ways its sequel. Indeed, this movement even characterizes the rhythm *between* the films; for there are films that are predominately static, films largely in close-up like *Alphaville*, and films that predominantly flow, like *Bande à part* and *Pierrot le fou*. But it is this deliberate ebb-and-flow within each individual film, this holding back then letting run-forward, that determines their physical effect upon us.

The most extraordinary sequence in this particular film is Episode VI – the encounter with Yvette, an old acquaintance also recently turned prostitute. Once again Susan Sontag has described how, at the opening of this sequence, the sound precedes the image. We hear the characters talking before we see who they are. 'It is as though Godard hears and then looks at what he hears.' The effect is somewhat similar to the opening sequence, forcing us to concentrate on the words while making us more aware of what is happening on the screen. Guaranteeing this alertness, Godard then proceeds to build up his view of life within the structure of the scene.

Nana and Yvette both question each other, but with no satisfactory answers. As in *À Bout de souffle* before it and *Alphaville* to follow, *pourquoi*, if it is answered at all, is answered fatalistically – *parce que*: 'Because that's the way things are,' as Nana says. Like other Godard characters, Yvette longs to escape to the south, while Nana seems to recognize that such a longing is self-deceptive. The other form of escape that seems open to Godard's characters is escape into the magic world of cinema, the world of making movies. Michel had worked (so he said in *À Bout de souffle*) in Cinecittà in Rome, and Yvette's husband had made it into the movies. Nana herself was hoping for a film part at the opening of *Vivre sa vie*; but in this scene she seems to have become more realistic. Unlike Yvette, she feels herself responsible for what she does, for what has happened to her.

Nana's disquisition on responsibility provides us with a curious moment in the film. Again it is a teasing moment like the many quotations and little stories that we find throughout Godard's films, teasing and rhetorical because the ideas expressed in them have little organic connection to the context in which they appear. What we have *seen* so far of Nana as a character is the complete reverse of what we now *hear*. Throughout the film we see what *happens to* Nana rather than what she *does* – the very reverse of responsibility as most of us would understand it.

This dislocation of characterization can have a double effect upon us. On the one hand, it is a part of the schizoid feeling that all Godard's characters convey, with their double names and the uncertain path they tread between real-life and fantasy, comic-strip roles. On the other hand, the same dislocation invites us, I think, to attribute to such a speech a certain choric force. When characters in a play speak out-of-character, we can assume, I believe, that they speak at least in part for the author himself. In any case, the ideas expressed, as in this moment in *Vivre sa vie*, gain the force of italics from the context in which they occur. More than that, as she delivers this speech in her self-absorbed way, the natural sounds in the café that are generally in Godard such a persuasive part of the naturalistic element of such a scene, these natural sounds for the moment are suppressed, thus adding emphasis to what Nana is saying and yet (like the movements of her hands and her head) giving it a slightly artificial air.

Is it as if Nana, the prostitute, doesn't really believe herself, we might wonder? Is it that Anna Karina, the actress, doesn't quite believe what Godard, at that time her husband, is telling her to say? We can never know.

> I raise my hand, I am responsible. I turn my head to the right, I am responsible ... I am unhappy, I am responsible ... It's like I was saying: to want to get away, that's a joke. After all, everything is beautiful. You've only got to interest yourself in things and find them beautiful ... A face is a face ... Men are men. And life is life.

There is simultaneously an absurdity in such a series of remarks considering their context; a beauty of a kind, representing a kind of ideal situation at odds with the world we actually see; and yet also a kind of passive acceptance of life as it flows over us, encouraging us to *think* we are in control when in fact we are not. *'Après tout, je suis con!'* Michel had said and acted accordingly, running at top speed throughout the film. *'Et la vie, c'est la vie,'* declares Nana and lets life wash over her, detached from external acts as if to preserve what Godard keeps offering us in this film as her soul.

But the scene doesn't stop there. Yvette goes to talk to Raoul, the pimp, and so to set up the next stage in Nana's acceptance of life. For a moment, Nana is left alone. But not really. After her speech, suddenly the natural sounds of the café burst in upon her and we see her, somewhat as in the second shot of the title sequence, lower her eyes as if embarrassed and then look up straight at us. Or at least that is how it feels at the moment. But Godard then cuts to a couple sitting opposite, so that Nana's gaze could be explained as having been directed towards them. Meanwhile, a jukebox has begun to play: Jean Ferrat has begun to sing one of his extraordinarily poignant songs, romantic in feeling and yet anti-romantic in the implications of its words – almost the reverse (one might say without too much sophistry) of so many of Godard's films!

He's singing about his girl-friend, who is no movie star but just a factory worker and yet (the song goes on) 'there is no girl I know that has more love in her eyes when she looks at her guy ... and that's me.' In a way that both parallels Nana's speech and yet provides a contrast to it, the song moves into its own mode of passive acceptance: 'There's no need to be sad, life's not so bad' (as the titles try to extract a rhyme from the French); but then before its cadence, the song is interrupted by the sound of a pinball machine, confirming (in my mind at least) the deterministic, pessimistic, hopelessly beautiful (or beautifully hopeless, to play with words à la Godard!) quality of this scene.

A burst of song like the unexpected blossoming of love can transform one's life. But for a moment only. The harsh realities of life are always there threatening to break in upon one with mechanical insistence, like the insistence here of the pinball machine. Worse than that: if the intrusion of the machine that interrupts the poignant song parallels the intrusion of Raoul into Nana's life (where Nana is to be bounced from man to man like the descending ball in the pinball machine – again the very reverse of 'responsibility'), the sudden intrusion of machine-gun fire from the street suggests a more-than-personal violence in the world outside. At the same time, even as we see Nana running down the street from this scene of political violence that has erupted without warning, it suggests the final yet arbitrary death that is to conclude with a similar abruptness Nana's own life.

All of Godard is in this one scene, it seems to me – just as every great moment in the work of a master seems to imply his complete works (and yet paradoxically requires his complete works to enable us to respond to it fully). As the fade-outs in this film get longer and longer towards the end of the film as if to suggest Nana's approaching death, so the juddering, freeze-frame pan to the right as we hear the machine-gun in this scene is a superb illustration of the freshness and inventiveness with which Godard responds to the simplest elements of film technique, enabling him to use them meaningfully, resuscitating the very grammar of his chosen medium.

The one great flaw in this film, everyone seems to agree, is due to the presence of private innuendoes that characterize the end of the film. 'He is mocking his own tale,' writes Susan Sontag, 'which is unforgivable.' I don't think so. Certainly, on a dramatic level, Nana's love with her voiceless young man is too insubstantial to be satisfactory. But the point is surely, whether we like it or not, that this young man provides the flimsiest of excuses for Godard to address himself openly and publically to the woman he loves. And this seems to me to be the point of the entire film. This *is* his tale, and the essence of his own romantic impulse, and, in a sense, his tragedy. Like Paul calling Madeleine in a record-your-own-voice booth in *Masculin-Féminin* or the same actor singing out his love from a telephone booth in *Weekend*, Godard seems best able to express his love through a public medium.

Yet in *Vivre sa vie*, at the very moment when he is striving to be most intimate in his presentation of himself as the young man reading Poe's *Oval Portrait* to Nana, he becomes most artificial in his handling of the scene. Not only is there the deliberate and obvious artifice of the young man's mouth always hidden by the book he is reading, the more easily to enable Godard to dub his voice over the scene; not only are there the sub-titles necessary to convey the speech of love, in order to keep the young man from having to speak; but, as he reads his story, Godard poses Anna about the room in quite artificial ways.

Like the opening title sequence, this scene gives us more the feeling of a hopelessly idealized love, the love of an image, of an appearance, than of an actual woman who has her own natural movement and way of behaving. Godard imposes *his* movement upon her as he poses her against walls and jump-cuts her from one position in the room to another without any sense of how she might actually move. And the cutting back in time as the two of them embrace and talk, through the titles, about going to the Louvre conveys the same feeling – a feeling of artificiality and unreality at the same time as our minds must recognize we are being offered a most private revelation.

For me personally, this scene creates a most troubling emotion, as if I am observing something too private in so public a medium. But there it is on the screen: the film, that's the film, I want to say! That is how Godard works and the whole film has been a preparation for this supposedly unsatisfactory end. Godard tries to distance this intimacy slightly through his characteristic wit in the reference to all the queues for *Jules et Jim* as we drive past the cinema on the way to Nana's death; but this doesn't quite work. As a gag it's just a gag but not disruptive enough to break the private and most personal tone which has been this whole film's *raison d'être*.

Throughout all of Godard's films, there is a most desperate feeling of anxiety, an anxiety which can be part of the pain we experience when we watch them. It is rather like the anxiety that we experience when in the presence of a highly sensitive yet over-insistent individual who matters to us: we want to be sympathetic, we want to understand, and yet we recognize that whatever kind of acceptance we might offer will be rejected as misconceived. So Godard in his life today has rejected many of the people who have most helped him create his own art – most notably his cameraman, Raoul Coutard, whom now Godard scorns for his willingness to put his talents at the service of a 'falsely bourgeois' political film like *Z*.

In the films themselves, the anxiety is almost physically created by this stopping-and-starting rhythm that Susan Sontag referred to. In Nana's long conversation with the philosopher Brice Parain in *Vivre sa vie*, not only do the glances she casts directly at us create a kind of anxiety, as if to embarrass us for eavesdropping on this personal conversation; but the way Michel Legrand's music flows in and then ebbs out creates what I think we must call a kinaesthetic parallel to Nana's own uncertainty about the meaning of life, the usefulness of words and the value of love. Similarly the episodic structure of so many of the films and the absence of causality between the scenes reinforces this feeling, the feeling of something lost. As Victor Perkins has put it:

> For it is the essence of his romanticism ... that in denying or destroying the expected connections and coherences he hints at a hidden (or lost) harmony. His manner of insisting on the absence of a visible pattern comes close to suggesting the presence of one that is invisible.[11]

This sense of loss and of something unseizable is at the centre of Godard's work, it seems to me. It is both the source of the anxiety his films can convey and the root of what Perkins has nicely called Godard's 'rich and gloomy romanticism'.

*

The films of Jean-Luc Godard seem split between two basic impulses, impulses that are completely self-contradictory: to achieve permanence through the unquestionable authority of his art; and yet to insist that everything is flux, in motion, uncontrolled, that so much in life simply happens *par hasard*. So the characters themselves fluctuate between two opposing tendencies: from *Le Petit Soldat* to *Masculin-Féminin*, his protagonists long for the reality of meaningful action outside themselves and yet long to retreat into a world away from action, a world given up to the celebration of personal love.

In the films themselves, this fluctuation is not at all clear. Peter Wollen has referred to the 'criss-crossing of roles between *À Bout de souffle* and *Pierrot le fou*'.[12] Sometimes, as in *À Bout de souffle*, it is the male character who both longs for action and yet longs for love; sometimes, as in *Une Femme mariée*, it seems to be the male characters who live out their lives in the world of action, while the female character longs for something certain in her love; sometimes, as in *Pierrot le fou*, it is the female character who longs for the greater excitements of the *film policier*, while the male character seems content with his Mediterranean idyll, his notebooks and his woman, trying to live out his love.

But the twin poles are there, throughout Godard's films, often irreconcilably, generally self-destructively. They parallel and partially embody the classic alternatives between action and contemplation. At times, in interviews, Godard himself has seemed well aware of this.[13] Yet there is a confusion about the intermixing and criss-crossing as it exists in the films, a confusion that suggests elements that Godard doesn't understand.

For instance, what is Godard's attitude towards the reflective intelligence? A gentle and beautiful moment in *Vivre sa vie* is provided by the conversation in the café between Nana and an actual philosopher, Brice Parain. The scene is unrealistic, in a way, as Nana is suddenly much more articulate herself and seems more intelligent than she does elsewhere in the film. However, this breach of realism, as I have argued, is in no way out-of-character with the rest of the film. Parain's talk is very French and very real, as he explains the necessity of language for the existence of thought, even the necessity of error in the effort to find the truth.

But does Godard now share the view of Parain that he claims some people had when they saw the film, saying 'they wished that old shit would shut up'? He might appear to, in the way he discusses the scene in that famous *Cahiers du Cinéma* interview a few years ago (1967).[14] Similarly, in the same interview, he seems to have little respect for the humanist position assumed by another actual philosopher, Francis Jeanson, in his anti-Maoist argument with Anne Wiazemsky in *La Chinoise*, although Godard recognizes that his audience can view the scene anyway they like, depending on their own political beliefs.

I want to reserve a discussion of Godard's political position for a later section; but the stylistic point about these scenes, it seems to me, as about Roger Leenhardt's disquisition on intelligence in *Une Femme mariée*, is that these old men all seem so real in the films, expressing with full conviction what they actually believe, indeed what they have lived for. In contrast to this, their interlocutors, whether Anna Karina, Macha Méril, or Anne Wiazemsky, are all obviously actresses, obviously being fed responses by Godard, all rather drained of direct, impassioned, personal involvement. So whatever one's political position, one's cinematic response (I should have thought) would have been more towards the greater reality of the thoughtful old men. But is Godard's? By the things he says about them, we must sense a contradiction between the persuasively realistic way he presents them – or, perhaps more accurately, allows them to present themselves – in the films and what he now feels to be the ultimate value of the things they say.

'Intelligence is to understand before affirming,' explains Roger Leenhardt during his monologue in *Une Femme mariée*; and he goes on to insist on the need to go beyond any simple understanding of an idea, any partisan concept of 'for' or 'against'. Set this beside the slogan so prominent in *La Chinoise* concerning the need to 'confront vague ideas with clear images' and what have we got? I'm not quite sure, but it appears to be a species of intellectual confusion. Yet it is also a kind of artistic richness, presenting us with experiences that need to be puzzled out.

It seems to me, however, that Godard's personal position, whatever we make of it, is much more precarious. The best he can do is to attempt to understand *by* affirming; and if this doesn't seem to lead anywhere, he goes ahead quickly and affirms something else. For Godard, to live is to make films; art is truth; the cinema, truth twenty-four times a second. In *À Bout de souffle*, when the celebrity Parvulesco (Jean-Pierre Melville) is asked whether Rilke was right in believing that modern life more and more separates men and women, his reply is simplistic and yet characteristic of many such replies in Godard: 'Rilke was a great poet. He was therefore undoubtedly correct.' Art is truth; the cinema is life; to live is to make films; to find truth is to make films. Truth is not something that exists out there, something that one understands before making films: one understands it, if ever, *by* making films, by thrusting oneself into an exploration of something that one doesn't understand. One searches for clear images with which to confront one's vague ideas.

There is, then, properly speaking, no longer any place in Godard's world for the reflective intelligence. It is outmoded, no matter how attractive it may seem. As in *La Chinoise*, action seems more urgent, even if badly planned and premature. Véronique (Anne Wiazemsky) sets off to assassinate a distinguished, but reactionary academic, perhaps one very much like the Francis Jeanson she was talking to earlier in the film. But she makes a mistake and kills the wrong man. She has to go back and do it all again. This might seem to relate her revolutionary action to the apishness of the soldiers in *Les Carabiniers*; yet it also might relate her action to Brice Parain's belief that 'Truth lies in everything, even a little in error.'

For Parain in *Vivre sa vie*, it was necessary to talk in order to think, to commit verbal blunders in the search for intellectual truth. Godard seems to have developed this position beyond that implied by Roger Leenhardt's speech, beyond the point of ambiguity or paradox to where it seems to result in its own self-destruction. Increasingly in his later films, Godard seems to imply that it is necessary to act *as if* without thinking, almost instead of thinking – as if thought might lead to indecision and paralysis, as it tended to lead Ferdinand in *Pierrot le fou* and Paul in *Masculin-Féminin*.

In *Pierrot*, Ferdinand kept turning away from the world of action, even from the physical reality of the world of love, to write in his notebooks, as if to use his intelligence in the effort to understand. But this leads him to disaster. Similarly, in *Masculin-Féminin*, Paul cannot really understand the world of action, whether the essentially selfish careerist action of his beloved Madeleine or the essential slogan-mongering action of his working-class friend Robert. In fact Robert explains the problem to Paul in a way that seems prophetic for the Godard films to come:

> I tell you that you'll never find an individual solution. There isn't any. You've got to throw yourself into the struggle, and being in it you end up by learning.

And then, referring to Paul's troubles with Madeleine, he continues:

> You put up with too much. That's impossible.

Yet Paul replies, with a sentiment that has not been heard of since in a Godard film:

> Listen, even so, I have the right to have problems with women.[15]

But these problems as Godard presents them to us have no solution and, one way or the other, lead to Paul's death, as they lead to the death of Michel in *À Bout de souffle* and of Ferdinand in *Pierrot le fou*.

The reflective intelligence, attractive though it may seem, encourages us to search for a private solution, as it encourages us to give in to the idealism of romantic love. In Godard's films invariably – even, ultimately, in *Bande à part* and *Alphaville* – it leads to a feeling of futility followed by death. Therefore the reflective intelligence must be shunned for the world of action (the syllogistic thinking of Godard's latest work implies), for the world of collective activity of whatever kind. For the Black Panthers, this means taking up arms; for the Maoists, it means political assassinations. For Godard, it means making movies – even though movies of an increasingly difficult and isolated kind.

But before Godard reached this position, he made *Une Femme mariée* and *Pierrot le fou*, two films that must be looked at in greater detail before we consider the implications of the austerity of his later work.

*

Une Femme mariée (1964) is simultaneously amongst the most stylistically controlled and yet most complex films that Godard has ever made. After the titles (and even the titles in Godard are more inventive, in the simplest possible way, than titles have ever been before), the film begins with a blank screen. Then the left hand of Charlotte (Macha Méril) – *la femme mariée* – creeps across it as we hear her say '*Je ne sais pas* (I don't know).' The rest of the film is dedicated to an exploration of her uncertainty – uncertainty about whom she loves, about who is the father of her child, about what she is interested in, and about her relationship to the outside world. In this particular film especially, but in Godard increasingly, the world is dominated by underwear advertisements and thoughts of efficient sex.

Je ne sais pas. The note is set for the first of the three love scenes that hold this film together, the opening and closing one with her lover, the middle one with her husband. And of course, in the way they are shot and in the things that are said, they are all very much the same.

So unusual is the execution of these scenes, so original in terms of cinema, that even now, after several viewings and a decent lapse of time, I still cannot describe accurately how these scenes affect me. In one way, they bore and exasperate me in what is really a visceral way, as so much of Godard increasingly bores and exasperates me. Yet it is not the boredom that we experience in the presence of something banal or slack, but more the boredom that comes from an overly insistent person, from someone who when talking to us moves in too close, whose manner is too unvaried, whose persuasions seem too imprisoning to be endured for very long. During these love-making sequences in *Une Femme mariée*, something in my body wants to tear away from the endless pattern of close-ups on the screen. At the same time, my mind is fascinated. The split nature of Godard's work invites a split response on the part of the spectator.

As a pre-title to the film itself, Godard offers us '*Fragments d'un film tourné en 1964*'; and as the physical embodiment of this fragmentary intention, all the love sequences are shot in bits and pieces, the bodies transformed into semi-abstract shapes. Any hint of passion is held firmly at a distance by the great formality of every scene and by the innumerable fades. Even the Beethoven is itself fragmented and so deprived of the flow of its intrinsic structural qualities and of all its ennobling associations. Yet the music succeeds in imparting a troubled passion to these scenes.

Nevertheless, what *really* is the music doing there? How do we respond to its particular appeal, which (especially if we already have a past relationship with the music) pulls us in the opposite direction from the two-dimensional, yet sculptural qualities of the images themselves? If from the evidence of so many of his films we are right in detecting a split in Godard between the mind that imagines and the body that feels, it is almost as if this split is imposed upon us by the films themselves, by the troubling efficacy of their forms. Hence the absorbed fascination of my appreciative mind and the exasperation of my physical fatigue. Godard's films seem to invite a kind of aesthetic schizophrenia, a splintered response which reflects something in Godard's own sensibility, certainly in his art.

Structurally, *Une Femme mariée* is a most controlled and balanced film. Like so many Godard films, perhaps indeed like Godard himself, it is built upon alternations. Within the complete works, I have already mentioned the alternation between films that stand still and films that move. Similarly, within each particular film, whatever its general mode, there is usually an alternation between moments of reflection that are usually stationary, frequently shot in the form of an interview, and moments of action, which assume various forms. Like the 14 July double parade in *À Bout de souffle* or the mad 'erotica' chase in *Une Femme mariée*, these moments of action are often bizarre and comic in the extreme; or else they seem futile and destructive, accumulating a sense of paranoia, as in all that driving about in cars in all of Godard's movies – the one American element that has remained consistently a part of his work right up until its culmination in *Weekend*. In *Une Femme mariée*, there is a further alternation between the scraps of dialogue and series of interviews, and Charlotte's troubled commentary that bridges the scenes.

This commentary too, like everything else in this extra-ordinarily unified film, is fragmented. It consists of lists of scattered words creating the sense of psychological confusion, of the desire for tenderness, the fear of rejection, and the hankering after oblivion. 'Not to be,' Charlotte says in despair as she wakes up one morning; and at other times we hear her thoughts as she runs from taxi to taxi, in flight from the furies both real and imaginary that she thinks are pursuing her:

> In the middle of the corridor, Hope ... The picture of a young girl. Who am I? I've never known exactly. The verb to follow, other reasons, I was once. Not her, a year ago. Only once, wasn't it? It's his fault. Always dream and then reality. A bitter satisfaction. I'll come back tomorrow. Friday or Saturday. He was afraid of me. I know he loves me. It's difficult. I'm on holiday. As the days pass. We met by chance. Happiness, I don't know.[16]

Like so much in Godard's films, these lines do not *mean* anything in any linear, rational way; but they most forcefully communicate their sense of confusion, of fragility and dread, of (in Laingian terms) Charlotte's 'ontological insecurity'.[17] It is this cumulative sense of dread that makes the final shot seem like an annihilation. The same left hand that we saw at the opening of the film *this* time withdraws from the frame leaving a totally white screen while we hear her voice: *'Oui, c'est fini.'* It's all over.

This ending seems more than simply the end of the film, or of her affair, or even of her marriage (as we might deduce from the *Bérénice* reference which forms part of this last scene). The end of the film is so total, leaving us staring at a blank screen, that it seems like the end of something absolute.

I for one always leave the cinema after seeing this film with the mixed feelings of exhilaration and despair. *C'est fini.* The combination that this film offers of abstraction of form and passivity of moral attitude add up to a nihilistic universe far more troubling and far-reaching than the detective spoofs of *À Bout de souffle*. Once the confusing physical impact of the film has ebbed away from us, we might also ask ourselves how Godard can go on making films of such freshness and energy about such inner insecurity and such total despair. What are his positives?

What really keeps him going? There are answers to these questions in all of his films, but they could be conveniently pinpointed by looking closely at another one of his most distinguished films – *Pierrot le fou*.

*

I read something by Borges where he spoke of a man who wanted to create a world. So he created houses, provinces, valleys, rivers, tools, fish, lovers, and then at the end of his life he notices that this 'patient labyrinth is none other than his own portrait'. I had this same feeling in the middle of *Pierrot*.[18]

By being the most organized structurally, the most abstract in general design, by having the paranoiac emotion most securely embodied in the distressed and uncertain Charlotte and to that extent being the most realized dramatically, *Une Femme mariée* might be said to be the most classical of Godard's films. Also, along with the snippets of Beethoven that both enrich and trouble the film, in *Une Femme mariée* all the literary allusions and neon-sign acrostics, its feeling for pop-art culture, seem most integrally a part of the total design of the film. They are both part of its uncertainty and of its keen observation of the human irrelevance of much of the modern world. But they also invoke the values of the things they represent. Like all allusions, they add to the film an aspect of themselves. From *Bérénice* to *Elle* magazine, from Beethoven to 'Erotica', from a Hitchcock poster to a Resnais documentary, from Roger Leenhardt's genial defence of the role of intelligence in civilized life to the sensational headlines in *France-Dimanche: Jusqu'où une femme peut-elle aller en amour?* – all these elements form part of the patchwork context for the central problem of the film, which seems very much a problem of identity, of Charlotte's relationship to the fragmented, uncertain world that surrounds her.

If, for all these reasons, *Une Femme mariée* could be called Godard's most classical film, *Pierrot le fou* (1965) might be called his most romantic. Like *Bande à part* before it and *Une Femme est une femme* before that, at first sight *Pierrot* scarcely seems to have been organized at all. So different from the static *Alphaville* that preceded it, *Pierrot* literally seems to flow before our eyes. If *Une Femme mariée* was statuesque in much of its movement and pervaded throughout by a sense of doubt and distress, *Pierrot* is a kind of ballet of colour and design. It has more the form of a lyric poem than any kind of conventional dramatic or narrative structure. Although the physical attractiveness of Anna Karina and Jean-Paul Belmondo makes both Marianne and Ferdinand a pleasure to behold, they scarcely exist at all in the film as comprehensible creatures who have an existence apart from the artist who created them. More than ever before, they seem to be projections of Godard's own thoughtful, beauty-craving, death-desiring mind.

More consistently personal than *Vivre sa vie*, *Pierrot* has no need of Godard's own voice to convey the urgency of its most intimate moments. In *Pierrot*, Godard seems to have discovered a form that has enabled him to express his most private and apparently autobiographical obsessions in such a way that by the end of the film they have the liberating quality of a work of art. It is also a form that enables him more than ever before to give the impression of capturing 'the definitive by chance'.

Like most of the films before it but here most consistently, *Pierrot le fou* achieves its power and coherence through its technique of allusion, allusion once again of a direct and literal kind. The extended epigraph about Velasquez sets the tone of the film:

... His only experience of the world was those mysterious copulations which united the forms and tones with a secret but inevitable movement ... The world he lived in was sad. A degenerate king, inbred infantas, idiots, dwarfs, cripples, deformed clowns clothed as princes, whose only job was to laugh at themselves and amuse those lifeless outlaws who were trapped by etiquette, conspiracy, lies, and inextricably bound to the confessional by guilt. Outside the gates, the Auto-da-fe, and silence ...[19]

While we're listening to these words, before we see Ferdinand sitting in the bath, absurdly reading these lines to his puzzled daughter, we see first a shot of a tennis court in full activity; then a shot of Ferdinand browsing in a bookshop (buying, in fact, the Élie Faure from which he is reading); then a shot of Paris by night, its street lamps reflected in the dark waters of the Seine.

None of these shots is related directly to what we are hearing, nor do they relate in any way to the rest of the film. At first sight, one might feel an element of arbitrariness; but by the end of the film, they seem superbly right as well. Not only do they combine with the commentary in setting the tone and declaring the imagistic style of the film, but they define as well the limits of Godard's world. Their apparent arbitrariness is part of the haphazard philosophy within the film (*par hasard* is always Marianne's explanation for everything that happens); while the tennis court suggests the sense of life as play, the night shot the final obliteration of death which, nevertheless, has something attractive about it, and finally, both in the book-buying and in the reading we get the sense that the only possible meaning in these two irreconcilable perceptions concerning play and death must be found through the unifying transformations of art, what used to be called the life of the spirit.

Similarly, leaping ahead a bit, we can explain the formal significance of the apparently gratuitous little cabaret song by Raymond Devos on the quay towards the end of the film. He sings of his romantic obsession, an obsession that has always been associated with a particular song, even though the female recipient of this amorous passion has changed. This song could serve as the theme of the film. (The novel by Lionel White which provided the source material for this film is called, in fact, *Obsession*.) The Devos character knows he is mad and seeks confirmation of this knowledge from everyone he encounters. Yet he cannot free himself from his fixation, even though he recognizes that it is absurd.

So too Ferdinand throughout the film is equally bound by a hopeless fascination: once he breaks free from the moneyed meaninglessness of his Parisian married life, the sole purpose of his existence springs from his addiction to Marianne, although she will never accept him for what he is, even to the extent of refusing to accept his name.

Like an aspect of *À Bout de souffle*, like the early short *Charlotte et son Jules*, like the puzzled face of the husband that further troubles the troubled Charlotte in *Une Femme mariée*, *Pierrot le fou* is basically a persuasion – a useless plea for masculine recognition. *Je m'appelle Ferdinand!* as he has to keep insisting, even at the moment Marianne dies. 'There is no such thing as unhappy love,' Michel has declared in *À Bout de souffle*: 'grief is always a compromise.' So too Ferdinand surrenders himself to the anarchy of his obsession, trying both to experience it and at the same time to record the process in a journal as if more fully to understand.

Once more, then, in *Pierrot le fou* there is this split between the body and the mind, a split that goes some way towards explaining why Marianne cannot remain true to him. As with so many of Godard's characters, we can see that Ferdinand gives himself to the object of his fascination, but we cannot *feel* that he loves, any more than we come to *feel* that Nana has a soul. Once involved with the creature of his desire, Ferdinand wants to read and write, to order his experiences intellectually in the effort to understand.

There is a short sequence on a beach in the south of France that beautifully dramatizes this situation in a way that seems crucial to more of Godard than just this particular film. Requiring too many words of too great a delicacy even to attempt to evoke its quality through language, it dramatizes the stalemate between Ferdinand and Marianne, which is at the same time the stalemate of Ferdinand's (and possibly Godard's) whole life.

Ferdinand is sitting on a ruined breakwater by the sea, a parrot by his side, writing in his diary. Marianne trudges along the shore towards him, throwing stones into the water and crying out her boredom in the winds: 'What am I to do? I don't know what to do.' He remains absorbed in his diary, scarcely noticing her distress. 'Why do you look unhappy?' he asks finally. 'Because you talk to me with words and I look at you with feelings.' They then decide to talk seriously to one another by listing all the things they like. Marianne mentions flowers and animals and the blue of the sky, while Ferdinand cites ambition and hope and the movement of things. They both conclude their list by saying 'I don't know ... Everything.' Then she moves off on her own again, still crying out *'Qu'est-ce que je peux faire? Je ne sais quoi faire.'*

This little scene seems to sum up the inability of Godard's characters really to talk to one another. We see them listing ideas of values more at the screen, we might feel, than at one another, with virtually none of the give-and-take of a real conversation, with none of the reciprocity that makes talk between people meaningful.

Godard's characters tend more to interview one another and then to say things that in the films themselves don't too solidly relate with what we have seen. Where in *Pierrot* have we seen Marianne's sensuous love of flowers and animals or Ferdinand's addiction to ambition or the movement of things? If anything, it would appear to be the other way round, part of this crisscrossing again that Peter Wollen has drawn our attention to and which distances us from any direct involvement with the characters as *characters*. At the same time, it tends to increase our involvement with the film *as a film*, as a most personal projection from Godard's own mind. For it is both the beauty and the intimacy of these private moments in the film that makes *Pierrot le fou* seem so romantic and so alive.

If *Pierrot* has a fault, it is perhaps to be found in its basic structure. Formally, it is less unified than many of Godard's films. There seems to be an uneven balance between the imagery and the plot. When Ferdinand and Marianne leave their *roman de Jules Verne* and return to their *roman policier*, the film sags a little. Up until that point, the surrealist association of the violence of death with the tenderness of love has seemed both comic and disturbing; for instance, a man lying stabbed in the adjoining room towards the opening of the film when Marianne sings her first song – *sans lendemain*, 'with no tomorrow'. But when the gun-running actually becomes part of the plot, with torture scenes in the bathroom looking like left-overs from *Le Petit Soldat*, I feel that it has begun to intrude.

No longer acceptable simply on the level of imagery, the violence begins to look as if we are supposed to be taking from it some social point, a point somewhat at odds with the very private, lyrical style of the rest of the film. Like the Vietnam sketch which strikes a falsely moralizing note in this film, the gun-running episodes imply a world of political struggles insufficiently explored in *Pierrot* to be effective in their own right.

But it is the intimate note that prevails and animates this extraordinary film, an intimacy made the greater by both Marianne and Ferdinand sharing the choric lamentation that punctuates the narrative. As in *Une Femme mariée*, although here without any psychological explanation to justify it, the lamentation, consisting of fragments of ideas and emotions, establishes the prevailing mood of hopelessness, despair, and inevitable death which counterpoints nicely the more abandoned sequences when the characters run about and sing songs. 'Life might be sad but it is always wonderful,' says Ferdinand in one of his more buoyant moments. This harks back to Velasquez again as it seems to sum up the final impact and (may I say?) the profundity of the film.

On the level of philosophic argument, I wouldn't want to call Godard's view of life profound. But as we experience it in a film like *Pierrot*, it takes on another dimension. The film embodies a recognition of certain basic facts that pertain to many people's lives. It recognizes that it is Ferdinand's preference for other people's written thoughts to clarify his own experience, this uncertainty of self, that helps to drive Marianne away from him. So, at the same time as we have in *Pierrot* one of the most literary and allusive films that Godard has made, we have, built into its structure, a critique of Godard's own allusive urge.

Also, I take from this film a feeling of profundity, as I took the same from *À Bout de souffle*, because of the sharp juxtaposition of conflicting images that seems to imply conflicting responses to life. Life is most beautiful when it is lived most freely as play; yet just around the corner is the arbitrary and meaningless destruction of death. Added to this is the feeling so intrinsic to Godard's autobiographical art and yet common enough in life to be applicable to us all: life takes on more meaning if we are deeply engrossed in something outside ourselves, even though this engrossment might be based upon illusion. From such a dedication to the follies of our mind (the film seems to say) comes not only much of a romantic richness of life but also much of our art.

So back to the opening images of the tennis court and the river at night and Velasquez again! In many ways, it is a sad and defeatist view of life that hovers on the brink of an easy sentimentalism. But as it is presented to us in *Pierrot*, with such a strong feeling of personal involvement and with such physical richness, it touches upon the profound. 'Pierrot le fou, was all Ferdinand was to Marianne – an essentially clown-like figure, solemn and foolish by turns, mad enough to believe in his own imaginings.

*

Montage will give back to the *pris sur le vif* all its ephemeral grace; it will metamorphose chance into fate.[20]

For the most part, throughout all the discussions in this book, I have been content to discuss problems of style by looking in considerable detail at only a *selection* of the films produced by any one man. Although there may be an arbitrary element in this procedure, I have not myself worried about it. Reasons of space dictate selection of some kind. With Godard, however, I feel my personal selection to be arbitrary in the extreme, very much the result of my need to condense. Certain films that I value highly and which are relevant to my theme – films like *Le Mépris, Bande à part*, and *Masculin-Féminin* – have not received the attention they deserve, while a film like *Les Carabiniers* has not been discussed at all.

I began this chapter by suggesting that I would be concerned to explore the conflict between love and politics throughout Godard's work. While I have not so far dealt explicitly with this conflict at all, I have indirectly, because the conflict in Godard between love and politics is yet another manifestation of the split nature of his sensibility, of the conflict between the mind and the body, between the desire for thought and the need for action. I have also suggested that these twin desires are mutually self-destructive. It is as if Godard recognizes that individualism is no solution, as Paul's friend explained to him in *Masculin-Féminin*, whether the individualism of reflective thought or of romantic love. Yet Godard has been unable to find a full commitment elsewhere. So his work now flounders. He remains as prolific as ever, and as inventive; but both the scale of his work and the size of his audiences are trickling away. As Richard Roud has suggested:

> It seems to me that Godard is uniquely unfitted to make the kind of films he thinks he ought to be making . . . it would seem he cannot do without the lyricism which recently he has been trying so hard to suppress.[21]

'Listen, even so, I have the right to have problems with women,' Paul once replied to his friend. Godard seems now to have given up this right. Yet he has not moved beyond it. As Roud suggests, he seems largely to have repressed that element in his work, impoverishing his films by denying them their most human qualities. With the rejection of love and the suppression (still not complete) of his lyrical style, there has disappeared as well any sign of what I have previously called the reflective intelligence, any sense of the characters trying to follow Leenhardt's principle of thinking *before* they act.

The political activists in *La Chinoise*, *Weekend*, *One Plus One*, and *Le Vent d'Est* act as if without reflection. Their thinking is a mindless slogan-mongering, as if in the effort to hypnotize themselves into believing that such slogans are the only truth. They are often seen declaiming from books or repeating phrases conned by rote from an imperfect tape-recorder. Thus they have more in common with the mechanical voice of Alpha 60 than they have with the absurdly romantic assertions of the stolid Lemmy Caution. Godard's political activists are the direct descendants of his ape-like soldiers in *Les Carabiniers*. And what, we must ask, are the *political* implications of this?

Standing to one side of his major work in the early days, *Les Carabiniers* (1963) now takes on a harsh prophetic quality. No one at that time would have seen in Godard's riflemen, if not the hope exactly, at least the only prospect for the future. The film was accepted by those who admired it as a grimly anti-war film, depicting with cool detachment the brutalizing processes of war and the futility of its ends. It seemed to me to be a kind of cinematic Dada, its uncharacteristic detachment partly the proof of the immense creative flexibility of Godard, partly, I have always assumed, the result of the direct influence of Rossellini. Viewed in isolation, the film can still seem like this; but in the light of his later work, certain ambiguities become, lamentably, rather less ambiguous.

The mindless, sub-human characteristics of Godard's riflemen lead directly to the cannibals that end *Weekend*, devouring (so to speak) the very society that has nurtured them. Similarly, in *Les Carabiniers* the execution of the beautiful partisan, who, like the sailors in *Potemkin*, calls out to her 'brothers' to save her from her fate, and who till the very end recites Mayakovsky, is simultaneously the execution of beauty and the extinction of poetry – the two qualities in which Godard, up until *Weekend*, has struggled to believe. With the extinction of these qualities, we have the extinction as well of the only humane values that have shone through the desperately uncertain world that Godard has created for us throughout his many, remarkable films, the only qualities (as Robin Wood has suggested[22]) that might make a revolution actually worth fighting for.

What have we left? Clearly, Alphaville. But the destructive mechanics lie less in the computerized technology that threatens human individuality, banning words like tenderness, conscience, and love from human contemplation, than in the characters themselves – in their mechanical, slogan-bound, loveless response to the world that surrounds them and in their passive acceptance of the need for brutality. Furthermore, the magnificently executed farm-yard recital in *Weekend* gives us the sense of Western art in total decline, Mozart fumblingly played and passively observed by a scattering of inattentive spectators.

Godard's cinema has become increasingly a self-destructive cinema. In *À Bout de souffle*, the presence of the impersonal violence of the world outside was constantly threatening to engulf the characters and disrupt their little recesses of talk and love; but by *Deux ou Trois Choses que je sais d'elle* (1966), these recesses have vanished. The violence of impersonal construction-noises almost totally overwhelms the soundtrack and obliterates the characters. The most human voice in the film is the voice of Godard, urgently whispering to us in his self-questioning way, wondering whether what he is showing us is what he ought to be showing us, wondering whether this tree or that is the right one to dwell upon.

In many ways, *Deux ou Trois Choses* is a remarkable film and, as Roud has suggested in concluding his own helpful and enthusiastic account, it does represent a 'summing-up of his career'.[20] But it is a summing-up that is more accessible on the viewing table with the script beside one, where one can stop and start the film at will and puzzle out what is going on (facilities that Roud enjoyed), than in the normal conditions of a theatre. If throughout Godard's work there has been this sense of the harsh impersonal realities of the social/political world impinging upon the inner life of the individual, in films like *Le Gai Savoir*, *One Plus One*, and *Le Vent d'Est*, there is no longer any inner life to impinge upon. The riflemen have triumphed. The human world has been destroyed. Art and beauty and the painful uncertainties of human love are no more.

What might we take to be Godard's political position? He would seem to believe now in the validity of revolution, but perhaps not really. Perhaps not really, because he nowhere shows that he fully understands what the issues of a revolution actually are, what the outcome might entail. Politically, he is an old-fashioned, idealist Marxist, offering us the over-simplification of the workers against the bosses as the terms on which a revolution must be fought. This might have been valid for Cuba and China – essentially agricultural communities exploited by foreign owners. But for modern, industrialized Europe and America, these comforting over-simplifications no longer have the validity they might once have seemed to have. As Theodore Roszak (among others) has convincingly argued,[24] the issues now would seem to be between the young of whatever class against their timid elders, the people against the technocracy.

This lack of clarity in Godard's political position can perhaps best be located in the Godard/Pennebaker footage, now called *1 PM*. Tom Hayden is an American radical with many things to say about the current situation. We actually see him in the film expounding his views in person to Godard, as we see Leacock's camera quietly recording what he has to say. Meanwhile Penne's camera is roving about with its characteristically restless inquisitiveness. Earlier on in the film, however, before we see Hayden talking out of the fullness of his own commitment to an ideal of revolution, the children against the parents, we have seen Rip Torn, an actor with a tape-recorder, walking out in the woods in full Indian regalia or up into a builders' lift in a superbly simple continuous take, the tape-recorder under his arm, playing back, with incomprehensible distortion, the very words of Hayden's that we are later to hear, playing them back and mouthing them mechanically, as if learning by rote, like the Black Panthers with *their* slogans in *One Plus One*.

It would seem from this sequence and similar ones in other Godard movies that the artist is now indeed 'Mocking his own tale'. His impulse is to make ridiculous what he apparently wants most to believe in, as if to protect himself from the futility of being wrong. As with Swift, in so many ways Godard's great predecessor (both in his creative energy and in the depth of his despair), Godard's protection against the fear and pain of life has always been a most derisive laughter. As Jean Collet has put it,

Godard's response to treachery and death, to the end of love – to man's pain – is ... hurtful laughter. A systematic denial of the serious.[25]

Often, quite courageously, Godard has directed this laughter at himself. Through his characters, he has frequently mocked the inconsistencies of his own position, the absurdity of his own romantic ideals. But more recently, while we still might feel from the evidence of the later films that he is mocking his own beliefs, there is nothing in his many interviews to suggest that he is himself aware of this. Moreover, this 'state of highly sophisticated confusion', as Ian Cameron has called it,[26] was a source of richness in his earlier films, where we could see a variety of forces opposing one another; in his later work, however, as in *Les Carabiniers*, everything seems to be pointing the same way.

Godard's professed espousal of revolution seems less the

result of an informed interest in the issues in contemporary society than a last-ditch gesture of total despair in the face of the complete incomprehensibility of the universe as he himself has experienced it. Since he has cut himself off from an idealized belief in the validity of beauty, the truth of art, and the liberation from the self brought about by human love, Godard's interest in revolution would now seem to be accompanied by a loss of faith in the processes of life itself. To my mind, this represents a most reactionary attitude.

The attitude is reactionary because self-deceiving. Like Bergman at his most rhetorical, in films like *Hour of the Wolf* and *Shame*, Godard is confusing his own inner distress with political reality. He is attempting to project outwards his inner tensions and split response to the complexities of life on to the more public world of political struggles. In his earlier work, when the personal seemed paramount, this was fair enough. Certainly there *is* a relationship between the senselessly impersonal urbanized society and the difficulties we find in establishing the inner security of love; and certainly in the violence around us we can find to a degree an impersonal counterpart for the violence that we might at times feel within ourselves. But in understanding such a relationship balance is everything. If we are ever to be successful in wringing some improvement out of the absurdities of this world, it will be necessary (so it seems to me) to separate our nervous and imaginative disorders from the more public issues that exist outside, interdependent though these two might be.

While certain films can give us a sense of profundity, there is at the centre of Godard both an emotional confusion and an intellectual facility which finally we have to isolate and resist. If in *À Bout de souffle* Michel seemed like a new kind of hero (as I have claimed), he also talked about cars and the material goods of life just like those guests at the party in *Pierrot le fou* that so disgusted Michel's heir, Ferdinand. (Indeed, Marianne might have talked in much the same way, in her own search for the excitements of material pleasure.) Godard has obviously a love-hate relationship with the glossy products of the American consumer society, just as he had a love-hate relationship with

American films, a relationship that has increasingly resolved itself into hate.

Similarly, while his most romantic films betray a fascination with the vocabulary of spiritual inwardness, *Vivre sa vie* and *Alphaville* abounding in words like 'conscience', 'soul' and 'love', there is a discrepancy between what we *hear* in these films and what we can imagine from what we *see*. When in *Vivre sa vie* Nana assures us that '*je suis heureuse*', her assertion is not accompanied by any physical exuberance that might give us the feeling that she is actually happy. Her words thus seem rhetorical in relation to the film or self-deceiving in relationship to herself. But there is no evidence that Godard is aware of this.

In his earlier work, Godard succeeded in disguising the uncertainty of his own position by a self-protective irony; and the jumble of collage that characterizes in different ways the complex achievement of *À Bout de souffle*, *Vivre sa vie*, *Une Femme mariée*, and *Pierrot le fou* (to mention only the films discussed here in some detail) seems to have served Godard well in creating an ambiguous balance between affirmation and despair. Now this balance, if we are to find it at all, would have to be between what he *says* he is doing when asked about his work and what we *actually see* when we experience the films.

The thin optimism that characterizes the endings of *Bande à part* and *Alphaville*, then, seems equally grim in the context of the complete Godard. While one or two of us might escape to the Outerlands or Brazil and carry on our comic-strip fantasy roles in 'cinemascope and technicolor', the world we flee from gets worse and worse and requires, one must finally argue, *constructive political action* in order to put it right. Even if things *are* so bad that constructive political action will have to involve violence and revolution, we would have to be clear *before* acting what some of the goals are that we are trying to achieve.

'For me, the time for action is over . . . the time for reflection begins,' declaimed Bruno at the opening of *Le Petit Soldat*. For Godard now, the reverse seems to be true. Reflection, as with Paul, would seem to lead to a romantic individualism which in turn leads to defeat and to death. Better the collective destruction of mindless revolution as in *Les Carabiniers* than the idealized suicide of romantic love: so implies the false logic that runs with such authority throughout the films of Jean-Luc Godard. It is a sad, grim irony for such a 'revolutionary' thinker about the cinema that a conventional 'bourgeois' film like *The Battle of Algiers* can convey to a far greater number of spectators both the hideous brutality of a revolutionary movement *and* something of the feeling of the actual victory that such a revolutionary movement might hope to attain. 'Trapped in an ever-present past,' Richard Winkler has written about Bruno in *Le Petit Soldat*, 'he has no future'.[27] These words could now equally serve to describe Godard.

*

However, I would not want to end this survey of the Godardian opus on such a negative note; for Godard's dilemmas, in many ways, take to extreme positions the dilemmas of us all. As R. D. Laing has beautifully said in explanation of his own interest in schizophrenics, creatures who have much in common with the characters that Godard has created on the screen: '... the cracked mind of the schizophrenic may *let in* light which does not enter the intact minds of many sane people whose minds are closed'.[28]

Godard's work remains fascinating for us, even when tedious, even when perversely muddle-headed, because of the nature of the issues it confronts, issues central to the world we live in, to the future of the cinema, and to Godard himself. Every formal detail in his films and every statement that each of his characters makes raises questions of the most far-reaching kind – questions not only of artistic procedure but of philosophical implication and political applicability. In fact, it is this questioning, this restlessly uncertain quality of every word and every image, that makes his films seem so much of our times.

Godard may yet prove himself to be one of those artists – like van Gogh or Artaud – whose uncompromising artistic sensibility drives them into the state that we conventionally call madness and who thus destroy themselves by their own art. But by so rigorously confronting the issues that obsess him, issues simultaneously aesthetic and political, he is at the forefront of the heroes of our time. We contemplate his achievement with fascination for his unrelenting ability, indeed his determination (as Susan Sontag has said of the philosopher Cioran), 'to be abreast of the incurable'.[29]

8

CONCLUSION:

a note on film style

Maybe a director sometimes doesn't know why he does the things he does. Maybe he does them subconsciously. After a picture is finished, perhaps a psychoanalyst could find out why a director did certain things.   *Fritz Lang, 1965*[1]

While there have been occasional cross-references in the preceding chapters, I have for the most part tried to keep each chapter independent, the better to be able to focus on the stylistic details of each director, to look at his work in close-up, so to speak. But if they are all held together in long-shot, certain elements stand out in relief against one another. I would like to conclude this study by speculating somewhat on what we might call the *meaning* of style. What, finally, is the lasting effect that each director has upon us? What value might we attribute to the distinctive *flavour* of each man's style?

Directors like Renoir and Fellini deliberately set out to please us, perhaps even to charm us into accepting the reality of their respective worlds, while others like Bergman and Godard, in their later works, seem almost to insult us. They appear to want to hurt us, as if to force upon us the reality of *their* particular worlds.

Renoir and Fellini are both traditionalists, as indeed is Buñuel in another way. Renoir's work is obviously rooted in the past. His values, as I have argued, are those of his father, those, indeed, of another and (it would appear) more beautiful age. He has brought to his film-making ideas of graciousness, of the supreme value of friendship, of gentleness, of an easy elegance, of the unalterable beauty of nature – ideas which sit oddly within films about murder and injustice as in *La Chienne* or about prison camps in the Second World War, as in *Le Caporal épinglé*. But these ideas are beautiful nevertheless. They are redolent of the leisured courtesy of certain aspects of the past and are very much a part of the atmosphere that we take away from Renoir's films. Yet, if his films are filled with beauty, they are also filled with sadness – as if in tacit realization that such beauty as he wants to believe in has less and less recognition in the contemporary world. These qualities find their occasional echo nowadays in the work of François Truffaut, who is in many ways Renoir's cinematic heir.

Fellini's traditions are different. They are less social and more interior. There is no sense of any hankering for the historical past in a Fellini film, but there *is* the sense of a man looking backwards, away from the responsibilities of a fully adult world, as if children have the answer. Up until *Satyricon*, any sense of a historical past could be located most specifically in his feeling for ritual, for religious processions and for many of the more ceremonial aspects of life. In fact, so important for Fellini are these collective celebrations that he tends to impose a ceremonial intensity on the most secular moments of life. The press conference that provides the pennultimate scene for $8\frac{1}{2}$ is, after all, not that different in feeling and treatment from the visit to the shrine in *Le Notti di Cabiria* or the bogus Madonna sequence in *La Dolce Vita*; the quality of each of these sequences involves the surrender of individual feeling to the collective feeling of the crowd, a collective feeling that in Fellini is always close to hysteria. This sense of loss of self in some form of transcendent reality is at the centre of Fellini's world and provides the core of what we must call, even if with distinctly pagan overtones, the religious impulse within his films.

Sharply different from Fellini's, Buñuel's traditionalism comes from his highly developed historical sense, his keen understanding of the past. By fastening on the surface reality of things and by possessing an unerring sense of place and time, Buñuel is the most *realistic* director discussed in this volume. Even more than Renoir, whose films seem to possess more a *feeling* for the past than an accurate *understanding* of it, Buñuel gives us the sense of creating an actual world objectively before us, a world of real people set in a particular place and time. Furthermore, he creates for us characters that to a large extent bring about their own destinies, gloomy though these may be. If they seem trapped, they are trapped as much by elements *within* themselves as by forces without. In contrast, Bergman's period pieces like *The Seventh Seal* and *Smiles of a Summer Night* seem more like excursions into an *imaginary* place and time, an excursion that allows him to waive many of the realistic expectations of the cinema to create an atmosphere where poetic licence may have free play.

Buñuel's films give us the impression of an unshirking intelligence and understanding brought to bear on the intricacies of human nature and on the political problems of the world. Yet the jokes that tend to end his films seem like an attempt to belittle the particularity of his own insights, as if in grim recognition of the fact that intelligence and understanding are perhaps not strong enough to make much difference in the affairs of life. This facetious espousal of absurdity also allows him to produce comparatively slight work – films like *Simon of the Desert*, *The Milky Way* and *Belle de jour*. There is a characteristically Buñuelian irony in the fact that *Belle de jour* should have proven to be the most *popular* film he has ever made – a state of affairs that goes a long way, sadly, to confirm the validity of Buñuel's own pessimism!

Yet, among the directors discussed in this book, only Buñuel gives us the sense of a man looking at cultures so diverse as those authentically created in the impoverished Mexican culture of *Los Olvidados* or the futile provincial French culture of *Diary of a Chambermaid*, seeing what they were like and creating characters *separable from himself* who work out their individual destinies within the net that their particular culture and historical situation have imposed.

Think of how real all conversations are in any Buñuel film, even in deliberately comic scenes, like the defeated old uncle talking to the supposedly hated priests towards the end of *Tristana*. Think of the many family scenes he creates for us, scenes of people eating together, talking together, and the strong sense of society his films thus convey. In comparison, Bergman and Fellini seem almost narcissistic; while Godard, aware though he is of all the surface details of contemporary life, is as confined within his own anxieties and cultural milieu as any Buñuelian personage!

Conversations and family life, of course, seem very real in Renoir as well, and to a certain extent in Bergman. But after *I Vitelloni*, talk in Fellini veers more and more towards monologue, and the characters seem to live increasingly on their own. In Eisenstein we rarely have anything more personal than declamation; and if there is genuine talk in Bergman, especially in late Bergman, his films nevertheless keep careering off into a monotonous rhetoric of self-pity and despair. Even if there *is* a strong sense of family life in films like *A Lesson in Love* and *Smiles of a Summer Night*, compared with Renoir and Buñuel, there is little sense of a society beyond.

Like Buñuel, Renoir too gives us the sense of a man taking delight in the creation of characters and epochs different from his own; and it is perhaps an indication of my own philosophical bias that, beautiful though Renoir's world appears to be, governed throughout by the perennial values of comradeship and acceptance, it seems somewhat inadequate for the contemporary world in comparison with Buñuel's. Given the themes that Renoir purports to deal with – passion, murder, war and death – his acceptance of life seems somewhat *imposed* on his material, something he *wants* to believe in, perhaps *needs* to believe in, more than something he has *seen* and *understood*. In Buñuel, on the other hand, we have a more tough-minded recognition of the actual effects of passion, murder, war and death. In some ways, the upshot of their world-views is not that different: after all, they both made versions of *Le Journal d'une femme de chambre*! But in Buñuel, the balance is distributed in a (to my mind) more realistic way. In Buñuel we get the sense that, however beautiful is the fitful compassion observable in life, given the odds against it, there can never be much hope.

Looking at these directors in this way, examining what we might call their historical sense, their sense of how the world has come to be as it is, in Godard paradoxically – with Godard, always paradoxically – there is little sense of history at all. For all his surface naturalism and avowed political concerns, there is almost no sense of the *reasons* for the intellectual and

Conclusion

economic conditions of everyday life that characterize the historical sense so strongly in Buñuel. Indeed, in comparison with Buñuel, Godard's films possess the sensibility of a perennial student. They are films of the Left Bank, of the excitement of ideas untested by action, of ideals unobtainable in the modern world. An entomologist by training, with a Swiss Calvinist background, Godard looks at life from a certain distance, making notes, suggesting juxtapositions, discovering puns and further student delights at the absurdities within the adult world; but he remains unable to effect a helpful synthesis. His films thus deliberately refuse to give us that old-fashioned sense of security available through art when we recognize that an artist has seen more than we have and has more totally understood – a feeling *especially* available, in my view, from the deep pessimism of Buñuel.

Godard seems so contemporary perhaps *because* he is so thoroughly a two-dimensional artist. His works lack perspective just as his characters lack depth. The fragmented surface of society is everywhere in his films – its poster, pop-art surface; but there is little sense of any social relationships. Rather, his people are seen in isolation from one another, related to things. Nevertheless, the feeling of extreme isolation that Godard's films can convey contravenes the deliberate superficiality of his characters to give his most personal films their extraordinary feeling of inwardness – at times (as I have argued) as confessional in feeling as anything in Fellini or Bergman. Oddity of oddities for a film-maker who thinks of himself as a revolutionary force for the future, Godard is in many ways the Flaubert of the cinema, far more so than Antonioni or Resnais who are most obviously the aesthetes. *Madame Bovary, c'est moi!*, Flaubert is said to have exclaimed. Godard has said the same about *Pierrot le fou*.

Godard's cinema is a desperate cinema because, at his strongest, he confronts us with our *own* inability to understand, with our *own* inability to effect a helpful synthesis out of the conflicting fragments of our own lives – a most gloomy confrontation! At the same time, Godard's world is confined to the realm of a highly personal perplexity, involving the relationship of his women to his men. Buñuel, on the other hand, no matter how hopeless his world might seem, does give us the sense of creating a world of people who actually exist *outside ourselves*, a world that is not just the projection of his private anxieties but is a real world, actually going on. Godard's world is static in comparison, without moral energy, even if in Buñuel moral affirmation usually meets with ignominious defeat. Buñuel's films can exhilarate us by the intensity of his own insights, even when, on a rational plane, there seems little to believe in. Godard's films, on the other hand, can drain us of all energy and leave us with a moral numbness (only rivalled by Antonioni!) that is the most anguished form of despair.

Fellini's world relates to Godard's in a peculiar way. Like Godard's, it too stands apart in time. Magical and irrational in most of its implications, sensory and anti-intellectual in its basic values, compared with the collage techniques that confirm Godard's inability to synthesize, Fellini's world represents a synthesis of the highest order. This much I must claim for it. All experience is filtered through his senses, transmogrified into grotesque shapes of a compelling plasticity, a world of perpetual amazement, a celebration of the marvellous, a delight in the incomprehensible, a faith that the most abject of human failures must in some way be divine. Released from the confessional where he has been warned that his sexual impulses are the prompting of the devil, young Guido in 8½ runs back to find the grotesque Saraghina shelling peas by the seaside. 'Ciao,' she leers at him as the wind blows her shawl about her face; and by the compelling authority of Fellini's art, she is transformed into a nymph.

In contrast with this sense of child-like delight, Godard's cinema gives us the sense of a lurking fear of life much more inhibiting than the mixture of dread and wonder that characterizes the films of Fellini. If Fellini has again and again returned to the affirmation of life through his children, Godard seems trapped in the uncertainty of an adolescent self-consciousness. Even his current revolutionary position seems more the text-book revolutionary attitude of an assertive young student than the practical, involved position of an adult systematically involved in changing the world. There seems in Godard's films a pervasive fear of the fullness of commitment, an inability in his characters to give themselves fully to anything outside themselves. This might seem true of Fellini too, but the effect is different. In Fellini, whatever failures his characters might endure, up until 8½ there was always the sense of something *beyond* these failures, of some ulterior purpose. Up until 8½ at least, there was always a sense of an espousal, of a celebration, of a welcoming – qualities embodied in the turbulence of his movement. In contrast, the tableau structure of so many of Godard's films gives us more the sense of life being held down, of experiences kept at a distance, of a self-protective, intellectual order imposed upon the unmanageable elements of day-to-day reality.

Fellini's cinema is one of physical responses, of imaginative delight at the promise of life. Godard's, on the other hand, is one of ideas and observations, but finally of fear – fear lest these ideas might be of no interest to anyone but himself.

Roaming this way from director to director, trying to clarify their inter-relatedness, I find the films of Ingmar Bergman difficult to pin down. Partly because he's Swedish and, especially in the past, Sweden have been so isolated, so far removed imaginatively from the intellectual and artistic centre of Paris, which in a study of this kind helps to unite the very different worlds of Renoir, Buñuel and Godard. Bergman's work is also difficult to encapsulate in the same way as the others because of his own image of himself as a conjuror; but perhaps this is our most salient clue.

Both in his public statements and in films like *The Face* and *All These Women*, Bergman has presented his 'artist' figure as a man skilfully cheating us, as a charlatan who is expected to have powers that in fact he fears he does not possess. Robin Wood has come to mistrust the rose-tinted affirmations of Bergman's earlier work, while I just as strongly mistrust the frantic declamations of his Baltic films. Either way, I hope I can argue, there is about Bergman's total output the sense of something not fully there, the sense of a man attitudinizing before his public, perhaps of a man ashamed of himself in some deep and inner way and yet, while insisting upon the validity of the shame, disguising the roots of it, amazing us with what, through the cinema, he has found he can do.

Like Renoir, Bergman is a man of the theatre. But if Renoir's theatre involves the feeling of adults at play, of his characters releasing their excessive energy through assuming roles, through participating in a masquerade, Bergman's theatre, while it also involves these elements, returns again and again to the lure of the limelight, to the sense of the theatrical man as an evil magician, of the artist as conjuror. His theatre is a theatre of special effects which some element in Bergman seems ashamed of using, as if aware of the fact that his power to move us is based on a sham. He is at his best, as I have argued, when he is least self-consciously theatrical, when he is absorbed in a quite conventional way by his story and his characters as in *Wild Strawberries* or *A Passion*, when his skill in conjuring is subservient to what he wants to say. At these moments, Bergman draws close to the cinematic world of Renoir and Buñuel, giving us a realistic sense of actual characters in a particular place and time, characters who have a life of their own that fascinates and involves us.

In other ways, of course, Bergman relates most obviously to Fellini. They are both fond of circuses, and in their early works especially, they both had a sense of life as a pilgrimage, as a journey or a search. But as I have suggested elsewhere, Bergman's journeys in his earlier, more directly allegorical days, were always quite specific, involving a particular geographical terrain with an actual goal at the end of them. From Stockholm to Lund in *Wild Strawberries*, from Stockholm to Copenhagen in *A Lesson in Love*, from Stockholm to Malmö in *A Journey into Autumn*, from Basle to Stockholm in the early *Thirst* – these specific journeys always had an exact destination and were always attended by an acceptance of some kind. In contrast, Fellini's journeys are less specified. Even at the end of *I Vitelloni*, when the hopeful Moraldo is leaving and the young station attendant asks him where he is going, '*Non lo so*' is his reply. He doesn't know.

If movement in Fellini tends to be circular, accompanied by

visions along the way, his characteristic delight in life and in his own powers as conjuror seem to express a delight in himself, in the potentialities of human nature that he feels within himself. Bergman's mistrust of these same powers and his unmitigable disgust with so many aspects of life seem similarly to express a mistrust and disgust with himself. There is something very Scandinavian about all this, but something that is peculiar to Bergman as well. His films, here like Godard's, give us the sense of a man working in increasing isolation, away from the possibilities of self-renewal that a less intense, less deliberately isolated world might provide.

More alienated culturally than Bergman ever was, Eisenstein is a man in whom the clash of temperament and historical situation may have prevented him from ever knowing fully who he really was or what totally engaged him. At the same time, this clash has produced the films that have come down to us and which have inspired the respect and excitement of four decades of film commentators. What the church has been for Fellini – a universalizing factor – the Bolshevik state might have been for Eisenstein had he not been temperamentally so much at odds with it.

It is probably as much Fellini's Christian background as his Italian temperament that, especially in his early works, enabled him to create the most humdrum characters with such detail and affection. The Communist Manifesto failed to provide Eisenstein with a comparable human concern. Rather it encouraged him to steer away from himself. As it is, the centre of attention in his films is so difficult to locate and when we do locate it, it appears different from what he himself would have claimed it to be. His silent films, especially, are so stylized that there seems no real 'subject matter' at all in the conventional sense of the word, which even the Godard of *Le Gai Savoir* allows us to a degree!

Eisenstein's prodigious artistic and intellectual curiosity manifested itself in the inventiveness and ingeniousness of someone who, finally, was not allowed fully to take himself seriously, who was not encouraged by his own culture to stand firm amongst his peers in the world. Reduced to an academic, he spent the bulk of his life expressing public regret for much of what he had done, a situation which must have made extremely uncertain his own sense of self.

By temperament and inclination, Eisenstein should have been a nineteenth-century enlightened man of letters, but the forces of history compelled him to believe he was a Bolshevik. Such an inner rupture might have happened to Renoir had not the greater security of his class and of French artistic life saved him to a degree. Though Renoir's world is full of moral *non-sequiturs*, it is not a world where the mind is divided against the sensibility in the way that Eisenstein's seems to be. We can't tell from *Ivan the Terrible* what Eisenstein actually felt about that man or about that period in time. We can respond to the film as pageant, as an oratorio, as I have suggested; or, through critical techniques akin to psychoanalysis, we can discover in it something of Eisenstein the man. Renoir's films, on the other hand, need no such cryptic approach to enable us to locate the human centre of his films. Charged with nostalgia though his best films are, Renoir's world is not a neurotically split world. Rather, it presents us with the most extraordinarily unified vision of a man yearning for the values of a world that has gone by.

*

Yearning for the values of a world that has gone by . . .

In a sense, this is the mood that unites *all* the directors discussed in this volume, to which could be added other distinguished European names, like Ophüls, Antonioni, Resnais, Truffaut. Even when happy it seems a melancholy world that all these men present to us, a world that has about it a recurring sense of loss, a recognition that the values which we have been encouraged to believe in are no longer sufficient to give meaning to our lives.

However, the acceptance of anxiety has characterized all significant historical periods. In fact, the coming to grips with despair has been one of the most productive aspects of civilizations of the past, whether through their art and ritual, or through their architecture and political structures. Yet in the contemporary European cinema, there is a difference. For all the profundity of vision into the plight of modern man that we find embodied in the films discussed in this book, the works are all sub-tragic. Perhaps more accurately, we should call them post-humanist. However we describe them, these films rarely provide us with that sense of elation which we can receive from serious works of art in the past, from authors as diverse in style and as far apart in time as Sophocles and Shakespeare – an elation which is obviously linked to the Aristotelian notion of catharsis.

It is beyond the scope of this volume to deal now with the therapeutic potential of great works of art, especially of the past; but such a discussion would involve a consideration of the kinds of hero possible in tragedy and of his relationship to the society that felt threatened by his qualities. Whether we think about *Oedipus Rex* or the more introspective *Hamlet*, we can find in both works a strong sense of community that carries on its own values after the destruction of the hero, no matter how outstanding his qualities might have been. In the traditionally humanist, tragic art of the past, there is invariably this sense of continuity, an aftertaste of social qualities, however timid and riddled with compromise, that will endure. In this way, the destruction of the hero seems to some purpose. Society itself will carry on.

In modern art, however, supremely in the cinema, this is no longer so. Our characters act out their roles in what often appears as a neurotic isolation from any sense of community. Philip Rieff has articulated an aspect of the problem:

> A positive community is characterized by the fact that it guarantees some kind of salvation to the individual by virtue of his membership and participation in that community.[2]

For the characters in a Godard and increasingly in a Bergman film, there is no longer any sense of a positive community. So there can be no salvation, neither for the protagonists nor for us. Except for Renoir and Fellini, with their sights set on either a historical past or on memories of a fantastic childhood, there is no longer any sense of perennial human values left to carry on. Instead, we have increasingly a feeling of uncertainty, uncertainty about the relationship of the characters to the world they inhabit plus an uncertainty on our part about our relationship to the characters on the screen. There is thus a kind of helplessness about the characters in most of the films we have looked at; and when it is absent, as in *Wild Strawberries* or in the gentler films of Renoir, we are tempted to describe the films as charmingly out-of-touch.

Perhaps civilization as we have known it is coming to an end. There is everywhere now the talk of revolution, yet unlike past historical periods, no one seems to have a blue-print for the future. Certain social thinkers like Theodore Roszak, while astutely accurate in analysing the problems, are forced back upon subjectivism and a Messianic hopefulness by way of solution – to my mind, just another form of despair.[3] Perhaps some future civilization will see in the films of Bergman and Godard evidence of the acuity of forlornness that signalled the approaching end.

Yet we should strive not to see it like this. As critics, thinkers, teachers, citizens, we should not play negative prophet in this way. To do so is to exhibit a failure of imagination with reference to contemporary problems which might end by so endorsing them that any constructive solution becomes impossible. If in traditionally humanist art the artist has led the perceptions of the citizen, has seen more and understood more, perhaps the time has come now for the citizen to discover sufficient resources within himself to enable him to take the lead. After all, it may be at least partly the death of their own art that the artists are singing about, their increasingly felt irrelevance in the technological world so persuasively described by Roszak and so acutely felt in the films of Bergman and Godard.

Decadence in art occurs when the artist, faced with the social and political exigencies of his time, withdraws into a compensatory beauty, self-contained. One of the great values of the cinema for us today is that it has been unable totally to do this. Even when we feel the individual artist is trying to create a compensational beauty of exquisitely wrought forms, as in Eisenstein and Resnais, the intrinsically realistic power of the photographic image never allows him to be completely successful. Even when apparently least concerned with it, the cinema seems to confront us with the realities of our time.

What has engaged me most thoroughly in the work of the film-makers discussed in this volume has been their sense of struggle in the face of the anguish at the centre of the contemporary world, a struggle which has involved not only the moral confrontation of all these social and political problems but also the creation of extraordinary cinematic forms. This act of creation might be the only kind of affirmation consistently possible to us now within a disintegrating society. Paradoxically, the act of creating, with force and originality, artistic vehicles that can contain our sense of loss *is* in itself a kind of affirmation. It implies that these issues are still worth considering, that perhaps there is someone out there who may appreciate and understand. The alternative would be perfect silence, as we see increasingly in Samuel Beckett, the total espousal of despair.

Contemporary cinema, especially in Europe, is a cinema of struggle – a struggle with ideas and with forms. Its achievement, the extent of which has only been touched upon in this volume, is prodigious. For many people today, it is *the* contemporary art form, the greatest source of international cultural unity that we possess. This volume represents both a celebration of its achievement and an examination of the inner workings of its form. But as I have said, film criticism, like the cinema itself, is still in its infancy. In spite of the references to gloom that have occurred in these pages, I still live with the excitement that the future lies ahead.

NOTES

Chapter One: Introduction

1. M. Merleau-Ponty, *Phenomenology of Perception*, trans. Colin Smith (New York, Humanities Press, 1962), p. xx.
2. Morris Shapira (ed.), *Henry James: Selected Literary Criticism* (London, Heinemann, 1963), p. 311.
3. John Berger, *Permanent Red* (London, Methuen, 1960), pp. 13–18.
4. Herbert Read, *Education Through Art* (London, Faber & Faber, 1949).
5. Siegfried Kracauer, *Theory of Film* (New York, Oxford University Press, 1965), p. x.
6. ibid., p. 16.
7. ibid., p. 40.
8. Robert Warshow, *The Immediate Experience* (An Atheneum Paperback, New York, 1970), p. 28.
9. ibid., p. 236.
10. 'Jean-Luc Godard', in *Cinéma 65* (Paris), No. 94, pp. 46–75.
11. Pauline Kael, 'Is There a Cure for Film Criticism?', reprinted in *I Lost It At The Movies* (London, Cape, 1966), pp. 269–92.
12. Susan Sontag, *Against Interpretation* (A Delta Paperback, New York, 1966), pp. 3–14.
13. Kael, 'Hud, Deep in the Divided Heart of Hollywood', *I Lost It At The Movies*, pp. 78–94.
14. George A. Huaco, *The Sociology of Film Art* (New York, Basic Books, 1965).
15. Karel Reisz and Gavin Miller, *The Technique of Film Editing* (London, Focal Press, 1963).
16. Richard Roud, *Godard* (London, Thames & Hudson, 1970), pp. 131 ff.
17. Berger, *Permanent Red*, p. 75.
18. W. K. Wimsatt, *The Verbal Icon* (University of Kentucky Press, 1954), p. 81.
19. Kenneth Clark, 'The Blot and the Diagram', in *Encounter* (London), January 1963, pp. 28 ff.

20. Suzanne Budgen, *Fellini* (A British Film Institute Publication, London, 1966), and John Ward, *Resnais, or the Theme of Time* (London, Secker & Warburg, 1968).

Chapter Two: Sergei Eisenstein

1. Robert Warshow, *The Immediate Experience* (An Atheneum Paperback, New York, 1970), p. 272.
2. S. M. Eisenstein, *Film Form* (A Meridian Book, Cleveland, 1967), p. 6.
3. ibid., p. 63.
4. ibid., p. 12.
5. ibid., pp. 195 ff. and pp. 169–70.
6. See Peter Wollen, *Signs and Meaning in the Cinema* (London, Secker & Warburg, 1969), pp. 19–73. Yet even here, for all the detailed understanding of Eisenstein's theoretical writings, there doesn't seem to be an increased respect for the films it supposedly justifies.
7. Ernest Lindgren, *The Art of the Film* (London, Dennis Dobson, 1963), and Ivor Montagu, *Film World* (London, Penguin Books, 1964).
8. S. M. Eisenstein, *Notes of a Film Director* (London, Lawrence & Wishart, 1959), pp. 53 ff.
9. See Warshow, *The Immediate Experience*, pp. 269–82, and William S. Pechter, 'The Closed Mind of Sergei Eisenstein', *Twenty-Four Times a Second* (New York, Harper & Row, 1971), pp. 111–22.
10. Marie Seton, *Eisenstein* (London, The Bodley Head, 1952), p. 385.
11. Eisenstein, *Film Form*, p. 49.
12. ibid., p. xi.
13. ibid., p. 12.
14. V. I. Pudovkin, *Film Technique* (London, George Newnes, 1937), p. xvii.
15. Jean Mitry, *S. M. Eisenstein* (Paris, Éditions Universitaires, 1955), p. 51.
16. I have already touched upon this point in answer to Charles Barr in 'What, indeed, is Cinema?', in *Cinema Journal* (University of Kansas), Fall 1968, pp. 22–8.
17. Pudovkin, *Film Technique*, p. 129.
18. Jay Leyda, *Kino* (London, Allen & Unwin, 1960), p. 209.
19. Eisenstein apparently felt that the montage principles could be

more scientifically discussed, while composition within the frame was too subjective for his objectivity-craving mind to dwell upon. See *Film Form*, p. 39.

20. Warshow, *The Immediate Experience*, p. 280.

21. See the British Film Institute Index Series No. 12 (London), compiled by Jay Leyda.

22. Mitry, *Eisenstein*, pp. 46–7.

23. From an unpublished paper by David Barraclough.

24. Charles Barr, 'CinemaScope and After', in *Film Quarterly* (Berkeley), Summer 1963; reprinted in R. D. MacCann (ed.), *Film: A Montage of Theories* (New York, Dutton, 1966), p. 321.

25. Warshow, *The Immediate Experience*, p. 271.

26. ibid., p. 280.

27. Pechter, *Twenty-Four Times a Second*, p. 118.

28. George A. Huaco, *The Sociology of Film Art* (New York, Basic Books, 1965), p. 149.

29. Warshow, *The Immediate Experience*, pp. 135–54.

30. Seton, *Eisenstein*, pp. 61–2.

31. Eisenstein, *Notes of a Film Director*, pp. 53 ff.; and Mitry, *Eisenstein*, pp. 87 ff.

32. Jay Leyda (ed.), *Film Essays* (London, Dennis Dobson, 1968), p. 15.

33. Sigmund Freud, *Leonardo* (London, Penguin Books, 1963).

34. Eisenstein, *Notes of a Film Director*, p. 108.

35. Freud, *Leonardo*, pp. 124 ff.

36. For the historical fact and actual disorder that did take place once the properly uniformed officers had been removed from the ship, see Richard Hough, *The Potemkin Mutiny* (London, Hamish Hamilton, 1960).

37. Seton, *Eisenstein*, pp. 195 ff., and 'Eisenstein's Unfinished Film', *Eisenstein*, a British Film Academy pamphlet (London), p. 20.

38. Eisenstein, *Film Form*, pp. 122–49.

39. As Marie Seton has argued in *Eisenstein*, p. 54.

40. See David Robinson, 'The Two Bezhin Meadows', in *Sight and Sound* (London), Winter 1967–8, pp. 33–6.

41. Leyda, *Kino*, p. 349.

42. David Robinson, 'The Boyars' Plot', in *Sight and Sound* (London), Spring 1960, pp. 87–8.

43. From David Barraclough again.

44. See 'Records of the Film', No. 2, by Roger Manvell (A British Film Institute Publication).

45. Seton, *Eisenstein*, p. 380.

46. ibid., pp. 436–7.
47. Eisenstein, *Film Form*, p. xiii.

Chapter Three: Jean Renoir

1. In *Premier Plan* (Lyons, 1962), Nos. 22–4, ed. Bernard Chardère, p. 29.
2. *Take One* (Toronto, 1967), Vol. 1, No. 7, p. 4.
3. From a TV interview on the BBC-2 series *The Movies*, originally transmitted 27 March 1967.
4. *Sight and Sound* (London), Spring 1968, p. 61.
5. Jean Renoir, *The Notebooks of Captain Georges*, trans. Norman Denny (Boston, Little, Brown & Co., 1966), p. 312.
6. ibid., p. 157.
7. ibid., p. 195.
8. ibid., p. 38.
9. ibid., p. 263.
10. In an interview between Huw Wheldon and Jean Renoir, *Renoir on Renoir*, part of the BBC TV *Monitor* series, Renoir explained: 'My father believed that each man had his role to play in life, each man his place. Renoir's was the artist's; another man's might be that of a servant . . . yet the bit player is as important as the great actor.'
11. Renoir, *Captain Georges*, p. 167.
12. ibid., p. 166.
13. See the review by Jean-Luc Godard in *Cahiers du Cinéma*, No. 78 (Paris, 1957), reprinted in *Jean-Luc Godard* (Paris, Pierre Belfond, 1968), pp. 98–9.
14. *Premier Plan*, pp. 16 ff.
15. Jean Renoir, *Renoir, My Father*, trans. R. and D. Weaver (London, Collins, 1962), p. 72.
16. ibid., p. 38.
17. Translated for a programme note for the National Film Theatre in London, from an interview with Jacques Rivette and François Truffaut in *Cahiers du Cinéma*, No. 78 (Paris, 1957).
18. ibid.
19. The entire *Premier Plan* has been compiled in this spirit of accusation, and documents the war years in distressing detail.
20. 'A good cook doesn't use recipes', Renoir recently remarked. 'He just uses his tongue and his nose' (*Take One*, p. 6).
21. See also William S. Pechter's suggestion that 'In Renoir's vision,

the impulse toward freedom seems always to lead away from community ...' (*Twenty-Four Times a Second* (New York, Harper & Row, 1971), p. 213).

22. Armand-Jean Cauliez, *Jean Renoir* (Paris, Éditions Universitaires, 1962), pp. 51–5.

23. From the *Cahiers du Cinéma* interview, translated by Sue Bennett for the notes for the Renoir Study Unit, available from the Education Department of the British Film Institute, London.

24. See Sue Bennett's careful balancing of all ingredients in her own note for the above Study Unit.

25. See Lee Russell (alias Peter Wollen) on Jean Renoir in the *New Left Review* (London), May–June 1964, pp. 57–60.

26. For a scholarly explication of the literary sources, see Suzanne Budgen, 'The Sources of *La Règle du jeu*', in *Take One* (Toronto, 1968), Vol. 1, No. 12, pp. 10–13.

27. For a discussion of the film in class terms, see Jacques Joly, 'Between Theatre and Life: Jean Renoir and *The Rules of the Game*', in *Film Quarterly* (Berkeley), Winter 1967–8, pp. 2–9.

28. However, many of these characteristics, including Octave's disappearance, are found in the sources. See Budgen in *Take One*.

29. From an interview in 1961 (quoted in *Premier Plan*, p. 405).

30. Roger Leenhardt, also in *Premier Plan*, p. 171.

31. Nino Frank, ibid., p. 290.

32. From the BBC TV *Monitor* interview.

33. Renoir, *Renoir, My Father*, p. 132.

34. ibid., p. 59.

35. BBC TV *Monitor* interview.

36. ibid.

37. For a thoughtful and detailed analysis of the film, see James Keirans, '*La Grande Illusion*', in *Film Quarterly* (Berkeley), Winter 1960, pp. 10 ff.

38. Pechter, *Twenty-Four Times*, pp. 208–14.

39. For a totally different view, see Pierre Leprohon, *Jean Renoir* (Paris, Éditions Seghers, 1967), p. 113.

40. Following the clarifications of a publicity hand-out, Antonioni's character is conventionally called Thomas – doubting Thomas, one might assume; but he is nameless in the film.

41. Renoir himself seems aware that his intentions have not been fully realized. See *Sight and Sound*, Spring 1968, p. 59.

42. In this way, as in occasional details of execution, the film bears a curious resemblance to André Cayatte's *Le Passage du Rhin*, whether intentionally or not I cannot say.

43. See especially *King Lear* (Act V, scene 3): 'Pray you, undo this button. Thank you, sir.'
44. Renoir, *Renoir, My Father*, p. 394.

Chapter Four: Luis Buñuel

1. Hans Richter, *Dada: art and anti-art*, and Patrick Waldberg, *Surrealism* (both London, Thames & Hudson, 1965).
2. Quoted in Julien Levy, *Surrealism* (New York, Black Sun Press, 1936), p. 9.
3. Anthony Hartley, *The Penguin Book of French Verse*, Vol. 4 (London, 1959), Introduction, p. xlvii.
4. Salvador Dali, *The Secret Life of Salvador Dali* (London, Vision Press, 1948), p. 11.
5. Quoted in Richter, *Dada*, p. 43.
6. Quoted in Waldberg, *Surrealism*, p. 16.
7. Ado Kyrou, *Luis Buñuel: an Introduction*, trans. Adrienne Foulke (New York, Simon & Schuster, 1963), p. 114.
8. Roger Shattuck, 'The D–S Expedition', *New York Review of Books*, 18 May 1972, pp. 24 ff., and 1 June 1972, pp. 19 ff.
9. J. H. Matthews, *Surrealism and Film* (Ann Arbor, University of Michigan Press, 1972).
10. Kyrou, *Buñuel*, p. 14.
11. Buñuel's son, Juan-Luis Buñuel, has now made a 22-minute documentary on this drumming ceremony – *Calanda*, 1966.
12. In *Luis Buñuel*, ed. Michel Estève, Francisco Rabal relates how once in Mexico, when Buñuel discovered that there were rats in his house, he would rather catch them in a cage in order to set them free in an open field than have to kill them (Paris, *Études Cinématographiques*, Nos. 20–21, 22–3, Winter 1962–3, pp. 11 ff.). See also Buñuel's sister's memoirs in *Positif* (Paris), No. 42, November 1961.
13. Luis Buñuel, from Estève, *Études Cinématographiques*.
14. For example, see any of the pieces in *Sight and Sound* (London), especially David Robinson, 'Thank God I'm still an atheist', Summer 1962, pp. 116 ff.; and Tom Milne, 'The Mexican Buñuel', Winter 1965–6, pp. 36 ff.
15. John Russell Taylor, *Cinema Eye, Cinema Ear* (London, Methuen, 1964), p. 85.
16. Frédéric Grange, *Luis Buñuel* (Paris, Éditions Universitaires, 1964), pp. 15 ff. Actually, all except the last section of this book is

written by Carlos Rebolledo. It remains the best all-round study of Buñuel's work to date.

17. Quoted in Freddy Buache, *Luis Buñuel* (Lyons *Premier Plan*, 1964).
18. See Pierre Renaud's analysis in Estève, *Études Cinématographiques*, pp. 147 ff., and Raymond Durgnat, *Luis Buñuel* (London, Studio Vista, 1967), pp. 22–38.
19. Taylor, *Cinema Eye*, p. 93.
20. For example, see Henry Miller's classic essay in *The Cosmological Eye* (New York, New Directions, 1939).
21. Jean Sémolué in Estève, *Études Cinématographiques*, p. 172.
22. For a description of these little-known films, see Jean-André Fieschi, 'The Angel and the Beast', *Cahiers du Cinéma in English*, No. 4 (New York), 1966.
23. From the filmography compiled by Rufus Segar in *Anarchy 6* (London), pp. 183 4.
24. Alan Lovell, *Anarchist Cinema* (London, Peace News, 1962).
25. ibid., p. 23.
26. For a comparison of these two films, see Grange, *Buñuel*, pp. 64 ff.
27. Durgnat, *Buñuel*, pp. 17–18, for Buñuel's attitude towards insects.
28. Quoted in Buache, *Premier Plan*, p. 51.
29. For a full and persuasive analysis, see Lovell, *Anarchist Cinema*, pp. 28–34.
30. Grange, *Buñuel*, pp. 103 ff.
31. Quoted in Kyrou, *Buñuel*, p. 120.
32. ibid., p. 127.
33. For instance, Tom Milne describes the film as 'a pure, devastating masterpiece of atheism' and refers to Ujo as 'the lewd and ugly dwarf who, simply because he wants her body, shows a charity to Andara which Nazario ... can never match' (London, *Monthly Film Bulletin*, October 1963), p. 141.
34. Again, see Lovell, *Anarchist Cinema*, pp. 34–8.
35. Durgnat, *Buñuel*, p. 20.
36. William S. Pechter, *Twenty-Four Times a Second* (New York, Harper & Row, 1971), pp. 215–25, and Tom Milne's 'The Mexican Buñuel' in *Sight and Sound*.
37. Durgnat, *Buñuel*, p. 16.
38. For a most thorough account of this film, see again Grange, *Buñuel*, pp. 152 ff. See also the script, published in *L'Avant-Scène*, No. 36 (Paris), 15 April 1964.
39. As Alan Lovell has argued (*Anarchist Cinema*, p. 26).

40. By way of small digression, we could note the troubling efficacy of evaded question that occurs at least twice in this film at crucial moments. *'Pourquoi?'*, which is followed simply by *'Parce que'*, in a way that cannot help but suggest Godard, suggests the breakdown of causality in a world of moral nihilism.

41. Tom Milne, in 'The Two Chambermaids', explains the facts: it appears that Chiappe was one of the key men responsible for the original banning of *L'Âge d'or* (*Sight and Sound* (London), Autumn 1964, p. 171).

42. For an informative and generally helpful article about Buñuel's Spanish background, see J. F. Aranda's two-part piece in *Films and Filming* (London), October and November 1961

Chapter Five: Ingmar Bergman

1. Ingmar Bergman, 'Qu'est-ce que "Faire des Films"?', in *Cahiers du Cinéma*, No. 61 (Paris, 1956), p. 18.

2. See Desmond Fennell, 'Goodbye to Summer', *Spectator* (London), 9 February 1962, and Kathleen Nott, *A Clean Well-Lighted Place* (London, Heinemann, 1961).

3. Bergman, 'Qu'est-ce que "Faire des Films"?', pp. 10 ff.

4. For Bergman's recurring 'symbols', see Jean Leirens, *Le Cinéma et la crise de notre temps* (Paris, Éditions du Cerf, 1960), pp. 99 ff.

5. 'J'ai composé beaucoup de scénarios avec mon cerveau; mais celui-là, je l'ai presque entièrement rédigé avec mon cœur' (quoted in Jean Béranger, *Ingmar Bergman et ses films* (Paris, Le Terrain Vague, 1959), p. 82).

6. Robin Wood, *Ingmar Bergman* (London, Studio Vista, 1969), p. 32.

7. John Russell Taylor, *Cinema Eye, Cinema Ear* (London, Methuen, 1964), pp. 138 ff.

8. Leirens, *Le Cinéma*, pp. 99 ff.

9. Wood, *Bergman*, pp. 66–72.

10. ibid., p. 70.

11. For a more detailed comparison between *Sawdust and Tinsel* and *The Seventh Seal*, see Peter Harcourt, 'The Troubled Pilgrimage – some comments on the films of Ingmar Bergman', in *Queen's Quarterly* (Kingston), Autumn 1961, pp. 459–66.

12. Steve Hopkins in *Industria International* (Stockholm 1958–9).

13. Peter Hall in *Gemini* (London, Winter 1959).

14. In these early days, Bergman acknowledged his belief in some

sort of God: 'Je crois en une idée supérieure qu'on appelle Dieu. Je le veux et il le faut. Je crois que c'est absolument nécessaire. Le matérialisme intégral ne pourrait conduire l'humanité qu'à une impasse sans chaleur' (*Cahiers du Cinéma*, No. 88 (Paris, 1958)).

15. Wood, *Bergman*, p. 81.
16. ibid., pp. 100 ff. But see also Wood's earlier account of the film, 'A Toad in the Bread', in *Definition*, No. 3 (London, 1961).
17. Wood, *Bergman*, p. 150.
18. Peter Cowie, *Sweden* 2 (London, Zwemmer, 1970), p. 95.
19. This seems to me more valid than Wood's extraordinary suggestion that it is the confused and apathetic little boy in *The Silence* who grew up and made *Shame*. See Wood, *Bergman*, p. 131.
20. See Susan Sontag, '*Persona*', in *Sight and Sound* (London), Autumn 1967, pp. 186 ff., reprinted in *Styles of Radical Will* (New York, Farrar, Straus & Giroux, 1969), pp. 123–45.
21. Wood, *Bergman*, p. 150.
22. Peter Harcourt, 'I, 182: an interplay of forces large and small', *Cinema* (Los Angeles), Fall 1970, pp. 32–9.
23. Wood, *Bergman*, p. 174.
24. Sontag, 'Trip to Hanoi', in *Styles*, pp. 205–74.

Chapter Six: Federico Fellini

1. Quoted in Delouche Dominique, 'Journal d'un Bidoniste', in Geneviève Agel, *Les Chemins de Fellini* (Paris, Éditions du Cerf, 1956), p. 129.
2. Agel, *Les Chemins*, pp. 5 ff. In the course of an immensely sensitive, predominantly Christian interpretation of Fellini's work, Madame Agel sees Osvaldo as marking one of the four stages in Gelsomina's development.
3. From an interview with Gideon Bachmann in Robert Hughes (ed.), *Film: Book I* (New York, Grove Press, 1959), p. 101.
4. For example, see Eric Rhode's review in *Sight and Sound* (London), Winter 1960–61, p. 34.
5. Hughes, *Film*, p. 105.
6. For a better understanding of the paintings of de Chirico, I am indebted to Peter Greenaway, painter and film-maker and himself a perceptive student of Fellini.
7. For Fellini imagery, see Agel, *Les Chemins*, or John Russell Taylor, *Cinema Eye, Cinema Ear* (London, Methuen, 1964), pp. 15–51.

8. From another interview with Gideon Bachmann in *Cinéma 65* (Paris), No. 99.

9. See Taylor, *Cinema Eye*, for the 'womb-like' quality of Fellini's affection.

10. This account of Steiner is adapted from Peter Harcourt, '*La Dolce Vita*', in *The Twentieth Century* (London), January 1961, pp. 81 ff.

11. Gilbert Salachas, *Federico Fellini* (Paris, Éditions Seghers, 1963), p. 2. With nice perception, Salachas sees Paola as 'l'hôtesse d'honneur' in Fellini's film.

12. For a more extended account of this film, see Peter Harcourt, 'The Secret Life of Federico Fellini', in *Film Quarterly* (Berkeley), Spring 1966, pp. 17 ff.

13. See Peter Harcourt, '*Satyricon*', in *Queen's Quarterly* (Kingston), Autumn 1970, pp. 447–52.

14. Federico Fellini, *Satyricon*, ed. Dario Zanelli (New York, Ballantine, 1970), p. 97.

15. For a compelling discussion of this sequence, see Suzanne Budgen, *Fellini* (London, British Film Institute, 1966), pp. 36–9.

16. From *Cinéma 65*, p. 85.

17. Deena Boyer, *The 200 Days of 8½* (London, Macmillan, 1964), p. 208.

Chapter Seven: Jean-Luc Godard

1. Quoted in Jean Collet, *Jean-Luc Godard* (New York, Crown, 1970), p. 37.

2. Ian Cameron (ed.), *The Films of Jean-Luc Godard* (London, Studio Vista, 1967), p. 10.

3. E. H. Gombrich, *Art and Illusion* (Princeton University Press, 1969), p. vii.

4. In several places, Godard has described the film as a kind of *Alice in Wonderland*. See, for instance, 'Le Dossier du Mois', *Cinéma 65* (Paris), No. 94, p. 50.

5. For a development of these traditional elements in Godard's films, see Robin Wood, 'Society and Tradition: An Approach to Jean-Luc Godard', in Toby Mussman (ed.), *Jean-Luc Godard* (New York, Dutton, 1968), pp. 179–90.

6. Jean-Luc Godard, *Masculine Feminine* (New York, Grove Press, 1969), pp. 72–3.

7. Richard Winkler, '*Le Petit Soldat*', in Cameron, *Godard*, pp. 17–20.

8. Nicholas Garnham, 'Introduction' to Jean-Luc Godard, *Le Petit Soldat* (London, Lorrimer, 1967), p. 13.

9. V. F. Perkins, *'Vivre sa vie'*, in Cameron, *Godard*, pp. 32–9.

10. Mussman, *Godard*, pp. 87–100, and Susan Sontag, *Against Interpretation* (A Delta Paperback, New York, 1967), pp. 196–207.

11. Perkins in Cameron, *Godard*, p. 36.

12. Lee Russell (alias Peter Wollen), 'Jean-Luc Godard' – a reply to Robin Wood, in *New Left Review* (London), No. 39, 1966, pp. 83 ff.

13. See Collet, *Godard*, pp. 82–94.

14. Translated in *Film Quarterly* (Berkeley), Winter 1968–9, pp. 20–35.

15. Godard, *Masculine Feminine*, p. 78.

16. Jean-Luc Godard, *Une Femme mariée*, translated by Sue Bennett and circulated in typescript by the British Film Institute, London.

17. R. D. Laing, *The Divided Self* (London, Penguin Books, 1965) – especially Chapter 3, pp. 39 ff.

18. Jean-Luc Godard, 'Let's Talk about Pierrot', in *Pierrot le fou* (New York, Simon & Schuster, 1969), p. 16.

19. Godard, *Pierrot le fou*, pp. 23–4.

20. Richard Roud, *Godard* (London, Thames & Hudson, 1970), p. 86.

21. ibid., p. 151.

22. See Robin Wood, *'Weekend'*, in Cameron, *Godard*, pp. 162–71.

23. Roud, *Godard*, p. 131.

24. Theodore Roszak, *The Making of a Counter Culture* (An Anchor Paperback, New York, 1969).

25. Collet, *Godard*, p. 12.

26. Cameron, *Godard*, p. 10.

27. Winkler, *'Le Petit Soldat'*, in Cameron, *Godard*, p. 20.

28. Laing, *The Divided Self*, p. 27.

29. Susan Sontag, *Styles of Radical Will* (New York, Farrar, Straus, & Giroux, 1969), p. 86.

Chapter Eight: Conclusion

1. Quoted in Peter Bogdanovich, *Fritz Lang in America* (London, Studio Vista, 1967), p. 60.

2. Philip Rieff, *The Triumph of the Therapeutic* (New York, Harper & Row, 1966), pp. 52–3.

3. Theodore Roszak, *The Making of a Counter Culture* (An Anchor Paperback, New York, 1969), pp. 239 ff.

INDEX

Films are generally listed under the name of their director.

281

Index

Index

Index

FILM AND REALITY
An Historical Survey

Roy Armes

Most contemporary film criticism does not take into account the relationship between artistic achievement and the historical context. *Film and Reality* sets out to redress the balance by offering both a broad outline of the cinema's development and a framework within which critical judgements can be made. Roy Armes explores in this book the varying relationships between image and reality in films from Lumière to the present.

The author first looks at film realism – from the early documentaries of Vertov and Flaherty to *cinéma-vérité* – and at the progress of fictional realism – from Stroheim's silent masterpiece, *Greed*, to the films of Renoir, Rossellini and the television work of Kenneth Loach. In the second part of his book he considers Hollywood and film illusion, showing how the work of Griffith and Chaplin finally gave place to a formalized system of studios, stars and genres. The book concludes with a discussion about the growth of film modernism and demonstrates how film, as a new and important twentieth-century art form closely related to such movements as Expressionism and Surrealism, has found its place as a genuinely new form of expression alongside the novel and the theatre.